The New
International Volur

The New International Volunteer

*A Hands-On Guide
to Sustainable and Inclusive
Development*

Elizabeth C. Medlin

Jefferson, North Carolina

LIBRARY OF CONGRESS Cataloguing-in-Publication DATA

Names: Medlin, Elizabeth C., author.
Title: The new international volunteer : a hands-on guide to sustainable
and inclusive development / Elizabeth C. Medlin.
Description: Jefferson, North Carolina : Toplight, 2023 |
Includes bibliographical references and index.
Identifiers: LCCN 2023006989 | ISBN 9781476691077 (paperback : acid free paper) ♾
ISBN 9781476649009 (ebook)
Subjects: LCSH: Voluntarism—International cooperation. | Sustainable development.
Classification: LCC HN49.V64 M44 2023 | DDC 302/.14—dc23/eng/20230221
LC record available at https://lccn.loc.gov/2023006989

BRITISH LIBRARY CATALOGUING DATA ARE AVAILABLE

ISBN (print) 978-1-4766-9107-7
ISBN (ebook) 978-1-4766-4900-9

Front cover image: © Daniel_Kay/Shutterstock

Printed in the United States of America

Toplight is an imprint of McFarland & Company, Inc., Publishers

*Box 611, Jefferson, North Carolina 28640
www.toplightbooks.com*

To my family—
I love you all big bunches,
whole wide world, forever & ever.

Acknowledgments

Dr. Richard Slatta, thank you for growing my mind in a way no one else has. I always look forward to our chats about Latin America. Without you, this book would be filled with passives and not nearly as informed.

Dr. Bob Patterson, thank you for encouraging me to follow my passion and to develop the material for this book. I wrote this book because you saw something in me and asked me to give a lecture to our class on this topic.

Dr. Dan O'Flaherty, thank you for helping me sculpt the ideas for this book. The Table of Contents, first chapter and graphs came to be thanks to your feedback during office hours. You show your students how exciting economics is, and I am lucky to have had you as my teacher. You do meaningful research and I hope to follow in your footsteps.

To Layla Milholen, my fantastic editor at McFarland. Thank you so much for sticking with me through the years on this project. You are an amazing editor and you are greatly appreciated.

To Drè Person, my other incredible editor at McFarland. Thank you for being there every step of the way, guiding me through the process of becoming a first time published author with grace and kindness.

To the McFarland and Toplight team for helping me make the best book possible. I truly appreciate you all. Thank you for all your work and this incredible opportunity to be published.

To my homestay family in San Lucas for the love, fun and protection and Bayron in Sololá for welcoming me, helping me and teaching me.

To all of the wonderful organizations and individuals mentioned in this book. Thank you for leading by example and making a positive impact in the international development and volunteering fields.

To Mom and Dad, words cannot express my thanks, but I'll try. Thanks for the unconditional support and love. Thank you for sticking with me, rooting for me, motivating me and helping me always. Love you big bunches.

To Mama Bina, Grammy and Austin for enthusiastically reading the rough draft, giving feedback and encouragement, and for supporting me always. I love you all very much!

Table of Contents

Table of Contents

Preface

The idea for this book grabbed onto me in 2013 and never let go. That summer I studied abroad and volunteered in the Lake Atitlán region of Guatemala. I got ill and decided to visit an international volunteer-run medical clinic to get help. That day in the clinic has stayed with me ever since, for reasons I did not expect.

The doctors at the clinic volunteered in Guatemala for a week at a time through an American church program. They saw as many patients as possible each day during the week and used a translator to communicate with patients. The doctors brought medicine with them and donations of used clothing. Each patient left the clinic with a diagnosis by a volunteer doctor, all the medicine they would need to treat the ailment and an article of used clothing.

While at the clinic, I had the opportunity to chat with two doctors and other volunteers who gave out clothes. I asked them why they volunteered and what they hoped to accomplish during their week at the clinic. Each of the doctors said they wanted to help at the clinic because they saw unmet needs in the community's healthcare. The volunteers in charge of handing out clothing stated that they wanted to give back. Despite these noble goals, I learned, from the patient's perspective, that the volunteers needed more than their best intentions to make the volunteer work successful.

This became apparent when the clinic doctors misdiagnosed me. In Guatemala, lab tests tend to be analyzed in a third-party lab before a patient sees a doctor. This allows the patient to give the results to a doctor up front, aiding them in making a diagnosis. The test results I gave the volunteer doctors said "No Parasites," but they diagnosed me with parasites anyway, without being able to specify which kind. I visited a Guatemalan doctor for a second opinion and she confirmed the test results' accuracy. I had an infection that needed antibiotics, not the anti-parasite medications the volunteer doctors gave me.

I could not help but wonder if the clinic doctors misdiagnosed other patients. Did they make these mistakes because they did not learn about common, location-specific ailments before arriving in Guatemala? If so, it could be easily remedied with preparation. Each misdiagnosis can prolong health problems and cause unnecessary suffering, making the stakes high for clinic patients and volunteer doctors alike.[1] Surely those who visit the clinic need medical professionals who can help cure them accurately, I thought.

The clinic had more problems than misdiagnoses. I went to the Guatemalan-run pharmacy across the street and asked the pharmacist his opinion on the volunteer-run clinic. He said it cost him a lot of business because patients no longer came to the pharmacy after going to the clinic. They did not need to since the doctors gave patients the medicine they needed before they walked out the door. Most families could afford medications in this area of Guatemala, so cost did not prevent most people from taking medicine, but the clinic provided it regardless.

A few streets over, many Guatemalans made a living by selling used clothes that they bought in bundles from donation stores in the United States. As the volunteers gave away clothes at the clinic, they took away business from the Guatemalan clothing sellers. The clothes sold for extremely reasonable prices, so cost did not inhibit people from buying clothes in the market. While at the clinic, I asked several women who brought their sick children there what they thought about the clothing donations. They said they did not need the clothes, but only came to the clinic because they did not like the quality of services at the local hospital.

Translation caused the last major problem at the clinic. Two doctors worked in separate exam rooms but only had one translator. Neither doctor spoke Spanish, so without a translator in the room, the doctors missed translations of vital medical facts that could help make a correct diagnosis. Additionally, they could not address any concerns patients had without the translator present. Doctor-patient communication and understanding required a second translator or for the doctors to speak Spanish themselves.

As I reflected on my unexpected clinic experience, it seemed that the doctors and other volunteers had the best of intentions but needed to change the way they carried them out. The quality needed to match their desire to help. Both matter in international volunteering. What if a new generation of international volunteers could use their desire to help as momentum to provide the highest quality healthcare to places that needed it? The doctors did a good job identifying a real need the community had, but they just did not meet that need fully effectively. What if international volunteers think not only about the needs they try to meet, but also about the consequences, good or bad, that come from the way they meet those needs? This book developed from these questions.

That day when I walked out of the clinic gates, with my inaccurate pills in hand, passing a line of Guatemalans waiting to get medical care, I knew there had to be a better way. My own journey in writing this book meant finding out how to volunteer the right way, so that next time, when I myself went to volunteer internationally again, I would be doing it right. And that the next time I saw volunteers trying to connect their goals to their actions and results, I could guide them through it. So that the locals and I who needed healthcare that day could have volunteers who excelled in quality clinics, while also strengthening the local economy. The first step to changing international volunteering begins with realizing what needs to be changed. The second includes learning how to carry out those changes. The new international volunteer will learn how to do both in the coming pages.

By reading *The New International Volunteer*, readers will gain new insights on the ins and outs of international volunteering and fresh perspectives on tried-and-true development methods. As readers analyze how an international development trip will play out in the long run, they will consider how to choose or create the ideal international volunteer trip, how to research it and how to approach it from an ethical standpoint. While picking from the best development tools for the job, volunteers will learn how to act sustainably and inclusively on every volunteer trip, how to evaluate the progress of an ongoing project and how to assess the success of the project after its completion.

Readers will understand how international volunteering fits into the greater scheme of poverty reduction, aid giving and global development efforts. As international volunteering comprises only a part of development, readers will learn how the individual fits into the volunteer role, how to maximize the volunteer role and the limitations of the volunteer role. Knowing this, new international volunteers will be prepared to face any possible challenges during a volunteer project. Volunteers will identify how to continue to help the host community after the project ends, how to best take care of themselves, how to prepare for a trip and how to reintegrate upon returning home. Finally, readers will learn common mistakes volunteers make and how to avoid them, how to find a good-fitting trip and, most importantly, how to succeed as a new international volunteer. New international volunteers will feel confident going into each volunteer trip with the capabilities to turn the local community's development vision into reality.

In this way, the future of development has the power to be filled with more success stories where international volunteers assist community members in every part of the world to eradicate poverty, eliminate food insecurity, let no one perish from a preventable cause, and raise up every child to be healthy and well-educated, regardless of gender, race or circumstance. In short, new international volunteers will truly and deeply understand the unique needs of the people they serve.

Part 1

*What Drives the New
International Volunteer*

I

The State of the World

World Improvements

Before the pandemic, more people experienced a higher quality of life than ever before.[1] Decreases in poverty were especially concentrated in Asia. The World Bank concluded that in 2000, 34.8 percent of the population in East Asia and the Pacific lived in extreme poverty (measured as living on less than $1.90 a day). Thanks to the economic growth of countries in the region, such as China, in 2019 the number of extremely poor declined to just 0.9 percent of the population. Concurrently, South Asia experienced a large decline in extreme poverty from 2002 to 2014, from 39.6 percent to 15.2 percent. Extreme poverty in Latin America and the Caribbean notably fell from 12.8 percent to 4.1 percent in the period from 2000 to 2019. In Sub-Saharan Africa, poverty declined from 57.8 percent to 38.3 percent over the same time period.

In fact, according to the World Bank, in 2000, 27.7 percent of the global population lived under the $1.90 a day poverty line, but in 2018 it declined to 8.6 percent.[2] This progress in poverty reduction indicates that people around the world have begun to see various improvements to their quality of life. For instance, the world population enjoys better health: 9 percent of people experienced undernourishment in 2019 compared to 14.8 percent in 2000.[3] Additionally, 87 percent of expecting women received prenatal care in 2017, up from 69 percent in 2000.[4] Outside of the health-care sector, the world has more electricity access than ever before. There were 90.5 percent of people who lived with electricity access in 2020 compared to 78 percent in 2000.[5] Also, children receive more education than ever before, as the percentage of students who completed primary school in 2020 rose to 90 percent from 81.8 percent in 2000.[6]

The major reduction of poverty came about due to many factors, such as policy actions taken by governments, shifts in the way the world functions, and the dedication of people living in poverty to escaping it. For instance, a first major cause of worldwide poverty reduction began when China decided to end a period of isolationism. China lived in a relatively isolated way before the great push to reduce poverty began in the 1980s. A factor in China's success occurred when the government opened up the country, specifically the financial markets, to international trade. By beginning to trade internationally on a large scale, China created many jobs for its citizens. While meeting a growing consumer demand for their manufacturing products worldwide, the influx of money into the economy has allowed the government to invest in improving infrastructure, education, and supplementing healthcare and wages when needed to reduce poverty. Taking advantage of strong economic growth helped China become the world's second largest economy.[7]

Advances in technology make up a second factor that contributed to the major reduction in global poverty. The single act of accessing the internet on mobile phones has allowed people to make their businesses more profitable with greater information and communication capabilities at their fingertips. Implementing the latest technology can help entrepreneurs grow their businesses in a significant way, increasing profit for owners and creating job opportunities for more employees. Take, for instance, the rise of mobile banking. Mobile banking has helped entrepreneurs and farmers across Africa grow their businesses. Accessing mobile banking on a cell phone can be more convenient than going to a physical bank as it saves time and supports efficiency. In fact, according to *The Economist*, studies have shown that rural Kenyans who use the mobile banking company M-Pesa as an alternative to traditional banks have earned 5 percent–30 percent more money. The rise in profit can most likely be correlated to increased business efficiency from using M-Pesa. Mobile banking services like M-Pesa improve the business environment in Kenya by offering people loans on mobile platforms, a payment system for employees' salaries and bill pay via phone.[8]

The rise of the mobile banking in Africa has created other helpful mobile tools for families and business owners. One such company, Pivot East, uses M-Pesa to make paying school fees more efficient by monitoring parents' late payments and by giving reminders that future payments will be due. Pivot East has also disrupted the farming industry to make poultry farming easier and more efficient by alerting farmers via text message about the health of their chickens. Before Pivot East, poultry farmers had to constantly monitor their chickens in-person. Pivot East frees up that time so the farmers can spend less time on poultry farming and more on expanding their other crop or animal offerings to earn more income.[9] M-Farm, another such mobile service, cheaply provides farmers with updated market prices for their goods via SMS. M-Farm also connects farmers to one another so they can sell their products together or buy crops as a group.[10]

Better paying jobs that allow for upward mobility and more purchasing power encapsulates the third reason why so many people have left extreme poverty. Countries such as India have seen a decline in traditional farming livelihoods as people migrate to jobs in the manufacturing and service sectors. The move from agriculture to service sectors, like IT support, helps grow the economy. Service sector jobs tend to be higher paying and come with better benefits than farming. India's tech industry signifies the shift from farming to high-skilled work that has become competitive in the global marketplace. For instance, India's strong IT sector has aided in economic growth and development by incentivizing universities to teach specialized computer skills as more Indians go to college.[11] When people get service sector jobs, they tend to do so in urban areas, thus migrating from rural towns to urban ones. Their increased purchasing power from service sector jobs allows them to demand other services and non-essential goods. As a result, service workers strengthen the economy in urban areas and fuel other service sectors in turn.[12]

The fourth factor that has helped people live better lives on a major scale includes government programs that have made a tangible impact on the populace. For instance, government healthcare programs in Rwanda help improve the quality and availability of healthcare for the entire population. Although better health gives people a reason to champion healthcare in itself, providing healthcare to a population also allows people to take advantage of better health to be more productive workers. More productive workers spur economic development by making (and spending) more income and as a result, live higher quality lives. Affordable healthcare access negates people being forced to choose between medicine and other essentials for financial reasons. In Rwanda, the poorest segment of the population does not have to pay for health insurance at all. After introducing a health insurance plan for those who could not afford to pay for clinic services, AIDS and Malaria rates declined while vaccination rates have gone up. Rwanda implemented their healthcare program by adding clinics and stocking them with medicine so that the system could be accessible in all areas of the country. To improve the quality of the healthcare system, Rwanda built more hospitals with surgical capacity and implemented a training program for medical staff. Additionally, Rwanda sought to expand the number of people getting healthcare access in rural areas of the country by funding staff to work in those areas. As a result, the percentage of Rwandan women giving birth in clinics has more than tripled, which has reduced child mortality rates and mother mortality rates.[13]

When businesses expand across national borders, they create

opportunities to match people's skills to new jobs not previously available. New industries in international locations oftentimes provide stable employment, opportunity for advancement and investment in human capital (marketable skills) of their employees. Issues can arise when industries like maquiladoras in Mexico pollute the environment, provide harsh working conditions and underpay their employees.[14] However, in successful and ethical international business expansions, people can benefit from employment of this type. When an international business chooses to open an office in another country and employ people locally, it can create an industry that offers people skilled jobs, an increase in wages and more job opportunities in their area. For example, according to *The New Yorker*, the call center Sykes employs approximately 3,000 people in El Salvador. The call center business has grown in El Salvador, where total Salvadoran call center employees number twenty thousand. Call centers expanded into El Salvador partly because Salvadorian deportees from the United States have English skills needed to fill these positions. Some call center employees get $150 a week, three times the minimum wage in El Salvador. The call center work experience has helped Salvadorans grow the economy in other ways as well, like by starting English language schools that train more workers for the call centers, run by former call center employees.[15]

Finally, a somewhat controversial factor in the worldwide decline of extreme poverty can be contributed to global aid. Historically, aid giving has not always been successful. In the past, money has been wasted on inappropriate or non-useful projects, contractors and vendors have acted inefficiently and officials have funneled aid money for their own corrupt uses.[16] However, when done correctly, aid can also act as an injection of money into an economy and go toward helpful projects that improve people's lives. For example, UNICEF helps children around the world by improving health, food security, water quality and sanitation, including in relief situations. UNICEF works in one hundred and ninety countries to further their goal that children everywhere live safely and healthily. UNICEF allocates much of their aid toward immunization drives to prevent children from dying of preventable diseases. They also fund efforts to end malnutrition. UNICEF USA gets money exclusively from donors— including NGOs, governments, individuals and companies. UNICEF's funding can be broken down into eighty-eight cents toward aid for children, nine cents for fundraising and three cents for administrative costs for every dollar spent.[17] UNICEF has Charity Navigator's highest ratings for transparency and accountability. They also meet all Better Business Bureau's standards for charity accountability. In this way, charities that act as good stewards of their funds can make a significant impact with aid money.[18]

As major progress in poverty reduction and improving quality of life have come about, the question can be asked: Who has played a major role in creating these changes? International volunteers have played a small part. However, people experiencing poverty do the most to reduce it. Many previously impoverished people have turned to entrepreneurship as a way to generate a large income and create jobs in their community. Bethlehem Alemu from Ethiopia did just that. Bethlehem started SoleRebels in her hometown of Zenabwork in Addis Ababa, Ethiopia, a place where few people could find jobs. As an entrepreneur, she started the company SoleRebels with $10,000 startup money from friends and family. SoleRebels sells fair trade shoes to 40+ countries worldwide. The company makes unique, handcrafted shoes from recycled materials, such as old tires for the soles. Employees hand loom locally grown cotton to give customers a low carbon footprint and an authentic Ethiopian shoe. In founding SoleRebels, Bethlehem created jobs for hundreds of people in her community and showcased Ethiopian fashion and craftsmanship to the world. SoleRebels jobs come with good employee benefits, including making at least four times the Ethiopian minimum wage. Employees also get medical insurance and a scholarship program to pay for their children's schooling. In this way, entrepreneurs can lift up the average income of their community and spread the benefits to their employees and families.[19]

Communities can band together to bring advancements to the collective group. For instance, people who lost their homes, possessions and electricity in Puerto Rico after Hurricane Maria fed their communities and lead the post-disaster recovery for their own towns. Puerto Ricans have created several community gathering spots, called Centers of Mutual Support, run out of closed schools, to feed the community after the hurricane. These women-led groups met a vital need as many people lived without power for months and so had limited cooking means. Volunteers delivered food to elderly or disabled community members who could not come to the center to eat. Centers even installed water purification in nearby rivers to provide what could be the only clean source of drinking water post-hurricane Maria. Some of the centers provided a need for socialization by starting a permanent community center with classes and services, like acupuncture and dance. Everyone who ate at the centers pitched in how they could—either by donating money, food, or cooking and cleaning. The centers exemplify an initiative that starts within a community to rebuild, where neighbors take care of neighbors. Many participants hope that the Centers of Mutual Support will spark changes in all of Puerto Rico as they reckon with post-disaster relief and the island's turbulent financial system.[20]

Although they do not always do this, governments have a unique power to bring about widespread improvements to quality of life and development initiatives. Governments can act as the dedicated entity to protect and assist the entire population of a country. National and regional governments tend to have structures in place to deploy programs and resources on a large scale to every part of their territory. These structures can be used for development means. Utilizing government power for wide scale development occurred in Cuba after the revolution when the new government made it a national priority to achieve full literacy on the island. At the time, many Cubans of all ages, especially in rural and mountainous regions, could not read. To change this, the Cuban government started a volunteer campaign where volunteers across the country signed up to teach people how to read and write. Volunteers received training and textbooks. The literacy volunteers lived in homes of residents of the towns they taught in so that people of every age could learn to read and write in the evenings at home. This campaign became so successful that after learning to read, many newly literate citizens went back to school and completed a primary education. The literacy campaign has a lasting legacy, as Cuba has a 99.75 percent adult literacy rate today, one of the highest in Latin America and the Caribbean. The Cuban government continues to prioritize education with limited class sizes, free education from pre-school through the college level, and providing students with meals and uniforms.[21]

Businesses have also made an impact in reducing poverty and promoting development, especially through their corporate social responsibility, or CSR, arms. More so now than ever, consumers demand that companies do no harm to the environment and contribute some of their profit to making the world a better place. Although businesses engage in CSR to garner support for their brand, their efforts have also made an impact on important problems in some cases. For instance, Ikea sells homes in a box to the UNHCR (The United Nations High Commissioner for Refugees) for families to live in. Ikea helps offset the cost to the UNHCR by donating money and by making bed linens for the families who will live in the houses. The Ikea shelter has several advantages over traditional refugee tents, such as durability—it lasts for years longer than traditional tents. Compared to other tents, the Ikea homes can be repaired using locally available materials when they start to wear down. The shelter keeps people more protected from the elements as well. A rooftop solar panel comes standard to allow families to have light inside at night and charge their phones, an impossibility in a traditional tent. The Ikea shelter gives refugees safety and privacy as each shelter comes with a lock on the door and slash proof walls. Most importantly, Ikea's design gives refugees a real home to have privacy, safety and solitude after trauma.[22]

Some of the world's wealthiest individuals have become dedicated philanthropists who seek to reduce inequality. In response, they have given most of their fortunes away and have done so in a way that does the most good as possible. Individuals like Bill Gates and Melinda French Gates, Jimmy and Rosalynn Carter, Warren Buffett, Mark Zuckerberg and Priscilla Chan have given substantial sums of money toward disease eradication and education, among other causes. Oprah Winfrey in particular focuses many of her philanthropic efforts on education. She founded a boarding school for girls in South Africa dedicated to teaching high school students from low-income areas. The school now has a network of hundreds of alumni, who Oprah calls her daughters. When a girl attends her school, The Oprah Winfrey Leadership Academy for Girls, Oprah covers every expense, including braces and uniforms, at a cost of over $140 million so far. Oprah herself grew up in poverty and that motivates her approach with the school. She makes sure to spend time at the campus often, teaching the students life lessons and meeting with them individually. Many of the girls go on to university after graduating from the boarding school, including to prestigious schools in South Africa, the United States and the United Kingdom, among others.[23]

International volunteers, the subject of this book, will be the last group of changemakers mentioned in this chapter. While volunteers make up only a small part of this global do-gooding coalition, they have made their mark. In fact, the United Nations celebrates International Volunteer Day each year on December 5 to commemorate and showcase the work of these volunteers. When utilized correctly, international volunteering can connect people in a world filled with need to people willing to help. We have a growing global consciousness of the unacceptability of poverty in a world where so many people have so much. New international volunteers see the way the world could be—without poverty and with less suffering—and this motivates them to volunteer internationally. At the end of the day, international volunteers acknowledge an inequity in the world and actively look for a way to disrupt this paradox.

The New International Volunteer's Role in World Improvements

International volunteers have been working alongside others to help spur major changes in poverty reduction and development over the past few decades. Worldwide, approximately ten million people volunteer internationally each year. This includes 1.6 million voluntourists. Of the people who volunteer internationally, over one million international volunteers hail from the United States and at least fifty thousand volunteers originate from the United Kingdom.[24] Australians, Europeans and Canadians make up another significant, but unspecified, part of the international volunteering workforce.[25] But it is not just people from Western countries who volunteer and the narrative should not be that international volunteering is a one way street from the Global North to the South.[26] In fact, due to all of the people who volunteer abroad, international volunteering has now grown into a two-billion-dollar industry.[27] This allows international volunteers to collectively make up a large, worldwide workforce committed to helping how they can. International volunteers contribute in several ways, from creating change quickly to supporting long-term preservation efforts.

In fact, international volunteering can act as a tool to quickly move forward development and lessen hardships, such as disease, famine and poverty. International volunteers have addressed these by bringing knowledge and resources to their volunteer projects and assisting locals with their development goals. These international volunteering strategies can be helpful because poverty occurs on a large scale but volunteering works on one project at a time to break down global issues into manageable, actionable chunks on a local level. Volunteers do what they can with what they have to make a difference here and now, instead of getting stuck with abstract, seemingly insurmountable problems. In this way, international volunteering acts on the hope that change does occur one person and one project at a time.

International volunteering has potential to meet people's most pressing needs around the globe. Sometimes individuals lack access to basics like food, clothing and shelter, and international volunteers can help fill those gaps. Casa de los Amigos, a Quaker-run shelter in Mexico City, does just that by taking in refugees, human trafficking victims, crime victims, asylees and immigrants that have nowhere to go. Casa de los Amigos supports people with temporary housing, food and clothing needs. They also focus on integrating residents into the Mexico City community with neighborhood orientation and Spanish language classes. Every single person who comes through the shelter leaves in a better situation, equipped with what they need to transition into daily Mexico City life. Although the shelter does not have capacity to help everyone, it still makes a difference one person at a time.[28]

International volunteers regularly act to implement practical and scalable solutions to large, systemic and urgent problems. In Haiti, one of these big problems consists of meeting the demand for maternal healthcare. Many Haitian mothers die while giving birth for multiple reasons, such as a ratio of one midwife per fifty thousand women, scarce resources, and, at times, lack of running water in hospitals. These circumstances contribute to Haiti having the highest infant mortality rate in Latin America and the Caribbean. Many Haitian women have seen loved ones die during delivery, which motivated them into midwifery with the organization Midwives for Haiti. International volunteers work with Midwives for Haiti to show local nurses how to become midwives with a specialty in maternal care. Midwives for Haiti gives their students standard tests translated into Creole and assesses their progress using the skilled birth attendant guidelines from the World Health Organization. The international volunteers with Midwives for Haiti must be certified and licensed medical professionals and can only volunteer in healthcare classes where their medical license allows. The volunteers do not provide midwife care themselves, but, instead, teach how to help at births at a rural hospital, a mobile clinic and at home births. Volunteers prevent duplication of classes by accessing the curriculum before traveling to see what previous teachers have taught. This also ensures volunteers have experience in the curriculum students will be focusing on. Thanks to Midwives for Haiti, over one hundred and fifty-five Haitian nurses have become skilled birth attendants since 2006. These nurses together help with twelve thousand births and sixty thousand prenatal checkups each year. Many of the graduates find work in rural areas and have seen declines in infant mortality rates because of their presence in areas otherwise understaffed with midwives. This is a tangible solution to a large problem in Haiti that volunteers can help with one class at a time.[29]

International volunteers make a positive impact by helping when no one else can. Volunteers often serve as the first point of contact during peacebuilding and in post-conflict situations. For instance, the United Nations has a volunteer program that aims to foster permanent peace in post-conflict situations. UN Volunteers help peacebuilding and peacekeeping efforts around the world. They build and strengthen institutions, advocate for human rights, monitor democracy and provide relief.[30] One such UN Volunteer, Marie Zamani, volunteered in Cote D'Ivoire to kickstart reconstruction in the country after long years of conflict. She did this by harnessing the power of public information. Marie performed outreach to relay concerns Cote D'Ivoire citizens had to the UN. She similarly disseminated important information to Cote D'Ivoire citizens by raising awareness about what UN peacekeeping hoped to achieve there. She focused her work in schools specifically because younger citizens particularly help maintain long-term peace through conversations about reconciliation. In this way, volunteers can help shape a path to peace by being the first to help after conflict.[31]

Similarly, international volunteers act as first responders, bringing assistance and relief to areas impacted by natural disasters. In 2004, American Red Cross and Red Crescent volunteers made a major impact after the tsunami in South Asia. Red Cross/Red Crescent volunteers helped meet survivors' immediate needs, such as food and shelter. Because the tsunami destroyed clean water access and sanitation systems, volunteers rebuilt clean water pumps. For sustainability, they made sure to then train people who lived nearby on how to use and repair the pumps. This effort ensures reliable water delivery in the future. So that public health did not decline after the tsunami, volunteers vaccinated more than one million children and built toilets and sewage systems to prevent the risk of disease spreading. After they addressed immediate needs, international and local volunteers partnered in a five-year tsunami recovery program. The long-term program focused on rebuilding houses and preparing people in case another tsunami hit the coast. Focusing on preparedness and sustainability, they trained many people in first aid, evacuation methods, and disaster response plans. Working side by side, locals and volunteers built new evacuation routes.[32]

International volunteers make a difference when they support people around the world during times of hardship. Major difficulties come in many forms, from weather-related natural disasters to human-made causes. For example, in 2017, a drought in Somalia caused a risk of famine when many livestock and crops died. To help prevent famine, UN Volunteers from all over the world got reassigned to support Somalians. UN Volunteers used communication methods, ranging from meetings with communities, radio shows, written reports and TV stories, to disseminate critical information of how, when and where to receive food. Overall, eleven million Somalians needed food assistance and UN Volunteers played a significant role in getting food to hungry people.[33]

Isolated areas present a challenge for international volunteering but volunteers can be useful in those areas as well. An organization called Missing Maps, born from a collaboration between the Red Cross and Doctors Without Borders, asks volunteers around the world to participate in mapathons. During a mapathon, international volunteers look at satellite images of isolated areas on their computers and then make maps where none previously existed. After creating a map from satellite images, international volunteers work with local volunteers to ensure the map's accuracy. Together, local and international volunteers add details to the maps that satellites do not pick up well, like water pumps, evacuation routes and street names. After volunteers put the finishing touches on a map, Missing Maps promises that volunteers and locals can use them by keeping them on open source software, accessible to all. NGOs have used the maps to help more effectively in refugee camps and to create vaccination campaigns in rural areas of Africa. In fact, organizations like the Red Cross and Doctors Without Borders have used the maps to spur major aid efforts such as disaster responses and ending Ebola during outbreaks.[34]

Additionally, international volunteers can erect necessary services where governments have not or cannot. The Foundation for International Medical Relief of Children works in Limón, Nicaragua, an area without much pre-existing health infrastructure, to reduce instances of diabetes and maternal mortality. Volunteers, especially pharmaceutical students, help develop the area's medical infrastructure by testing people for diabetes, despite insulin not being available in the area. Volunteers also raise awareness about an insulin alternative, a pill called Metformin, available over the counter in Limón. Diabetes patients who take Metformin do not have to do regular insulin testing, helping to lengthen the lives of people in the area who do not have access to diabetes testing kits. Pharmacy student volunteers educate pharmacists in the area about the risks of diabetes and the signs of the disease, while demonstrating the benefits of the commonly available alternative pill. Volunteers also use their knowledge to conduct in-home prenatal visits because pregnant women do not have many other options for prenatal healthcare in the area. These routine visits by volunteers help prevent maternal and infant mortality by ensuring that pregnancies progress smoothly and by addressing any health problems before delivery.[35]

International volunteers often teach in demand skills that people desire. Lyla Fujiwara used her computer science degree as a Peace Corps volunteer to teach computer skills to girls and entrepreneurs in Rwanda. She did this by teaching and organizing a camp for girls, exposing them to computer technology. Local IT professionals led many of the camp classes. By the end of camp, the girls learned how to create blogs and to program games, allowing them to eventually choose careers utilizing computers. Lyla also taught in a school's computer lab and generated a computer literacy curriculum for students. The computer lab had donated laptops but teachers did not have enough training to use them. Lyla applied her IT skills to get the laptops working and showed teachers so they could teach the students as well. After her volunteer tenure in Rwanda, Lyla met her goal of helping people in rural communities create an IT community. Lyla's work helped reduce a gap between IT skills, training and career options between urban and rural areas in Rwanda.[36]

Each international volunteer brings unique skills and knowledge to each project, as do locals. When the two team up, the combination of specialized knowledge can create positive change. One such partnership between locals and volunteers occurred in Panama. Farmers teamed up with Peace Corps volunteers to improve agricultural outputs by changing cropping practices. Together Panamanian farmer Nico and volunteer Laura Sofen transitioned from a slash and burn technique and chemical fertilizer to composting. Composting gave higher crop yields than previous methods. The material composted included local decomposing trees to help the soil become more nutrient rich. Nico and Laura then worked with other farmers in the area so they too could experience higher yields using the new, but proven, composting approach.[37]

Similarly, volunteers have successfully helped locals achieve their development goals. The Carter Center, founded by former President Jimmy Carter and First Lady Rosalynn Carter, focuses on eliminating diseases from the world. The Carter Center helps people in Sudan eradicate Guinea Worm, a disease caused by drinking from a contaminated water source. The Carter Center made headway in eradication via educational, treatment and preventative approaches. To achieve Guinea Worm eradication, The Carter Center relies on locals to remind their neighbors about transmission risks and to give out replacement water filters regularly. The water filters allow people to drink from a contaminated water source if needed without contracting Guinea Worm. As a result, the joint effort has reduced transmission rates in the area.[38]

Similarly, several women in Ghana volunteered through the Red Cross to end Guinea Worm in their communities. They have made an impact on advancing women's status in their communities by taking the lead in Guinea Worm eradication. Typically, men had more authority than women in holding meetings about the disease. Program participants noticed that other women would share their concerns and comments in women-led meetings more than they would in meetings led by men. Women in Ghana spend more time in their villages then men and typically gather water in the division of labor, so they see who got sick from Guinea Worm the most. Also, since humans contract Guinea Worm by drinking contaminated water, women volunteers had a direct role in stopping transmission. However, over time women volunteers made a large impact by getting more cases reported by meeting participants. This allowed individuals to receive treatment and stopped community spread. In this way, international volunteers can help support local volunteers as they make public health and social strides in their communities.[39]

Lastly, international volunteers support preservation efforts to protect ecosystems around the world. Fundemar works in Bayahibe, Dominican Republic, a fishing and tourist town on the Caribbean Sea, to advocate for marine protection through a wildlife conservation campaign. The campaign focuses on the harm in touching or consuming endangered animals in the area. International volunteers at Fundemar advocate for best practices in ecotourism by partnering with local dive shops and hotels to encourage divers to preserve and restore Bayahibe's coral reefs. Fundemar strives to prevent coral reefs in Bayahibe from dying out by building coral gardens in the ocean and transplanting reefs. The lionfish, an invasive species, threatens Bayahibe's marine life in the coral reefs. Fundemar promotes lionfish consumption so fishermen and women catch them and sell them. Restaurants buy lionfish for tourists to eat and to educate them about the dangers of invasive species to marine life. This strategy simultaneously reduces the risk of lionfish hurting the ecosystem and makes a profit for local businesses and fish workers.[40]

The Dark Side of International Volunteering

Sometimes, any help can seem beneficial at first glance. The words "help," "aid," "development" and "volunteering" bring positive connotations to mind. But, occasionally, the way people go about volunteering internationally does not lead to the intended benefit that they hoped to achieve. Indeed, international development volunteering has not been perfect up to this point. As humans, volunteers can be fallible. Many volunteers with the best of motivations try to create positive development, but accidently cause economic turmoil instead. However, mistakes in the development arena can have disastrous consequences. People's livelihoods can be at risk if international volunteers and development organizations do not have a thorough understanding of how to properly develop and overcome challenges in development.[41]

For example, aid money has been mismanaged by development actors in the past. In 2012, according to the former Secretary General of the United Nations, Ban Ki-moon, 30 percent of aid money disappeared due to corruption. This caused problems when funding vanished that needed to go toward education in Nigeria and civil society groups in Tanzania. Consequences for aid money mismanagement can be severe for intended recipients. This occurred when the World Bank canceled a loan for a bridge in Bangladesh due to corruption.[42] When aid money goes to its intended place, international volunteers can make the most impact. International volunteers need to consider economic and financial development tools in their work, as responsible finance can be a powerful means to promote long-term economic growth. So much of poverty revolves around a lack of money, therefore, international volunteering must revolve in part around improving the way aid money gets allocated.

Another problem in international volunteering has been inefficiency and wastefulness. For instance, the One Million T-Shirts Project for Africa shone a spotlight on inefficient international volunteering efforts because the one million tee shirts would not be made by people who would be wearing them, thus not creating local jobs. An outside intervention of this kind could have hurt the local clothing industry by reducing demand for their goods. Thus, the creators abandoned the idea before completing it.[43]

Sometimes international volunteering projects do not function as intended. For instance, when medical volunteers diagnose parasites in patients and give them anti-parasite medicine, the parasites will usually die and the patient will feel better. However, this will only be effective for a little while as people can get re-infested through continued exposure. If volunteers leave after treating people for parasites but before addressing the root causes of infection, the goal of eliminating parasites does not fully get met. To achieve the goal, medical volunteers must treat people who already have parasites and also eliminate continued exposure to them. For waterborne parasites, for example, volunteers would need to sanitize contaminated water sources, educate people about the dangers of waterborne parasites and how to keep water sources safe.[44] Therefore, volunteers make a real difference when they take the time to ensure the project's outcome matches its intentions.

Sustainability cannot afford to be overlooked on international volunteering projects. Some international volunteering trips for medical care do not prioritize sustainability by not providing continuity of care for locals. Medical volunteering can be discontinuous when volunteers fail to diagnose patients correctly, forcing them to seek care elsewhere, or leave before patients get better. Medical volunteering requires continuity of care, which means there needs to be ample opportunity for follow up appointments. If a patient's condition does not improve, but volunteer doctors have left, then they have to find medical care with someone else. New doctors oftentimes do not have access to records of previous visits with volunteer doctors, compelling the new doctor to guess the diagnosis made and treatments they already tried. The patient may not be able to tell a new doctor much about the diagnoses and medications prescribed by an absent volunteer doctor if they did not explain it to them.[45]

Even short-term international volunteering affects future development. By not considering the long term before, during and after all international development volunteering, volunteers do not ensure that their contribution will be sustainable for the host community in the long term. For example, *The Economist* reported that at a mental hospital in Sierra Leone, European Union workers built five toilets for the patients. However, they left without a long-term maintenance plan. All of the toilets broke, obliging the patients to go to the bathroom in buckets next to their beds. This unsanitary alternative negatively impacts their quality of life.

None of the people who completed the project ensured the functionality of the system in the long term, and had no quality control monitoring after. A sign advertising the EU funded toilet project acts as the only still operational result from the work.[46]

Successful development volunteering requires two cultures and communities coming together to solve the direst problems facing humanity. When one of the communities, or both, does not consider the importance or potential impact of the other, development projects can go awry. This happens when volunteers lose the focus of volunteering by making it about the experience rather than the people they volunteer for.[47] Some volunteers go to orphanages abroad and benefit from the time they spend playing with kids and the pictures they take with them. However, in reality, the orphanage experience does not help the kids, it hurts them. Orphanage volunteering has created an industry where sometimes kids who live there have families, but get sent there to bring in more volunteers for funding. Even in legitimate orphanages, volunteers might walk away feeling like they benefited meeting the kids. However, kids who grow up without exposure to the same long-term caregivers can have a hard time making attachments, which negatively effects their mental health and stability.[48] These unintended consequences show a pressing need for pre-project preparation for all international volunteers. Pre-project preparation includes learning how to utilize best practices in development and researching the host community's economics, government and culture. The new international volunteer has come about to help each project use proven development methods, be sustainable, focus on the community and to be successful in the long term.

The New International Volunteer's Place in the World Today

International development has become a defining issue of our time. With each passing day, disease, war, climate change, crop failure, drought and crime work against development efforts around the world. Nonprofits, Non-Governmental Organizations (NGOs), regional groups (like the Organization of American States and the European Union), Bretton Woods institutions (The World Bank and the International Monetary Fund) and the United Nations constitute major stakeholders dedicated to ending world poverty in our modern society. Nevertheless, much work remains to be done, and the new international volunteer can support it. In a globalized twenty-first century, the focus on international development projects and volunteers' impact on communities they assist has become ever more important. Indeed, in a world filled with poverty, inequality, famine and war, international volunteers have a unique power to step in and help bring about positive economic and social change. Volunteers can influence better government policies, support new development projects, and assist with complex economic and social solutions in the international community. In short, the new international volunteer will play a pivotal role in international development as we know it.

I have grasped that the world of international volunteering has not always been as picturesque as it may seem. Going into my first foray as an international volunteer trying to make an impact, I quickly learned through observation and personal failure that some development methods do not help when volunteering internationally. However, when international volunteering goes wrong, it can be corrected. Volunteer and aid systems can be improved. Most importantly, the new international volunteer can prevent issues before they happen, via thoughtful planning, insight of the pros and cons of various development methods and by embracing best practices.

Everyone who has previously volunteered internationally or wants to in the future has the potential to be a new international volunteer. Previous international volunteers have inspired this movement by acting as new international volunteers and/or speaking out and educating others about what has and has not worked for them while volunteering. They assisted in this transformative process by frankly discussing errors they have made and witnessed, so that future volunteers do not make the same mistakes. This openness and willingness to improve started the foundation for building the new international volunteer concept from the ground up. However, those who wish to act as a new international volunteer do not need prior experience. In fact, someone becomes a new international volunteer simply by pledging to ensure that all volunteering they take part in will be ethical, sustainable and concretely help.

The phrase "global citizen" has been popularized in recent years. People who consider themselves global citizens can join the new international volunteer movement. The new international volunteer actually goes further than being a good global citizen, although that remains part of it. This new kind of international volunteer practices best development methods and rejects approaches that have not worked in the past. They distinguish themselves by their knowledge about why they volunteer and know how to maximize their efforts to help those around them. The new international volunteer pledges to do no harm (even accidently), prioritizes the people they volunteer for over their own interests and changes development norms through innovation and a commitment to sustainability. The new international volunteer knows how to utilize the unique role of the volunteer position to leave long-term and sustainable progress behind.

Volunteers need to transition to the new international volunteer way starting now. It seems paradoxical that the volunteering industry needs the new international volunteer in an age where people all over the world generally live better off than ever before. But the world needs them now, and for a few reasons. First, new international volunteering methods will maximize the efficiency and helpfulness of those who already act as international volunteers and aid workers. I have heard it said that an aid worker needs to work themselves out of a job. That happens by using best practices and by advocating for others to utilize them as well. Secondly, still to this day, some people around the world feel sick, hungry or thirsty, need shelter and education and live in war or disaster zones. New international volunteers have the potential to reach out to offer a helping hand. Their principles will help future volunteers maximize their impact while working with people who still need support.

New international volunteers can be beneficial everywhere around the globe. Every ongoing and future international volunteering project can somehow benefit, in ways either large or small, from the new international volunteer movement. New international volunteers can assist in every part of international volunteering organizations as well. They can contribute in all kinds of organizations, from small non-profits to multinational NGOs to voluntourism companies to governments that make international aid policies. New international volunteers can guide future aid efforts from the CEO's desk all the way to new volunteers in training. New international volunteer principles also apply to every type of international volunteering, from short-term trips to study abroad/volunteer abroad combos to long-term assignments. They additionally can enact best practices in trip specializations ranging from agriculture to medical clinics to post-natural disaster cleanup and animal welfare.

A Note on the Covid-19 Pandemic

The first sentence of this chapter states, "Before the pandemic, more people experienced a higher quality of life than ever before." But the pandemic changed everything. People around the world have suffered in many ways, from dying because of lack of a supply of ventilators, to suffering a painful illness for a long time, to grieving the loss of loved ones, to children missing out on an education and more.[49] This has directly translated to a drop in quality of life, a rise in poverty and we cannot say, at this moment in time, that statistically, more people in the world are better off than ever before.[50] While the pandemic continues, the goal of the new international volunteer is to help ease suffering, in what ways they can, and to help us again be able to say, as quickly as possible, that more people experience a higher quality of life than ever before.

The pandemic has highlighted systemic problems exacerbated by the pandemic in many societies around the world. It has taught us that everyone needs a safety net that includes unemployment insurance with a livable wage and quality free medical care, keeping in mind all the workers who work informally. Structural changes needed include guaranteeing equity between countries as well. The worldwide vaccine rollout has prioritized the richest countries first, to the detriment of others.[51]

Although so much in the world has changed, the methods for international volunteering that new international volunteers will use remain tried and true in most situations. (Readers will see throughout the book that it is noted when special care needs to be taken to adapt the methods to be Covid-safe.) The needs of people in host communities around the world, however, may very well have evolved during the ongoing pandemic. For instance, individuals who had escaped poverty may have become unemployed and fallen back into hard times. Communities may not have the medical care they need to handle surges in cases. Many people need food aid. In fact, in September 2021, the United Nations stated that food aid was running out for Afghanistan during its famine and asked for $600 million.[52]

International volunteers are needed now more than ever. Climate disasters will keep happening, refugees will seek safety from wars still being fought and Covid complicates those efforts. With that in mind, new international volunteers will need to consider some pandemic-specific principles when volunteering until the pandemic ends. First and foremost, volunteers cannot infect members of the host community by bringing Covid-19 with them. This will involve using Personal Protective Equipment (PPE), such as masks, and social distancing, but it could also include community-specific safety measures, such as quarantining.

For example, an employee at a non-profit told me that the towns in Honduras where they work are so remote that no one had been exposed to Covid-19 at that time, several months into the pandemic. No outsiders arrived in those towns, essentially creating a bubble. The non-profit's representatives are locals who have been working in the communities and making progress during the duration of the pandemic with minimal disruptions.

The safety measures to protect locals will also protect volunteers as well. International volunteering in this time cannot be successful if community members or volunteers contract Covid-19. For some volunteers, including myself, volunteering internationally effectively during the pandemic could mean volunteering virtually instead of in person.[53]

II

Making an Impact

The Difference Negative and Positive Project Methods Can Make

International volunteering projects can be seen as economic shocks that affect the outcome of locals' development efforts over time. Shocks, in the economic sense, can be defined as events that create a disruption that leads to change. These shocks can be either positive or negative, leading to improved or worsened development outcomes. This means that international volunteering can create positive shocks to improve economic outcomes in host communities. By using best development methods, international volunteers can avoid negative shocks that worsen development outcomes for host communities. In this way, international volunteer trips act like shocks because they have either a positive or negative impact on the host community's future. They also disrupt, in either a positive or negative way, locals' efforts to develop their own communities, businesses and economies.[1] Awareness of how much a project can affect people can change the current state of international volunteering by ensuring that each trip uses positive development methods. This positive or negative potential will be graphically represented in this section.

Each graph has the same characteristics that change slightly in each scenario. In every graph, the solid line represents the host community's economic growth trajectory prior to the contributions of volunteers. The unshaded circle attached to the end of the solid line signifies the final output before volunteers begin working in the host community. The shaded circle denotes the first amount of output that volunteers have contributed to. The dotted line that juts out of each shaded circle represents output after the contributions of volunteers over time.

In this graph, the upward sloping solid lines signifies that in this case, before volunteers arrive, locals have created a growing industry, business or economy. The growth has a positive development trajectory. In this situation, the international development volunteer project helped provide a positive boost to growth, strengthening the industry even more. Thanks to the positive effect of the international volunteering project, locals' output could increase significantly in the future. The dotted line could alternatively represent an improvement in quality of life or increased economic demand. This first graph signifies the ideal best-case scenario of the impact an international volunteer project can have on the host community. In real life, this graph could represent a successful agricultural project that volunteers assist with. If a productive cocoa farmer in Colombia asks international volunteers to repair the farmer's second plow, and they do so successfully, the second plow will increase the farmer's crop yield.

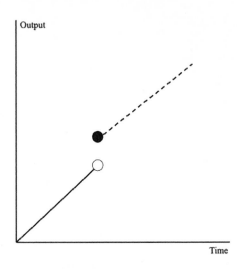

Positive international volunteering project.

In this graph, the solid line demonstrates a growing industry, business or economy on a positive development trajectory. However, in this case, the international development volunteer project did not work as intended, lowering growth and weakening the relevant industry. After the volunteers finished their project, output decreased. The dashed line could alternatively mean that quality of life decreased, or economic demand decreased. This graph embodies the worst-case scenario of the impact that international volunteer projects can have on the host

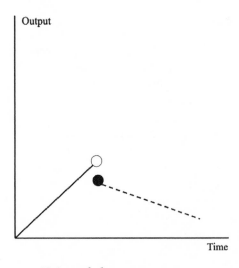

Unintended consequences.

community. To also use an agricultural example, this graph would represent a scenario where international development volunteers lowered demand for local corn crops by providing everyone in town with free corn for a year. No one in town would need to buy the farmer's corn so the demand for corn would significantly decrease, hurting the farmer's source of income.

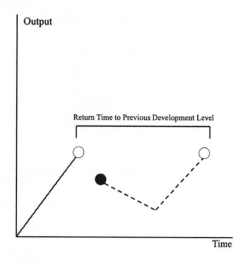

Return time to development in the long run.

This final graph also demonstrates the effort required to get an industry, business or economy in the host community back on track. It can take time for the economy to grow back to its original point before volunteers arrived. When locals eventually bring their community back to the original development level after some non-zero-time interval, it signifies *return time to the previous development level,* or return time to development for short. Return time to development shows the time and effort it takes for locals to fix volunteers' mistakes. It demonstrates the real impact unintended consequences have, causing the host community to endure a significant loss of time and economic output while they get the industry, business or economy back to pre-volunteering development levels.

In agriculture, if volunteers helped farmers implement a new cropping technique but it failed, the lowest point on the graph would represent the loss of crop yield. The return time to development would signify how long it would take to regain the original crop yield and the profits from it before volunteers introduced the hurtful cropping technique. The return time to development could have been spent increasing the crop yield instead of raising crop yields to their original level.

Unintended Consequences

Unintended consequences in international volunteering can occur if volunteers have the intention to help a community and improve lives through international development volunteering, but despite best efforts, hurt the host community. Well-meaning thoughts do not always lead to beneficial actions due to mismanagement, inappropriate development methods and focusing volunteering on the volunteer instead of on the community.[2] Locals may have to work even harder to move forward than they already needed to, making even short-term harm untenable.[3] In this way, helping only helps when the output concretely aids local communities. Because of this, only locals can unanimously and unwaveringly decide that a development project helps because they know their needs the best. To ensure that positive development will occur, volunteers have a responsibility to know what their impact will be and specifically how it will help.

I myself have made mistakes as an international development volunteer. Volunteering in Guatemala involved going to local elementary schools and reading a book to each class as a library representative. I hoped that I could encourage a love of reading while promoting the library to the kids. I read a Spanish fairy tale picture book that seemed popular with the children and told them they could read this book and others like it at the library in town. I wanted to pass on enthusiasm for reading, an unreasonable goal for one day, as a love of reading builds over a lifetime.

This prompted a cause for reflection. Did I possess a full awareness of my responsibilities as a volunteer? Or did I assume that simply by volunteering that everything would work out fine? What expectations did I have for volunteering success? Did I set the bar too low at "fine"? And why did my efforts have unintended consequences? In the end, I realized that I tried to do too much in the time I had. Even though the librarian asked a few of the elementary schools for permission for me to read to their students, I only had time to go to one classroom at one elementary school because of my study abroad commitments. This taught me the importance of scale when thinking about how to maximize time spent volunteering abroad.

Additionally, I attempted to center the experience on what I could do instead of what would be the most helpful. This did not elevate locals' development goals. With shorter trips, temptation can creep in to focus on what volunteers have time for instead of committing to more lengthy projects that locals could use assistance with. A good short-term trip marries both concepts to execute a to do list that can reasonably be completed within the time frame that volunteers will be working with. If volunteers concentrate on one or the other instead of both, then unintended consequences can happen quickly. Effective volunteers will understand the discrepancies between what needs to be done and what the group has time for. If new international volunteers can come up with a plan to address those discrepancies, then the short-term trip will model good development practices.[4]

If these trips still cannot guarantee that the project will create positive change, then volunteers can work with the host community to complete the needed project in phases with other volunteer groups. Or, if the project needs more consistent workers, then the host community and volunteers can work together to recruit more volunteers from the local community and from volunteers' network of family and friends. Since this requires planning, volunteers should communicate with the community prior to the start of the project. This allows everyone to have the same expectations for what work will be completed in the designated timeline. Not only will this facilitate smooth communication once volunteers arrive, but it will also ensure that enough people will volunteer to complete the project in a sustainable and high-quality way.

The dynamic of unintended consequences can be remedied by volunteers who actively work to cultivate sustainable development practices when they volunteer internationally. This begins with setting a high bar for quality standards that prioritize communicating with the community above all. Prior communication and research will allow volunteers to educate themselves on the particular obstacles a project will bring and how to overcome those with good development methods. However, when helping could have unintended consequences mid-project, volunteers should stop what they are doing immediately and solicit the local community for advice, explaining the difficulties they face. Then the issue needs to be fixed by approaching volunteering differently and implementing advice the host community gives to correct the problem. Being accurate and thinking ahead can make the difference between volunteering that helps or has unintended consequences.

Volunteers can fuel positive change by volunteering where locals need them to. When I volunteered at a library in Guatemala, I learned why I should volunteer where I am asked, instead of going where I decide. The government does not usually run libraries in Guatemala; banks run them. Practically, this means that libraries have a profit mandate. To make a profit, banks install libraries only in the most populous towns with a university and many schools. The library I volunteered in had one employee. Children checked out books for school projects or borrowed a textbook to do homework. I never saw any adults as patrons in the library. No one could leave the library with a book—they all stayed at the library permanently. The library had one copy of each book; therefore, it had to stay in the building so every student had a chance to use it each night to do their homework. I found this setup to be markedly different from libraries I frequented at home.

Also, the Guatemalan library never had volunteers before me. To volunteer I had to get permission from the mayor, who did not quite see the point of me volunteering, but let me do it anyway. To be fair, I did not know what I was doing either. At home I had always volunteered at my local library for as long as I could remember. I worked my way up to the position of Teen Advisory Board President during middle school, I put on programs like a murder mystery night, I hosted discussions about popular books and I taught young English as a Second Language (ESL) learners how to read in English and in Spanish.

To me, because these experiences felt central to my life, the library seemed like a natural place to start volunteering at in Guatemala. I wanted to help, and I felt comfortable assisting at the library, even if this felt like only a vague notion at the time. I think I assumed that people would need help everywhere and that I could just insert myself where it felt best to me. Volunteering internationally mistakenly felt like a conga line at a middle school dance—inevitable and I could jump in at will. At this time, I thought generally about volunteering internationally and I thought of it in terms of myself. As I specified my ideas about volunteering at the library, I aimed to assist people with finding and checking out books (an impossibility), to help kids with their homework and to teach English classes. Despite this plan, the library essentially did not need a volunteer. Kids did their homework completely independently, and knew where to find their books. Their self-reliance taught me the importance of logistics as a volunteer. It additionally showed me how to step back and listen instead of throwing myself into an unknown situation as a leader on a mission, with a rather inflexible plan. If I would have asked how I could help the library instead of telling how I was going to help at the library, then I could have learned right away that I did not need to assist in this capacity.

When volunteers choose to volunteer where locals need them to instead of where they decide to volunteer at themselves, they can prevent unintended consequences. They can ensure that they spend their time meeting real needs in the host community, rather than designing tasks that they hope will help, as I did. Ideally, volunteers will take an interest in volunteering where locals need them to, because the overlap can create the best outcomes for volunteers and for the host community. The needs of not only volunteers, but also of the host community where volunteers will work, matter. When volunteers choose to volunteer where locals ask, then the host community's needs can most readily be met.

Best volunteering methods can allow new international volunteers to make solid progress on eliminating poverty, increasing quality of life and making the world a better place to live. New international volunteers care about more than volunteering—they also care about the well-being of the people they work with, the Earth and the long-term impact they make. These knowledgeable professionals will deliver high quality work that everyone can take pride in. The new international volunteer movement guides people to functional and ethical volunteering methods. Together we can stop and even reverse the damage done by harmful volunteering. Even one project with new international volunteers makes an impact on the quality of life of the homestay community. Just one new international volunteer on a trip with volunteers who do not know best practices can boost the team's quality of work by educating the rest of the team about how to do the project well.

Best Development Tools vs Best Development Practices

This graph illustrates common pitfalls that volunteers could face that prevent development success. To be successful, the new international volunteer must stay within Quadrant I on the graph. Quadrant I represents both quality and helpful development tools (best practices) and also development solutions (the project methods). The x-axis on the graph represents development tools. Development tools include best practices, such as sustainability, ethics, women and minority inclusion and letting locals lead and create. The y-axis denotes development solutions. Development solutions encompass the development methods that volunteers will use. Relevant techniques include development versus relief, education and microfinance, donations, and committing to solutions that will still function well in the long term. If a development project does not already meet Quadrant I criteria, then moving from either Quadrants II, III, or IV to Quadrant I and staying there becomes volunteers' goal.

Quadrant I, as mentioned above, denotes the intersection of good development tools with good development solutions. Quadrant I constitutes success because these projects start with

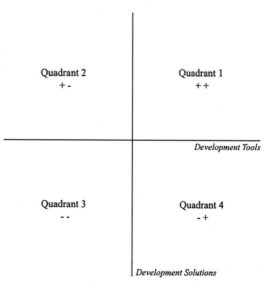

Best development tools vs. best development practices.

great ideas and volunteers implement them well. Imagine a group of volunteers who will go abroad to assist with installing a new microgrid. The microgrid will give electricity to a town that previously had none. A good project that falls within the realm of Quadrant I would be if the team helped install a microgrid that includes solar panels and a battery to capture and store any extra energy. The Quadrant I project, using both good development tools and solutions, would, in the process, create a few jobs for technicians. The battery and solar panels would be made locally with readily available materials. Since volunteers locally sourced the parts, then locals can easily fix it. Locals would find the system to be useful in the short term and a reliable source of electricity in the long run. A microgrid international volunteer project like this would be a true partnership between local mechanics, residents and volunteers.

Quadrant II still boasts strong development solutions, but volunteers do not implement the good ideas with best practices. In other words, the project has a sound premise but lacks in implementation. In order to move to Quadrant I, volunteers should try to create more sustainable, inclusive, ethical and local-led solutions. In an international volunteer microgrid project, a Quadrant II project would hypothetically occur if the solar panels would work well, but volunteers manufacture them in their home country and locals cannot replicate them with available materials. Although solar panels power the microgrid at first, when the grid inevitably breaks, the host community will either need to improvise with other, possibly non-clean energy options to source their electricity, or go without like they did before the microgrid project.

Quadrant III represents the farthest quadrant from international volunteering success. A project in Quadrant III would have inappropriate development solutions implemented without best practices. When dealing with a Quadrant III project, volunteers need to go back to the drawing board of ideas to assess the weaknesses and eliminate them. Checking with locals to determine best technology and best practices for the project will help move the project toward Quadrant I. A microgrid project in Quadrant III would have volunteers set up a microgrid based on wind turbines in an area only windy during a part of the year. The corresponding battery would not be capable of storing enough excess energy to meet the host community's demand during non-windy times. This project does not accurately assess locals' energy needs and does not keep sustainability in mind.

Quadrant IV has Quadrant II's opposite traits. Rather than good development solutions but bad development tools, Quadrant IV has inappropriate development solutions implemented with best practices. Projects in Quadrant IV usually mean that volunteers have the right intentions but the main project method needs improvement. To get a Quadrant IV project into Quadrant I, volunteers can change the approach to the development methods the project will use. Volunteers participating in a Quadrant IV project would have great practices, such as training locals to repair and maintain the microgrid and source the microgrid parts locally. They would be on the right track. However, they would choose the wrong technology, like hydropower in an insufficiently large body of water. Thus, the overall development solution would not maximize its potential to be helpful.

III

Success

Measuring Success

Volunteers want to facilitate solutions to problems that compelled them to assist. Traditionally, volunteers consider projects to be successful based on a finished project's final numbers. In fact, the international volunteer industry often relies on reporting final figures since they universally measure projects that vary so much in scope, aim and location. Many international volunteers want to volunteer in order to help achieve commonly cited metrics, such as getting everyone to $1.90 a day or hitting the top level of the Hierarchy of Needs Pyramid. In fact, the United Nations made their first Sustainable Development Goal to live in a world without poverty. The UN aims to reduce the number of people living in poverty by half by 2030.[1]

Most people have heard of the World Bank's International Poverty Line as a common way to measure poverty. The International Poverty Line defines poverty as people living with less than $1.90 a day in low income countries, $3.20 a day in lower middle-income countries, $5.50 a day in upper middle-income countries and $21.70 a day in high income countries. This current system has been improved because it now considers many levels of poverty instead of just one. Also, the International Poverty Line used to be a single metric of $1.25 a day, and then changed to $1.90 a day to adjust to the strengthened dollar. Now it differentiates between poverty lines in low, middle- and high-income countries.[2] People criticized the old method because those who fell just above the international poverty line of $1.25 a day still experienced poverty, but tended to get overlooked.[3] However, this method's advantage lies in its ability to quantify poverty. Societies can use the number as a baseline for ending extreme poverty. By revising the international poverty line to include different numbers for different countries, the World Bank hoped to give more specific and applicable metrics to apply to more people.

A second measurement system stems from psychology: Abraham

Maslow's Hierarchy of Needs, often depicted in a pyramid shape. Maslow based his system on the idea that people have more urgent needs than others and that less urgent needs cannot be taken care of while the most urgent remain unfulfilled. Maslow posturized that most urgent needs must be taken care of before the next most urgent needs can be addressed too. The most urgent biologic needs like food and shelter sit at the bottom of the pyramid. Safety and security, including physical safety but also economic safety as well, follow biologic needs. Friendship, love and being part of a group come next; then esteem, such as self-esteem and respect from others, follow. Finally, the top has self-actualization, such as fulfilling one's potential, as the least urgent need. The Hierarchy of Needs Pyramid can be applied in international volunteering by considering someone's place on the pyramid to help them boost up to the next level of the pyramid, and the next after that. This more holistic method can be more comprehensive than reducing poverty to a single number, but it does not account for people who have shelter but not food, for example.[4]

The common systems used to measure poverty help but can be improved to be more comprehensive and well rounded. Poverty cannot be fully measured by these common methods because they do not paint the entire picture of what people suffer and would like to change. Poverty encapsulates more than how much money a person makes or their unfulfilled needs. It also includes a lack of opportunity and how that impacts lifestyle. Similarly, in international volunteering a project's final numbers and statistics may not be the best gauge of success. This is because a number cannot include all the variables needed to determine success, such as sustainability and quality. An international volunteer project can report large final numbers saying it gave x amount of something to Y people, but the entire project could be based on bad development practices, and the x can be hurting Y people. In this way, a number or statistic cannot tell the quality of the things volunteers completed nor how locals feel about them (if they find them helpful) nor how the things completed will hold up in the long term.

Some international volunteering programs that focus mostly on the numbers revolve around volunteers congregating in a certain place for a short time, like packaging meals for international distribution. An event of this type only lasts an afternoon, but the x number of volunteers could package 18,000 meals during that time. The 18,000 meals packaged does not necessarily equate to an international volunteering success, however, because it does not help solve the bigger problem of food insecurity in the area where the food will be delivered. After people eat the 18,000 meals then food insecurity will be a problem again. Even if more and more food shipments get sent to them, eventually they cannot be sent anymore or there could be problems with receiving shipments, leaving people hungry. Instead, if the program revolved around helping international communities to achieve food security while the initial meals get delivered, it would provide both temporary and permanent relief. Reaching permanent relief would be a true international volunteering success that does not focus on quantifiable statistics.

Also, a project's final numbers say nothing about the quality of the results. Therefore, the new international volunteer looks beyond the numbers to determine the quality of the results of the project. Hypothetically, if an international volunteering group travels to Panama, bringing building materials with them, and builds ten houses in seven days for twenty Panamanians, their endeavor may not necessarily be successful. It sounds like a success because volunteers built ten houses in seven days. However, the materials used to build the houses will sooner or later wear down and break. Replacement parts might not be available locally. Since volunteers built so many houses so quickly, they may not have been built to last. Additionally, by bringing building materials with them, volunteers took away business for the local builders. The building materials may also not adapt well to the Panamanian climate. Since traditional results do not always indicate that success has been achieved, the international volunteer industry needs to scrutinize each project's results. Host communities need quality international development projects that utilize sustainability and ethics.

I found success with the English lesson I taught at the library in Guatemala by giving accurate and helpful answers to Guatemalans' questions about the English language. The English lesson attendees spent the evening asking me their burning questions about English. People did not want me to teach the basics, an impossible task for a two-hour time slot. Participants wanted to see how to expand their vocabulary, how to use various words correctly, and to figure out what certain words mean in a larger cultural context. As a Spanish tutor and former English as a Second Language volunteer, I felt qualified to answer these questions. For example, based on student questions, I taught an example about the lack of gender notation when people talk about pets in English. We do not say *el perro macho*, or male dog, usually, but rather we use the gender pronoun he for a male dog, as we would use with a human. The language difference brought about an intense discussion about how the English language notates our cultural intimacy with household pets in a way that has a different cultural and lingual meaning in Spanish. Even though teaching an English lesson in Spanish may not be quantified as a traditional success, I counted it as a success in a nontraditional way. I used best practices, such as being qualified and not over committing to do more than the time slot allowed. I also defined success as that at the end of the night no one had any additional questions. Success additionally came from the fact that we had an engaging discussion where we all learned from each other and participated in a cross-cultural exchange of ideas and insights.

Success by numbers does work in some specific situations. Guinea Worm, for instance, can be classified as a Neglected Infectious Disease, caused by a parasite that harms their human hosts. Since the Carter Center has focused on eradicating it, Guinea Worm has achieved 99.99 percent world eradication, down to 15 known people with the parasite in 2021. They started the countdown from a high of 3.5 million people in 1986. By focusing on the numbers, the Carter Center could track outbreaks in various locations and target their eradication strategy to those areas.[5]

If an international volunteer project has achieved its stated goal, then it can be quantified as a success. Instead of reporting final numbers, success can be determined by whether volunteers met the goal by the end of a deadline or not. This method benefits abstract projects that do not have final numbers they can report. However, this success measurement can still have flaws. If volunteers set a lofty, impractical or unsustainable goal, but still meet it, then the project would not actually be successful despite completing the goal. Donors who back international volunteer projects can perpetuate this standard of success. Donors can put external pressure to produce quantifiable results, measured by goal achievement. Good pressure can act as motivation to get the job done without wasting donors' money. Donors often give more money as positive reinforcement when volunteer organizations meet certain goals.

However, if donors apply too much pressure, then people can take shortcuts and cut corners to meet the goal. This hurts the host community as a consequence. Donors like to see success measured as results produced to ensure organizations spend their money wisely. But the current mainstream donor financial system can skew the international development industry's standards of success. International volunteers sometimes focus on results to keep donors happy and to continue getting money from them to finance more development work. Without donors, many international development organizations could not fund staff or buy supplies, so they recognize the importance of demonstrating success to donors. Donors may not continue to fund an organization that does not appear successful by traditional metrics. Donors could divest from an organization or project that seems like a waste of money. With limited funds, donors must allocate them in a way that makes a maximum impact for their investment. This can disincentivize donors to shy away from projects with intangible results or projects that demonstrate returns only in the long term.[6]

Donors' motivation to see goals met and measure success works with short-term projects that provide quick wins for everyone involved.

However, long-term international volunteering projects constitute a fundamental part of development. Development does not happen overnight, so goals for a long-term project may not come to fruition for a while. If results can be expected in the long term then volunteers and donors cannot judge the project's success by the results seen in the short term. It stands to reason that if a project's structure aims to create long-term change, then success may happen in the long term too. Some projects could be discounted as a failure because they did not show success during the short term, while actually producing successful outcomes in the long run.[7] This means that donors could use different metrics to evaluate the success of a project.

Success in a long-term project can be measured in the short term by examining how much progress has been made at various times. A long-term project often has several phases that get completed along the way. Each milestone completed could be considered success in the short term. For example, Doctors Without Borders runs a hospital in Jordan that focuses on healing people injured by warfare in the Middle East. The hospital emphasizes holistic health, including physical and mental health. Since 2006, the hospital has cared for many long-term patients, who tend to undergo multiple rounds of surgery. Mental health issues also take a long time to heal. Every surgery and mental health therapy session gets each person closer to healing and gives patients back greater levels of mobility and independence. In this way, the hospital has been successful at various points in the short term by hitting milestones that add up in the long term. Each surgery, counseling and physical therapy session a patient goes through in the short term can be counted as successes for the hospital. Together they lead to the long-term goal of rehabilitating the patient. After patients heal, the hospital achieves long-term success by helping them get well enough to leave the hospital. Even the hospital itself, as it treats each patient and finds new solutions to treat infections, has short-term wins that lead to long-term quality success as a specialized healthcare provider.[8]

Personalized Success Metric

A project can be a success with a nontraditional impact. The intangible, unquantifiable results that happen when caring for someone or launching a long-term project can be profound yet unmeasurable. This means that the new international volunteer and host community need an alternative way to declare an international development project a success. An alternative would consider intangible and difficult to quantify results. Therefore, international volunteering success can be defined as the quality of the process, instead of the quantity of the results. If volunteers and donors define international development success through the quality of the process, then a successful project will be appropriate, sustainable and follow ethical practices.

The following system carves out a workable way to quantify this new measure of international volunteering success. It targets what specifically needs to be done to bring every category to fair, good or great. This method targets needs with precision. It recognizes that different people within the same community need distinctive things. It also acknowledges that different towns face disparate obstacles. When a system can be used to differentiate between family units, the community and the region as a whole, then each individual can receive the attention they deserve. When volunteers focus on assisting households to meet their specific needs, it can revolutionize volunteering methods by aiming to help what people care about the most. In order to be precise and target individual needs, the scale has several categories, from poor to great. The rows comprise the major tenets of development, i.e., the chief components of development and economic progress. Economic growth cannot succeed without these categories at the core. Many categories, like freedom from slavery, do not need elaboration, but the categories that do can be found in the following paragraphs.

	Poverty		Developing	Mostly Developed	
	Poor	*Inadequate*	*Fair*	*Good*	*Great*
Job Market					
Transportation					
Market Access					
Energy Access					
Property Ownership					
Education					
Shelter					
Healthcare					
Potable Water					
Food					
Free from Slavery					
Clothing					
Safety					
Bathroom Access					
Child Labor					
Emergency Services					
Public Sanitation					

The local economy cultivates the ecosystem of development. A good job market gives people consistent employment with fair pay and fulfilling work. Employment contributes to society in a larger way, whether by working at a corporation that contributes to overall GDP, as the government which provides services to citizens, as farmers that feed people, as vendors that sell individuals things they need, or as people who raise children, etc.

Transportation ability and energy access directly help with market access, and market access allows the economy to grow. Transportation ability considers the state of the roads, the cost of vehicles, the propensity for large trucks to be able to traverse the roads, and the reliability and safety of roads. It also includes access to roads, such as discounting a too expensive toll road that acts as a barrier to entry for some people. Economic growth relies on the ability to use transportation to meet the needs of the people and to provide physical access to market. To test how transportation ability affects economic growth, ask: Do the roads connect to major places where people can buy and sell goods? Can people get there reliably, affordably and safely?

Market access drives the local economy. It permits people, goods and services created in the local economy to meet competitive prices in the region. Lack of access will limit the scope of economic growth because goods will not potentially reach new consumers, disallowing the customer base to grow. Many rural communities have limited market access because they live far away from the main market areas in the region or country. They could also lack reliable ways to bring their goods to the distant markets, creating economic isolation. Additionally, abolition of child labor majorly drives progress and economic growth. Child labor takes young individuals away from school and injects them into the work force. This will leave lasting and depressed educational levels throughout the community for the foreseeable future.[9]

Similarly, energy needs to be reliable and cost effective for true and universal access. The economy cannot grow based on temporary or intermittent energy access. Electricity access can come via the traditional grid, a community microgrid or a household grid from a solar panel on the roof. Energy also needs to be clean because without clean energy, the community will have to deal with the negative externalities of climate change and expensive and polluting energy.

Property rights legally allow individuals to build economic and financial assets. Property rights define ownership and thus provide a basis for growth for any nation or community. Throughout history, people have had to farm land they do not own, using seed and fertilizer they bought themselves to eke out a meager profit which they then have to spend at a store landowners own. Landowners often kept people in a cycle of working land they do not own by forcing them into debt over the farming materials and supplies they bought. Property ownership stimulates entrepreneurship and economic independence—an impossibility under a land renting latifundial-like scheme.[10]

Many people have access to running water but not to potable water. Many other people do not have in-home water at all. Drinking unclean water can lead to parasite ingestion and also cause many illnesses, depending on the water source. Similarly, food needs to be affordable and plentiful, comprised of a diet rich in vitamins, minerals and protein. Without a well-rounded diet, children and adults can suffer from vitamin deficiency, stunted growth and malnutrition.[11]

Without safety, not much else can be done economically. Safety provides an environment for businesses to thrive in and stability for the workforce. An unsafe area causes major stress and trauma to the community. Each locale needs to be able to enforce the rule of law. Emergency service access comprises the ability to quickly reach police, firefighters and emergency healthcare workers, such as ambulance personnel. Without emergency services, people become vulnerable to calamities, many of which emergency services can mitigate. A lack of emergency services can contribute to a breakdown of the rule of law, preventable death from injuries and fire, along with destruction of properties from crime and fire.[12]

Public sanitation can be seen as a communal good that benefits the entire community. The state of the streets can impact economic growth. For example, dirty streets create a sanitation problem and a health hazard. Dirty streets can also be inaccessible when it rains and often lack proper drainage and sewage disposal. Economically, dirty streets can be a burden for businesses if they cannot properly operate due to bad city sanitation. Garbage collection can also be an issue if garbage overflows in the street. Exposed garbage attracts vermin, smells bad and negatively affects health.[13]

* * *

I am now going to give an example for a household in the town of San Lucas Tolimán, Guatemala, where I studied abroad in the summer of 2013. In an effort to protect privacy, this example will not be of any particular household, but a composite of households in the town. Afterward, I will explain disparities between households within the community.

Job Market—Fair

The job market for the composite household in San Lucas can be labeled as fair. Most people can find employment, but it can often be unsteady, temporary, and a part of the gig, or informal, economy. Many people leave San Lucas during the work week to teach in the surrounding area, or to go to a steady job in Guatemala City. These people return to their families in San Lucas on the weekends. Many persons seek to supplement their income through working multiple jobs and selling items out of their houses. Major sources of employment include the town market, agriculture, housework, and in education and transportation.

Transportation Ability—Inadequate

Many locals consider transportation to be the biggest barrier to economic growth in San Lucas. San Lucas, located on the far side of Lake Atitlán, has only one main road that connects it to other towns on the lake. This road cannot accommodate eighteen-wheeler trucks due to its small width and many mountainous turns. Large trucks could import goods from other areas of Guatemala and export goods from San Lucas to major markets throughout Guatemala and internationally if roads allowed them access. Additionally, the road can be dangerous to traverse during the rainy season as mudslides can cause injury and death. If San Lucas had a better way to connect itself physically to the rest of Guatemala, it could experience major economic growth.

Market Access—Inadequate

The lack of transportation ability severely limits San Lucas' market access. Residents mostly market their goods and services to others in the town. To a lesser, but still crucial, extent, some sell products to the surrounding towns on the lake. Many people who live in San Lucas travel by car to other major towns between the lake and the capitol in order to shop. Goods can only be brought in and taken out of San Lucas in small batches, since only small vehicles can safely navigate the road. Many townspeople take only the goods that they can carry with them each day on the public buses and boats. They sell them in nearby towns, particularly towns that attract more tourists, like Panajachel.

Energy Access—Good

San Lucas has a strong grid with electricity access for each house and business. The electricity access satisfactorily powers multiple appliances in each room of every house. Many families have household internet and computers, and those without frequent several public internet cafes around town.

Property Access—Great

Families own most property in San Lucas instead of large shareholders. Most people who farm work the land that they own.

Education—Fair

The education quality differs by school in San Lucas. Locals generally believe that the private schools offer the best education and educational resources for students. However, many families cannot afford the cost of private school tuition. In the public schools, children learn to read and write, but the quality of education varies from teacher to teacher and school to school. Many children leave school after the elementary level, and many do not complete middle or high school. Teachers only need to have a high school education, and not a college degree, to be qualified to teach.

Shelter—Good

Everyone has shelter in San Lucas. Each home has space to cook and do laundry, and people generally do not live in crowded conditions. Locals see home as a center for family life, and most homes have a designated family dining area and living room. Many homes have multi-generational family members living together. However, some homes are not made with long-lasting materials while others have dirt floors.

Healthcare—Inadequate

People do not have many health insurance options, so they deal with overcrowded, distant and under par public health services. Many people in San Lucas do not like the quality of healthcare. Some choose to pay for private hospitals if needed. International volunteers run healthcare clinics but these have unreliable quality. The town needs more and better doctors, along with better quality public healthcare workers and medical facilities.

Potable Water Access—Poor

Every family in San Lucas has access to unpotable tap water. Locals must pay private companies separately to get potable water delivered in jugs to their homes. Some families choose to purchase filters for the unpotable tap water but need to replace the filter frequently, which can be prohibitively expensive. The government does not purify the tap water sourced from Lake Atitlán, one of the most polluted lakes on Earth. Drinking the tap water can cause a variety of health problems, although lifelong San Lucas residents have more of an immunity to the water than visitors do. The government shuts off water access at unpredictable times during the day and night. Even after purchasing potable drinking water, families do not have ways to make water from showers and sinks potable.

Food—Great

Most everyone finds corn tortillas, the main food staple, very affordable and easy to make or purchase in San Lucas. Most families eat meat, such as beef or chicken, once a day, for lunch—the biggest meal of the day. People regularly purchase fruit and vegetables at affordable prices from the market. San Lucas has many bakeries that most families buy breads from daily.

Free from Slavery—Great

San Lucas has no known cases of slavery, indentured servitude or human trafficking, based on the research I conducted.

Clothing—Great

Almost everyone finds clothing to be very affordable and readily available in the San Lucas market. People in San Lucas tend to wear traditional Mayan clothing made by women and sold in the market. Alternatively, they purchase used clothing from America that sellers buy at wholesale prices and sell cheaply. Many clothing sellers set up shop in the market, and thus have a healthy competition that keeps clothing prices down.

Safety—Fair

Organized crime is not a major problem, but crime occurs in many forms. Locals feel safe to walk alone in town during the day and in groups at night. Many people go out at night to watch sporting events, such as soccer and basketball, or to spend time at the edge of the lake. Families guard their houses with barbed wire fences, guard dogs and steel doors, due to a lack of police presence. Corruption runs rampant.

Bathroom Access—Great

Every house has indoor plumbing and the town has an adequate sanitation system.

Emergency Services—Poor

San Lucas does not have a 911 or equivalent. Police rarely patrol the town and if an emergency occurs, many people will hire a driver to take a loved one to the hospital in a nearby town, because ambulances can be too expensive and slow to arrive, if available at all.

Child Labor—Great
(for this household)

Most children in San Lucas do not work and instead go to school. Some help around the house and in the fields after school, but many also play sports and spend time with friends and family and do homework in their spare time. Some children in other households, however, work in the fields instead of going to school.

Public Sanitation—Inadequate

Streets in San Lucas tend to be dirty and have trash on them. During the rainy season, locals cannot traverse most streets during storms, bringing daily life to a halt until the rain stops. The streets do not have gutters for rainwater to pass into. San Lucas also has an abundance of street dogs, leading to feces and carcasses in the streets.

Discrepancies exist within the town of San Lucas, as within every town. I created this scale to reduce differences within communities and so that volunteers can help each household meet their needs. Needs vary from house to house, family to family. However, improvements to major categories can benefit the entire community. For instance, if one household connects to the grid, it will be easier for other neighboring houses to connect too.

Within the community of San Lucas, in some households, child labor ranks as poor. Some parents feel that their children can better provide for the household by working instead of going to school. Education can range from inadequate to fair depending on which school a child attends. In some schools, children come out knowing only the very basics of reading, writing and math. Many parents in San Lucas choose to forgo public schools and send their children to private school instead, in an effort to give them the best education possible.

Many households in the area experience food security but some do not. To help alleviate this, the schools provide breakfast and lunch to students. Some parents instruct their children to work instead of going to school because more children working on the farm can produce more food for their families. Based on interviews I conducted, a correlation exists between child labor and food insecurity in San Lucas.

Finally, transportation access ranges from household to household, depending on the household's transportation needs and what methods of transportation they have available to them. Public transportation includes bus, boat and riding in the back of a pickup truck. The government does not run public transportation. Rather, individual entrepreneurs own their vehicles or boats and charge passengers a fee. For some families, this transportation suffices, but for others, particularly agricultural workers who sell their own food, the cost of purchasing a vehicle to drive the crops to various markets outside San Lucas can be a large barrier to entry.

The new international volunteer must justify the category ratings. Volunteers can gather quality information for the scale by surveying people, conducting interviews, doing research, reading the local news, etc. If volunteers do not justify their ratings, then they can be subjective and arbitrary. This can be avoided if volunteers explain why they chose each rating and give evidence to support them. For the scale to be accurate, locals can rate instead of volunteers.

Local Feedback

International volunteers can gauge their success by asking the host community for frequent feedback. The opinion of locals matters most with every aspect of an international volunteer project. Locals will be the ones who will make use of the final product a project creates. In other words, only members of the host community can unanimously and unwaveringly decide that a volunteer project actually helps in the intended way because they know their needs the best. After testing the volunteer project, local community members will decide how it affects their lives and if the project constitutes an overall worthy investment. Success can be measured by the quality of the benefits that the volunteer project adds to their lives.

An international volunteer project has a better chance of success when volunteers talk with locals to find out about their needs before work on the project begins. Then the project can focus on meeting those needs. Well-meaning volunteers can lack a full understanding of the problems at hand but can understand them when they solicit candid feedback from locals.

Therefore, the new international volunteer can use a survey to determine success of international development projects. The survey below conveys the host community's satisfaction (or lack thereof) to volunteers and can be adapted to solicit feedback for any international volunteering project. Completed surveys by members of the host community helps volunteers to understand the consequences, positive or negative, of their actions on the people they try to help. Sometimes it can be difficult to understand the cause and effect of one's own work while in the middle of it. The people who will be impacted by the work will have a much better and fuller understanding of the potential consequences and effects of the work on their lives, community and economy. Distributing a survey to locals will allow volunteers to better assist because they can adapt to any feedback in real time.

The new international volunteer understands that they cannot fix problems that they do not know about, and so they make every effort to understand all current and potential problems an international volunteer project might have in order to fix them. Troubleshooting with locals who use the services or products from an international development project helps volunteers understand problems the best. Volunteers have a certain perspective on the project that they help with, which can be limiting. Locals have a different perspective and vantage point of the potential benefits, pitfalls and improvements of the project. A holistic perspective from all possible viewpoints will allow volunteers to minimize and eliminate problems that prevent success.

This survey, unlike the rubric above, does not include a scale by which to judge each category because the scale should be applicable to each unique project and host community. The scale volunteers choose for the survey should be familiar, comfortable and user-friendly for everyone involved. The rubric will need to be translated to each applicable language spoken in the host community. Volunteers can discuss with locals whether it would be beneficial to change the wording of the survey to make it specific to the situation. For example, perhaps instead of asking locals if the project seems high-quality or not, the question could be phrased as "Do you think the doctor gave you a quality diagnosis?" or "How satisfied do you feel about the doctor's examination and prognosis?" This encourages each response to be as specific as possible. The scale could differ to meet the needs of the project, such as choosing one of the following: Very Satisfied, Somewhat Satisfied, Neither Satisfied nor Dissatisfied, Somewhat Dissatisfied or Very Dissatisfied, with the option to write-in what went well and what did not. Or, if appropriate, the scale could be Yes or No. Some people who have vision problems, differently abled individuals or those who cannot read could need the survey read out loud to them in a confidential setting.

Survey Categories

1. Usefulness
2. Beautification
3. Reliability
4. Quality
5. Added-Value
6. Accessibility
7. Safety
8. Understanding
9. Dignity
10. Friendliness

The survey includes ten main categories volunteers can report on. A good survey will ask questions about each category to make sure that each one gets addressed. Sometimes each category will need just one general question (such as "Is the project useful?") but other times, in order to determine the project's usefulness, the survey will need to ask several questions relating to different aspects of usefulness. This allows differentiation between very useful, somewhat useful, or only useful in certain aspects. For instance, if a project provides multiple services, then in order to determine overall usefulness, the survey would need to ask questions about the usefulness of each service. I have compiled a list of general survey questions for each category below.

General Sample Survey

Category	General Questions
Usefulness	Is the project useful to you?
Beautification	Does the project look nice?
Reliability	Can you and your family rely on this project? Is it consistent?
Quality	Is the project high quality? Does it serve its purpose?
Added-Value	Does this project make your life better in any way? If yes, how so?
Accessibility	Can you and your family easily access this project whenever you need to?
Safety	Do you feel safe with this project?
Understanding	Do volunteers answer all your questions? Do you know everything you need to know about this project?
Dignity	Do volunteers always treat you and your family with dignity and respect?
Friendliness	Are volunteers always friendly and obliging to you and your family? Do you feel comfortable using the project?

Usefulness—Do you find the project useful?

It may be helpful to ask how survey respondents find the survey useful to ensure the project's aims are being fulfilled. Also, it can be helpful to know if some individuals find the project useful for different reasons than others. The data collected from these questions can allow volunteers to maximize usefulness or pivot if needed.

Beautification—Does the project look nice?

Beautification puts the icing on the cake of an international volunteer project. Beautification exemplifies the adage "If you are going to do something, do it right." Beautification applies mostly to construction focused international volunteering projects. Some projects revolve entirely around the concept of beautification, like projects that clean up trash. Beautification remains important for two reasons: it shows pride, and volunteers should take pride in the work that they do. Secondly, everyone deserves a nice community to live in. Since volunteers often participate in projects that add to the community in some way, it would be nice if they could contribute to the community through beautification. Sometimes beautification can be as simple as a new coat of paint or keeping a space clean and bright. A beautiful place evokes feelings of welcome and comfort, and volunteers want that for the people who will be partaking in the project's final product.

Reliability—Can you and your family rely on this project? Do you find the services consistent?

This question is similar to the usefulness question above, but it goes a step further. For instance, the project may be useful but may need improvements with reliability. For example, with the medical clinic, the clinic's services may be useful, but farmers may not be able to rely on the clinic due to the hours it is open during the day. By asking this question, volunteers have the potential to make their work as helpful as possible by making it reliable for as many community members as possible, even if it means adding more hours to the daily schedule.

Quality—Do you think the project is high quality? Does it serve its purpose?

Many important aspects in a volunteer project revolve around maximizing quality. A high-quality, effective and efficient project will make the most difference in peoples' lives. If a project is useful and reliable, but not of the highest quality, then there is still room for improvement. By asking about usefulness, quality and reliability together, the survey paints a fuller picture of how the project functions.

Added-value—Does this project make your life better in any way?

Added-value can essentially act as a litmus test to see how useful a project can be in people's lives and to the host community as a whole. Added-value or value-add means that the project creates something helpful that did not exist before. It could be something intangible, like making a process more efficient or the free time a person now has because of efficiency. Or it could be something tangible, like a healthcare service.

Accessibility—Can you and your family easily access the project whenever you need to?

Accessibility means that everyone can use the project, not just select people. An accessible project accommodates people's needs and eliminates obstacles to people using the project. For instance, each building should have disability access. A clinic should accommodate the schedules of second and third shift workers who need it. There should be no barriers to use.

Safety—Do you feel safe with this project?

Safety should be a priority. If needed, volunteers can ask third parties like a security firm or a building inspector for help in making a project safe. In many cases, safety can be built into the plans for a project, such as in the physical design or by purchasing an item, like a backup generator for a medical clinic.

Understanding—Do volunteers answer all of your questions? Do you know everything you need to know about the project?

Understanding in this context means that locals know what volunteers do. Volunteers need to be ethical and aboveboard by providing access to information about the details of the project to the host community. The project should be transparent and use an outside auditor for the project's finances. A project should also promote understanding to individuals, in addition to the entire host community. Volunteers need to make a point to take all the necessary time to explain everything to locals and answer all questions they may have, fully and completely. This can be a problem at medical clinics where volunteer doctors do not answer all of their patient's questions.

Dignity—Do volunteers always treat you and your family with dignity and respect?

Dignity can sometimes be a problem on international development trips if volunteers accidently insult locals. This can happen either if volunteers unintentionally say something insulting, or if the structure of the project offends locals. An insulting project can harm the trust between locals and volunteers. To prevent this, volunteers can work with locals side by side on the creation and implementation of the project. Many times, if a project insults, it does so accidently when volunteers create and execute the project without accounting for cross-cultural differences or local perspectives.[14]

Friendliness—Do volunteers always act friendly and obliging to you and your family? Do you feel comfortable using the project?

When volunteers act friendly and accommodating, locals can feel comfortable. Friendliness helps build strong relationships between volunteers and the host community.

* * *

I am going to present a survey example based on the medical clinic I attended as a patient in Guatemala, which I wrote about in the Preface. Patients have several criticisms about this volunteer-run medical clinic. If they filled out this rubric, volunteers could create the positive changes needed to get the clinic functioning at its very best. When I received treatment at the clinic, it struck me that locals talked openly about the problems, but volunteers did not catch on because they did not think to ask locals if the clinic worked for them. Volunteers could have known locals experienced problems if they spoke Spanish, but they did not. In fact, if the volunteers spoke Spanish, then it would have solved a lot of the problems locals faced there. In this example, the quotes represent what the rubric would look like filled out with customer comments. Patients said these quotes to me about the clinic. The lessons the volunteer team can take away from each quote can be found in parenthesis following each answer. I am adding in Author's Notes in some sections of the rubric to give readers pertinent background information that clinic volunteers would know that explain some of the comments.

Usefulness—Do you find the clinic to be useful for you and your family?

Answer: "Yes, I like coming here instead of the hospital." (The clinic met an urgent need for alternative healthcare in the town.)

Beautification—Does the clinic look nice?

Answer: "The clinic is nice to come to. It is always clean." (The clinic looks clean and sanitary.)

[Author's Note: Beautification seems less applicable to a medical clinic, but the building itself looks well maintained and fits in amongst the nearby buildings in the town.]

Reliability—Can you rely on the clinic when you need it?

Answer:

- "I have to wait outside in the heat and stand in line for hours. I have to get up early in the morning to get in line to be seen by a doctor." (Patients cannot make appointments, which would help the clinic run smoother. Patients do not know when they will be seen by the doctor and how long they will have to wait in line, because of the first come, first served method and high demand. People have waited in line through high temperatures and rain despite being sick. People who arrive at the clinic early in the morning sometimes wait for hours before seeing a doctor.)
- "If I am still sick when I finish the medication the doctor has given me, then I have to come back and see a different doctor. They don't know my medical history." (The clinic does not promote continuity of care due to different doctors volunteering every week. The volunteer doctors do not keep records, so each patient does not have a medical chart that doctors at the clinic can look at for greater continuity of care.)

[Author's Note: From these comments, and from attending the clinic myself, I can tell that the clinic runs more like an urgent care facility because it does not focus on long-term health, preventative care and wellness. It does not offer wellness-related appointments or annual physicals.]

Quality/Effectiveness—How would you rate the quality of healthcare at the clinic?

Answer:

- "The doctors get me in and out but there are still long lines." (The clinic workers act in an efficient manner, but lines remain a problem.)
- "The doctor gave me medicine but a month later I am still sick." (Doctors misdiagnose patients.)
- "The doctor did not take the time to answer all my questions, so I do not know what I am sick with or why he gave me this medication." (The doctors do not take enough time per patient.)

Added-Value—Does the clinic add value to your life and to your healthcare?

Answer: "I like that they give me the medicine I need and show me how to take it." (The clinic gives patients the medicine they need.)

[Author's Note: Giving out free medicine can harm the local pharmaceutical market. Patients do appreciate it, though.]

Accessibility—Can you and your family access the clinic when you need it?

Answer: "My husband cannot come to the clinic because he has to go to work early every morning and cannot take the day off to wait in line." (If someone feels sick but still has to work, then they will have a hard time visiting the clinic to get the care they need.)

Safety—Do you feel safe at the clinic?

Answer: [Author's Note: This does not directly apply to the clinic. The rubric and survey can be adapted to make each category and question asked applicable to each volunteer project. Additionally, any missing category can be added.]

Understanding—Do you leave the clinic knowing all you need to know and with all your questions answered? Does the doctor explain things to you?

Answer:

- "The doctor did not speak Spanish, so he could not answer my questions during the examination. The clinic did not have a translator for the exam room." (Whichever patients have a translator in their exam room get the information that they need from the doctor but the other patients do not.)
- "I do not know what I am sick with." (Many times, doctors do not answer the patient's questions nor explain things to them that they want to know. Patients do not leave with an understanding of their diagnosis nor an explanation about their illness, and what they can expect while they recover, how they can prevent this sickness again, etc.)

[Author's Note: The clinic only has one translator for two doctors who work in separate exam rooms at the same time. Therefore, doctors sometimes explain diagnoses to patients without a translator present. Alternatively, patients need to explain things in Spanish to the doctor who cannot understand them without the translator present.]

Dignity—Do you feel like the volunteers at the clinic treat you with respect?

Answer: "I feel like giving us clothing is insulting. We have plenty of clothes. We came to the clinic because we need medical care."

Friendliness—Do the clinic volunteers act friendly and kind?

Answer: "The ladies who give out the clothing and medicine always act so nice to us. They always smile, and even though they don't speak Spanish, they always try to ask us how we feel and say hello." (The kindness of its volunteers remains one of the clinic's strengths.)

To recap, the major problems at the clinic, based on patient feedback, include the lines to get in, the discontinuity of care, misdiagnoses, not explaining things to patients, a language barrier, lack of access for people who cannot wait in line, and clothing donations. Beautification, friendliness, safety, usefulness and added-value make up the clinic's strengths. Although, from an economic perspective, the pharmaceutical added-value harms local industry and economy.

Some simple changes would make a big difference in addressing patient's concerns at the clinic. Volunteers could build a waiting room with many chairs so that sick people would not have to stand in the elements to wait for the doctor. This would allow patients greater comfort. The clinic could also start making appointments so that people would not have to wait in line at all. If the clinic makes afternoon appointments, then people who have to go to work early in the morning can still access the clinic. Additionally, the clinic could keep medical records for each patient so that when new doctors come in, they can see what medications the patient has already taken and what the next step in treatment should be, based on previous treatments. To address patient concerns from the survey, the clinic can stop giving out clothing donations and focus on excelling at giving medical care instead. The doctors themselves can take more time with each patient in order to explain everything to them and answer any questions they may have. They can also break the language barrier by learning Spanish and by always having a translator in the room.

Actually, fixing one problem might tackle many issues on the list, such as spending more time with the doctor with a translator present. This would address many of the unsatisfied answers on the rubric, such as taking more time per patient and improving both quality and understanding. If the doctors and clinic volunteers spoke Spanish or hired enough translators then that would also improve the quality and understanding as well. After volunteers take the critiques from the rubric into account, then the clinic will be the highest quality and most preferred healthcare option in the area. People could trust clinic workers to help them feel better and stay better. Now that would be a successful international volunteering project.

IV

Motivations

Motivations for Volunteering Internationally

Motivation is important in international volunteering because motivation leads to action. Most motivations can be good, but the actions the motivation drives matter most. No one will always get every action perfect, though. The key is to know how to adapt and correct as necessary. This book teaches overarching principles on how to volunteer internationally, so that one, volunteers can assess if their motivations and actions align with those principles, and two, to recognize when a course correction is needed and how to make it happen.

There are as many motivations to volunteer internationally as there are volunteers. Each volunteer is a unique individual and their motivations and life experiences are equally as unique. One strength of international volunteering is that everyone brings a distinct perspective that helps the group. A study in Switzerland found that there are three main categories of motivations for international volunteers. These include "a first group called 'Achieving something positive for others,' a second group named 'Quest for the new,' and a third group of motives labeled 'Quest for oneself.'" The study noted that participants often had motivations that fit into multiple categories.

New international volunteering tends to orient toward the first category of "achieving something positive for others."[1] But why does the international volunteer want to achieve something positive for others? For instance, achieving something for others from a paternalistic, colonization and/or savior motivation would not fall under new international volunteering.

It can be beneficial for volunteers to conduct a thought exercise that gets to the heart of what motivations drive them to volunteer abroad and why. This can clarify not only the why, but the how, in order to determine the route toward volunteering that would be most helpful for the volunteer organization or host community. Getting clarity on motivations also ensures that the volunteer chooses a volunteer organization that has a similar motivations as they do. It harmonizes the volunteer with the mission of the volunteer trip and with the other members of the volunteer team. Additionally, if any motivations are discovered during the thought exercise that do not align with the principles of new international volunteering, then that can be helpful in its own way. Exploring the thought patterns and history of those motivations can clear away limiting beliefs before volunteering begins.

Initially, I was motivated to volunteer internationally for two reasons—so that I could leave the world better than I found it, and so that I could give back to the community that was hosting my study abroad. Now though, that several years have passed and I have learned more, my motivations have evolved. My motivations now are to meet unmet physical needs in the world (both at home and abroad) and to answer calls for volunteering, such as when a non-profit needs a project done that could help them expand their good work. This leads to the question: How will I do that?

I have decided to focus on eliminating hunger via donations of funds, time and activism. The other "how" is to use my data skills to assist non-profits who need data help. This includes data cleaning, analysis, visualization and reporting. Many organizations have questions that can be answered by data analysis, or they have data and would like to derive insights from it. Since non-profits are focused on providing services, some do not have data sets to answer questions with or analysts to sift through the data they produce. Data analysis can give insights that add value to the organization's day to day work.

There are some outside forces that can influence motivations for volunteering internationally. Two main forces that can change our thinking around international volunteering include social media and culture, including the people around us. The rest of this chapter will cover these non-intrinsic motivations volunteers can encounter.

Social Media

Social media has come about with globalization and keeps everyone connected, allowing globalization to flourish further. International volunteering has created social media norms and opportunities to share volunteering activities. Volunteers spread information widely because of technologies like smart phones with state-of-the-art cameras that have made it possible to capture important moments. The images and videos international volunteers post online get transmitted widely due to platforms designed to share our lives with each other, such as Instagram, Facebook and TikTok, to name a few. The internet has led to more people viewing materials online that volunteers have posted on social media. Many times, volunteers do not personally know all their followers, who can live all around the world. In the past, international volunteers would only have been able to share their trip photos in-person to friends, family and colleagues. But today, international volunteers can disseminate their experiences to outlets like tv stations and news organizations. The information shared by volunteers on social media can inspire their followers to volunteer internationally as well.

In fact, some people volunteer abroad because they see other people having a positive impact on today's most pressing problems.[2] In the era of social media, it has become difficult to ignore when disaster strikes or previously unknown problems move to the top of the news cycle. In response to learning about those problems, many people volunteer internationally in order to personally contribute to improving the world or to meet an urgent need. Volunteers mobilize in droves after difficult world events to pitch in. For instance, in 2015, two earthquakes hit Nepal. They killed almost 10,000 people and destroyed or damaged over 900,000 homes. Habitat for Humanity sought volunteers to remove rubble, give families temporary shelter, assess the safety of houses still standing and rebuild homes over the long term.[3]

With volunteering, social media can either be an advantage or a hindrance. Social media becomes most beneficial when volunteers use it as a tool to raise awareness and ask followers to pitch in. But social media can be a double-edged sword because some international volunteers have used it for personal gain. Even when volunteers share their experiences on social media without bad intentions, some have posted pictures and videos that eliminated the privacy of the people they helped. In this way, social media can be problematic when it comes to international volunteering because of its propensity to be misused and the normalcy with which it seems to be misused.[4]

International volunteers have misused social media by posting poverty porn on their accounts.[5] Poverty porn can be defined as images and videos that depict poor people suffering, usually used in advertisements to solicit donations. The images try to elicit an emotional response that will lead viewers to donate money or feel sympathy. Poverty porn leads to one-time donations but it does not address systemic situations. It gives viewers the idea that donations will fix a problem and that only charities can implement solutions. This mindset can be damaging because these images bring simplicity to non-simplistic situations. It does not give the complex problem of poverty the attention it deserves. Poverty porn can trivialize people's situations and show them in their worst or most vulnerable moments. Poverty porn promotes the assumption that the images represent the subject's normal or day-to-day life, but they do not. Since it exploits these vulnerable moments, it doesn't treat people in the images well.

In fact, people often post poverty porn without the permission of the people in it. By objectifying and simplifying for advertising purposes, poverty porn decontextualizes the images while reducing the dignity and respect of the people in it. This makes people in the images seem helpless without revealing the entire truth. According to Theo Sowa, "When people portray us as victims, they don't want to ask about solutions. Because people don't ask victims for solutions."[6] This appearance of helplessness puts a blanket stereotype that everyone experiencing poverty is the same, regardless of any differences.

In international volunteering, when people put up poverty porn, they oftentimes include themselves in the images, so it looks like they saved people or solved poverty. This type of international volunteering poverty porn gives followers who have not traveled to that area the idea that the poverty porn represents an accurate depiction of life in that location. It misrepresents the location, the role of the international volunteer and acts as a disservice to the people who live in the host community. The stereotypes insinuated by the images can create an inaccurate, incomplete and degrading view of the place and the people international volunteers assist.

Some international volunteers like to take selfies of themselves with people who live in the host community and pictures of themselves doing the actual volunteering. Many volunteers post these pictures on social media to share what they did, encourage others to volunteer internationally and capture memories of the experience. However, while it can be okay to take pictures on social media and post them, it can be harmful to post selfies with children or while volunteering. This type of picture can be popular on social media, but it misses the point of international volunteering. Keep in mind that when volunteers take a lot of pictures of themselves at the worksite, they spend their time not actually working. The pictures can also perpetuate the stereotype that international volunteers fix things while the host community gets placed into a passive participant role.

To challenge this notion, volunteers can take pictures that combat poverty porn images. These pictures would show the host community accurately. It helps to focus on the work and not on potential pictures for social media, enabling volunteers to be fully present and engaged. I personally try to only post pictures of scenery during my travels. This gives my followers an idea of what the area is like, but does not take away anyone's privacy or perpetuate harmful stereotypes. As a rule, volunteers need to get verbal permission before posting a picture on social media featuring anyone other than themselves. New international volunteers not only ask permission before posting pictures of people in the host community but also ask themselves questions to gauge the appropriateness of posting it at all. Some of these questions include: Would posting this image be respectful, fully accurate and meaningful? Does it show nuances? Would it be better to post something else?

Taking pictures with kids abroad can make volunteers seem internationally savvy, compassionate and good with kids, leading some people to post pictures with kids on their dating profiles and social media accounts. However, this benefits volunteers and not the kids in the pictures. Images of this type take away kids' privacy at the personal gain of the volunteer. In most places, it would be considered strange if a stranger came up to a playground and took a picture of kids playing, or if they came up to a group of kids and tried to take a picture with them. This would not be okay, and in most situations, it should not be seen as acceptable while volunteering internationally as well. In the past, some international volunteers have taken pictures of children in vulnerable situations, such as when they live in an orphanage or lie sick in a hospital bed. As minors, children cannot give volunteers permission to take or post these pictures of them. They may grow up to find these pictures of their most vulnerable and difficult moments captured by volunteers online, but they should be the ones in control of their online presence, instead of volunteers.[7]

Some organizations and social media accounts seek to bring awareness to poverty porn in international volunteering. Radi-Aid, a Norwegian students and academics fund, disrupts how people portray poverty porn in an effort to end stereotypes in international development. It creates satirical videos to raise awareness of the dangers of poverty porn. Radi-Aid gives awards for the best and worst NGO and nonprofit ad campaigns each year. The worst-ranked ads feature poverty porn since many international development organizations use it to solicit donations on TV. Radi-Aid created a social media checklist so that international volunteers can be sure each image they would like to post online meets a ten-point criteria for ethics. The checklist includes double checking intention, consent, the subjects having access to the photo, respectfulness, appropriateness, and specificity, and absence of stereotypes and generalizations.[8]

An Instagram account, Barbie Savior, shows mock posts to impress upon followers how harmful perpetuating stereotypes can be in international volunteering. Barbie Savior poses Barbies with a Photoshop background to joke about common poverty porn images international volunteers put on social media. The account promotes Radi-Aid's social media guide for ethical posts. For instance, one post shows Barbie with a tattoo of the continent of Africa over her heart with the words "Te Amo" inscribed in the tattoo. In the caption Barbie Savior says, "The country of Africa has captured my heart" and "Te Amo means love in African." While this post is funny, it shows how some international volunteers perpetuate stereotypes with posts that glance over nuances and overgeneralizes their volunteering.[9]

Social media holds tremendous potential to be used for good in international volunteering. Social media can be utilized in many creative ways, such as raising awareness. A student I went to Guatemala with raised awareness after the trip finished by setting up a Go Fund Me page to finance his homestay sister's private education. He promoted the Go Fund Me to the people in his network so followers could raise money. A private education for the girl felt important to his homestay family as a way to give her the best future. He raised some money and contributed to his homestay family thanks to fundraising on social media.

International volunteers can use social media for good by volunteering remotely and by providing virtual community support. Some volunteers choose to not stop volunteering with their host community after returning home. Social media can be a tool to garner international support, a way to practice remote volunteering and to deepen relationships with the community. Virtual volunteering has become popular as many non-profits, both international and domestic, need extra staff but do not have the means to hire additional personnel. Volunteers can help fill this gap by taking over the organization's social media accounts to start campaigns that showcase the work of the non-profit. Volunteers can even use foreign language skills to post in multiple languages, an especially pertinent idea for international non-profits. Virtual volunteering can be a healthier and more beneficial way to use social media for good in international volunteering.[10]

Virtual volunteering became more popular during the Covid-19 pandemic. Many domestic and international non-profits had to quickly adapt to a virtual volunteering approach in order to continue or increase their operations safely.[11] Non-profits and NGOs around the world received soaring demand for needs such as healthcare, food security and shelter.[12] This meant that many organizations needed more volunteers, and the virtual environment allowed them to pull in volunteers from anywhere with a solid internet connection. It also enabled volunteers to work during lockdowns and around their work or school schedules. Virtual volunteering during the pandemic demonstrated the power of helping each other in times of crisis, despite limitations and restrictions.

Finally, volunteers can stay in touch and build long-term relationships with the people they met abroad while volunteering due to widespread social media use in this era of globalization. It used to be difficult or impossible to continue a relationship with people in the host community after volunteering when mail and telephone calls served as the primary mode of communication. International mail, even today, can be unreliable in places where people do not have formal addresses, and it can also get delayed for months in customs. International calls can be expensive, bad service can make it difficult to hear, and calling restricts people without access to telephones. However, thanks to widespread internet availability internationally, most volunteers can regularly interact with the people they meet while volunteering. I have had the good fortune to maintain a relationship with my Guatemala homestay family for over nine years. Through conversations with my homestay family on Instagram, I have the privilege to see their children grow up.

Acting Globally and Locally

Today there exists a growing movement to be both good citizens and good global citizens. A global citizen applies principles of good citizenship to the whole world. This includes respecting the rights of others, helping make the world a better place, being involved, caring for others, and participating in society. Global citizens do not place importance on man-made borders and embrace all of humanity, recognizing shared oneness. Former Prime Minister of the United Kingdom Theresa May once stated after Brexit "if you believe you're a citizen of the world, you're a citizen of nowhere." But a growing amount of people believe they can be global citizens and citizens of their country; that these do not represent mutually exclusive concepts. European Union citizens practice global citizenship daily by partaking in freedom of movement within the Schengen passport free zone, living and attending university in other countries, making decisions as a continental unit and supporting each other. In order to be both a good citizen and a good global citizen, individuals can embrace their community, country and the world. By volunteering both internationally and locally, people practice citizen values of caring for others in many forms. Other ways to be both a good citizen and a good global citizen include being a conscious consumer so that local and global producers receive a fair wage for their work, encouraging the benefits of globalization in one's home community and donating to both domestic and international aid organizations.[13]

The coolness factor of international volunteering represents one reason some individuals may choose to forgo volunteering domestically for volunteering internationally. International volunteering can be cool because people who have done it have fascinating stories to tell, have experienced something others have not and can post beautiful pictures of it on social media. The coolness factor often can appear to lack in domestic volunteering. If someone volunteers internationally, many people will hear about it, but not necessarily so if they volunteer locally. The coolness factor can be a motivating influence for choosing international volunteering over local volunteering, but it does not have to be. People can choose to volunteer in both settings, or forgo the coolness factor as a decider in choosing between volunteering locally and internationally. For instance, many college students volunteer internationally over spring break, but they could spend that week helping out locally instead, even though it would not be as glamorous. Or they could volunteer internationally over spring break but volunteer in their college town during the semester, as many students do.

The coolness factor can impact how and where to dedicate volunteering time, internationally and domestically. For example, a group traveled for a week from North Carolina to New York to volunteer picking up trash. They had a long drive to pick up the trash but could fundraise and advertise their trip to New York. It seemed like more of a sacrifice to travel to New York than it would be if they spent their time picking up trash in their own community. If they spent their volunteering hours picking up trash in North Carolina instead of New York, then they could do so without telling anyone.

The coolness factor can be summed up by this question: If a person volunteers but does not tell anyone about it, does it matter? The non-cool volunteering option would be beneficial for one's home community if volunteers chose it, however. Trash exists for volunteers to pick up in the greater Raleigh area, which would beautify the volunteers' hometown, and that could be a more beneficial, sustainable choice. Over time the group could monitor trash build up on roadways or start a do-not-litter campaign in their own community for lasting change.

When people think of poverty, they usually envision people living in poverty in other countries around the world. However, poverty can be found in every country around the world. For example, in the United States, and according to the book *One Nation, Underprivileged: Why American Poverty Affects Us All* by Mark Robert Rank, most people in America who experience poverty usually do so for a spell instead of for a long time. Children are most likely to be impoverished in America, especially children who live in female-led single-parent households, even if the female head of household has a job, according to povertyusa.org. Women in America do not usually get paid as much as their male counterparts, so children with two employed parents or with a male single head of household have more income to work with. Domestic volunteers and community assistance programs can be vital to ending American poverty, especially with temporary support to help people through spells of poverty, such as a job loss.[14]

Donating to and volunteering at food banks represents one way to build a safety net to catch people who fall into poverty domestically. In the United States, Feeding America, a national food bank, feeds over 46 million Americans each year. That amounts to almost 14 percent of the population, for a total of 4 billion meals annually. They gather food that would otherwise be wasted from food companies and build nutritious meals for those who need them. Already over two million Americans, or 0.6 percent of the population, volunteer at food banks or other meal assistance locations every month, but 51 percent of food programs in the United States completely operate by volunteer labor. America has a large untapped volunteering force that could help through food assistance programs and other essentials. The Stanford Center on Longevity found that only 25 percent of Americans volunteer but 90 percent would like to. However, the Corporation for National and Community Service found that more Americans volunteer now than ever before. Potential exists for this trend to continue upward to create a major volunteering force in the United States.[15]

We need to give love to our own communities. Our hometowns deserve our volunteering focus, in conjunction with our international volunteering. Volunteering in our own country represents a patriotic act that says we want to invest in where we live by giving of our time and talents to serving our fellow neighbors. Volunteering in our communities shows deep love and caring. When we take time to take care of others at home, it builds a sense of togetherness for the whole area.

Local volunteers keep their communities running well. They are the backbone of meeting community needs, whether from a religious institution, a non-profit, a school or firehouse. Each action takes care of neighbors. Local volunteers provide essential services to maintain quality of life, and they do so in many ways. Volunteers in schools help individual kids who need help catching up in reading or math. Firefighter and EMT volunteers save lives, and every family whose loved one has received medical attention from them that made all the difference greatly appreciates them, including mine. Volunteers run community homeless shelters, feeding people who would otherwise go without. These volunteers and many more fill in gaps of need that the government or individuals cannot or do not. Everyone, in some time of life, needs a helping hand from a volunteer. Local volunteers have touched every one of us in some way.

Volunteers can split their volunteering time within their community in two ways. Both are important, yet distinctive ways to help meet needs in the community. Firstly, volunteers can establish a consistent volunteering routine with an organization that they believe in and identify with. Regularly volunteering in this way maintains the ongoing work of the organization, allowing them to produce a consistent output in helping the community. When this happens, people in the community can rely on the organization, thanks to the work of regular volunteers. For instance, in some places, homeless individuals rely on local homeless shelters for food each day. When volunteers make and serve dinner one night each week, the homeless community does not have to go hungry and can depend on the shelter to help them get through a difficult time in their lives. These regular and reliable volunteer interactions strengthen the human connection between members of the community. They also give volunteers insights that help them better understand existing needs of the community.

When volunteers understand the needs of the community better, they have a chance to meet them. Therefore, the second prong of local volunteering encompasses finding innovative solutions to unmet needs. Sometimes, the organizations in place to help the community do not meet all the needs present in the community. That can be changed by volunteers though. For example, Boy and Girl Scouts who do their Eagle Scout or Gold Award projects often use their projects to innovate and implement solutions to unmet needs in the community. I know an Eagle Scout in high school who noticed that a nursing home in our community had outside space but nowhere for residents to sit in it. That meant that residents could not fully utilize the yard to enjoy the outdoors as much as they wanted to. To fix this, the Eagle Scout built benches from scratch and stained them for the residents, ensuring that they would be able to use them for many years to come. One-time projects like this can meet many needs the community has, but it may require regular volunteering to fill a gap in an unmet need.

Local volunteers represent an especially important component of volunteering where little safety net exists for sick people or those experiencing poverty. Sick people may not be able to hold down a job, losing employer-sponsored health insurance and leaving them with unaffordable bills. Even people who work full time can still experience poverty because of insufficiently low wages and lack of affordable housing.[16] Some people also become impoverished because they become unemployed. Without volunteers, people without housing, food, shelter and medical care would go without basic necessities. For instance, when a young woman in my community began cancer treatment, she could not work. Her church congregation pooled together its collective resources to help pay her mortgage for several months. Without acts of kindness by the community such as this, people would have few other options to meet their needs in a trying time.

In this way, innovative volunteering can be done with an event when needed. An event can raise enough money or bring together enough people to be sufficient in and of itself. Past community events have raised funds for medical treatment, built a house for a family, held a back-to-school supplies drive and provided Christmas gifts to kids who would otherwise not get any. These events do more than meet a physical need, they also provide critical support and an outpouring of love when people need them the most. In this way, a major advantage of the local volunteer force is that they show that the community will look out for its members in times of need.

Local volunteers can also try to make individuals' lives better through gifts, visits, companionship, encouragement and support. These small acts can make a huge difference to people having a hard time because it reminds them of love, care and community. This could mean volunteers set up a meal schedule to bring food to a family after a funeral so they do not have to cook while grieving or by making gift baskets for children in the hospital. Regular companionship for people without many visitors, such as people in the hospital without family to visit them, homebound elderly individuals who spend most of their time alone, and elderly living in nursing homes, can take little time out of a volunteer's schedule but make a huge difference in the quality of life of the people they give companionship to. Sometimes local volunteering can be as simple as showing support and letting others know that they matter.

Volunteers can bring together the global and the local to help support others in domestic volunteering. For instance, the Refugee Community Partnership (RCP) in Raleigh, North Carolina, helps refugees and asylees settle into their new home. Refugees feel integrated into the community thanks to local volunteers who guide them through the transition process and build a long-term relationship with them. It can be difficult for newly arrived refugees to adjust to such a large life change after experiencing trauma. All volunteers help to support refugees for a minimum of one to two years by visiting them for a few hours each week. This gives refugees a sense of stability and a close relationship with volunteers. Many volunteers and refugees take part in weekly family dinners. Volunteers cook for refugees and refugees cook for volunteers to strengthen community and preserve the refugees' culture. The organization and its volunteers closely listen to refugees' needs and address them during the transition process. According to Refugee Community Partnership's website, "Parents, children, volunteers, and staff design Family Field Days to address social isolation and redevelop a sense of safety in public spaces. While kids and volunteers play, parents and staff discuss community needs, brainstorming ways for RCP to adaptively fill gaps. Here, communities are playing a lead role in addressing the issues that profoundly affect them." The Refugee Community Partnership helps give families the best new start possible due to the partnership with local volunteers.[17]

Local volunteers can come together to change circumstances that affect the entire country. When systemic problems keep people from getting their needs met volunteers can rally to fix things by protesting, raising awareness, changing local laws and spreading the word to make change. Equal pay for women, improving the situation of the homeless and benefits for families in poverty represent some of the issues volunteers advocate to change. In bringing awareness to problems, volunteers can make changes on a large scale that can positively impact many people. For example, in the United States, EpiPen prices rose to about $600 in 2016. EpiPens, a self-injectable medicine, save the lives of people living with food and environmental allergies when they go into anaphylactic shock. When EpiPen prices went up, some families had to choose between purchasing EpiPens and buying food for their family. Over 500,000 people signed a petition demanding the drug company Mylan change the price of EpiPens. Volunteers helped organize the petition, spread the word and delivered the petition to Mylan's headquarters. The public pressure urged Mylan to act and it created a generic version of the EpiPen that cost 50 percent less, making it more affordable for more families. Although at $300 the price still remains unaffordable for many people, volunteers mobilized to make a positive change.[18]

Additionally, international volunteers can combine the global and the local. When international volunteers come back home, their community and country can benefit from the cultural knowledge they learned. If volunteers share their newfound perspectives and experiences, others can understand fellow humans more and have more compassion for our shared humanity. Community members can also benefit from an expanded global awareness and have the potential to assist the host community further. Returned international volunteers can begin this knowledge transfer by talking to family and friends, holding a community meeting or even by becoming a teacher and passing wisdom to students.

Part 2

Best Practices for New International Volunteers

V

Local Involvement

The Volunteer Role

We need to begin this chapter by stating what the international volunteer role does not include before defining what it does. For one, the international volunteer role does not necessarily mean that volunteers go to fix things. The word "fixing" implies that locals cannot improve matters but volunteers have the power to do so. This notion takes away the agency of locals and puts them into an unjust narrative of being incapable. Fixing also implies brokenness, which does not hold true. Locals may simply need more resources or manpower to make their goals happen. The international volunteering role also does not allow volunteers to monopolize the project with their perspectives. It does not include digressing from locals' vision for the project. Similarly, international volunteering does not mean making the local community like back home because that takes away the culture and unique life of the community.[1]

Additionally, international volunteers' mandate does not include ending poverty alone. Poverty manifests as a complex and often systemic phenomenon that looks different in different places. If poverty could be ended that simply, then locals would have done it already. No one could be more motivated or more capable to end poverty than the people experiencing it. In this way, international volunteering cannot be a band-aid that fixes all poverty, but rather a tool to facilitate the goals of locals to improve quality of life. However, if many people volunteer internationally using best methods, then poverty should lessen over time.

Some volunteers have a vision in mind of what would be best for locals, but that does not embody the volunteer's role and objectives. By definition, international volunteers do not live in the area they volunteer in, and cannot know what would be best for locals. Therefore, the international volunteer's role does not include convincing locals that the volunteer's development idea would be best for them. *The Economist* tells a story of an NGO trying to stimulate ecotourism along the Kapuas River in Indonesia, saying "[I]t is hard to convince locals to build bamboo homestays when gold mining is so much more lucrative."[2] It would be much better if the NGO focuses on what locals need—in this case, a high, stable income—versus what it thinks locals need—bamboo homes for tourism. This would align the locals' vision with the NGO's work instead of making them in conflict with one another. In this way, international volunteers must help locals with what they actually need assistance with.

While volunteers perform different activities on each international trip, the overarching purpose of volunteering—and what the volunteer role means—ultimately remains the same. Using one definition of the volunteer role will eliminate uncertainties and unify the international volunteering community around the core purpose of the role of the volunteer. The international volunteer's role is to serve, to be a liaison, and to be an extra set of helping hands for whatever locals need assistance with in development. Development means growing in a way that complements the community's values in various areas such as the economy, politics, etc. This oftentimes means that volunteers contribute resources and create awareness as needed.

The new international volunteer fulfills this role by one, listening, and two, by committing to assist the locals' vision. Listening effectively acts as a roadmap for international volunteering because it helps volunteers perform optimally as they learn about the needs and ideas locals have. Listening also reveals obstacles locals face. If volunteers do not listen, they will come into the project at a disadvantage without knowing all this information. They will not understand the entirety of the situation surrounding the international volunteering project. Sometimes, international volunteers start a project with clear goals of what they want to implement and accomplish. However, listening to locals will allow volunteers to focus on the community in order to truly assist them. Listening permits the new international volunteer to challenge the notion of the volunteer—instead of the community—running the project.

Listening has a place during each part of the international volunteering experience. Before the trip, volunteers must listen to community members during pre-trip research in order to formulate a plan of assistance based on locals' feedback. Volunteers also need to listen during the project to make sure that any progress helps as intended. The feedback locals give during the project acts as a compass of sorts to keep volunteers going in the right direction. However, volunteers ultimately need to still listen to locals after the completion of the project, even after returning home. A follow-up with the community allows volunteers to see if their work turned out the way they planned. It also allows volunteers to identify if the community needs ongoing help in the future. If problems arise, post-project feedback lets volunteers know if they need to change anything or do troubleshooting if something does not function as intended.

When international volunteers commit to assist locals' vision it benefits the community by aligning volunteers' actions to their wishes. When international volunteering loses focus on the community's wishes and desires, it subverts the intended meaning of volunteering. Sometimes, volunteers have worked separately from the community, unilaterally worked without involving the community, or even without being invited into the community. Instead of committing to the locals' vision, some volunteers decided to volunteer without involving the community's opinion whatsoever. This can insult the community as it ignores their wishes, desires and autonomy. It assumes that the volunteers know better than locals and that locals cannot do what the volunteers want to do.[3] By committing to assist the locals' vision, the new international volunteer destroys these assumptions and aligns their volunteer work with the development plan of community members.

The new international volunteer must commit to assist with the locals' vision for the future of international volunteering to be optimized. The new international volunteer works with the community at their invitation. They will work side by side with community members to fulfill a shared vision and mutual understanding of a common goal. Therefore, volunteers will not go off on their own to create and lead projects for people they do not know and whose needs they do not understand. To commit to the locals' vision, the new international volunteer must comprehend what locals envision for the international development project. After asking for clarification when needed, volunteers can help enact the vision by obtaining approval from locals for the plan of work that will be conducted. During the project, volunteers commit to locals' vision by working alongside the community with a team that consists of locals who lead and international volunteers who assist. Post-project, international volunteers should periodically ask locals for feedback to see if they view the project as a success.

The Blueboys, the Instafamous Staffordshire Bull Terrier dogs Dazzy and Philly, exemplify what it means to commit to the locals' vision in international volunteering. The Blueboys raise money every year for one Staffordshire Terrier and/or Pitbull dog rescue organization in Australia, the United Kingdom and the United States. The Blueboys' owners, Jennifer and Lachlan, dedicate themselves to supporting these dog rescues each year. When the rescues need help getting a dog adopted or need emergency funds for surgeries to save a dog's life, Jen posts an appeal to the Blueboys' followers on social media to help meet those needs. Jen and Lachlan visit as many of the shelters as they can to learn about the operations and needs of the rescue, including Players for Pits in Chicago. One year, Players for Pits invited Jen to be a guest speaker at its annual fundraising gala. Donations were needed to pay for medical care for the dogs brought in from kill shelters in Chicago. The annual gala raises money for this. After the gala, Players for Pits leaders took Jen and Lachlan to Chicago Animal Care and Control, the local dog pound. Chicago Animal Care and Control euthanizes dogs when the pound reaches maximum capacity. Players for Pits rescues dogs from the shelter so they will not be euthanized and pays for all necessary medical care before putting rescued pit bulls up for adoption. Players for Pits showed Jen and Lachlan the dire conditions of the dogs at the pound, which motivates their work. Players for Pits wants all Pitbull–like dogs to be adopted into loving homes, especially to end the dogs' stress they experience from living in cages at the pound.[4]

On the trip to Chicago Animal Care and Control, Jen and Lachlan helped Players for Pits rescue a Pitbull they named Cooper for care and adoption. Rescuing Cooper meant that he would no longer have a chance of being euthanized. Players for Pits placed Cooper into a temporary foster home so he could stop living in a cage. The experience with Players for Pits in Chicago led Jen and Lachlan to create a Blueboys Christmas Appeal to their social media followers, with the goal of raising 60,000 AUD for dog rescue organizations. The money raised got divided among six dog rescue organizations, two each in Australia, the United Kingdom and the United States, including Players for Pits. They raised 68,319 AUD from 2,569 followers around the world in less than two days. In fact, in the year 2017, The Blueboys raised a total of 95,386 AUD for the rescue organizations.[5] They have continued to raise money each year after as well.[6] Jen and Lachlan represent the international volunteer role well by listening and responding to the needs of the international dog rescue organizations they sponsor in whatever way they can. They also exemplify the international volunteer role by committing themselves to the vision of the rescues through fundraising and social media exposure.

I have personally learned the importance of committing to locals' vision. During my time in Guatemala, I volunteered at the library in the place where I lived. The librarian would tell me about how he wished his town could cultivate a stronger culture of reading for fun every day. He stated that almost all of the school children who either borrowed a textbook or did homework at the library did not tend to read for fun. Almost all adults in the town read the daily newspaper, but many people did not read fiction or nonfiction books for fun and leisure, according to him. The librarian thought that reading for fun every day offers the town several benefits, including continuing education, encouraging children to read by their parents' example, spending more family time reading aloud to improve children's reading skills, and providing an opportunity to relax and unwind.

No books could be checked out or taken outside the library, so the librarian wanted to create a book box outside in the main plaza. He thought that since the families use the plaza to relax and to have fun, then having books available in the plaza would encourage this shift toward reading for fun more often. Guatemalans and tourists alike visit the plaza often to soak up the sun, spend time with family and meet up with friends. Because so many people with different interests utilize the plaza, the librarian wanted to build a small structure that would house a few shelves of many different kinds of books. He wanted everyone to find something they enjoyed reading in the book box. People could read the books in the plaza, and then return them to the box when they left. He wanted to put a sign on the box in both Spanish and Kaqchikel, a Mayan language actively spoken in the town, that explained the premise for the book box. In the box, there would be books appropriate for all age levels and about various topics of interest and also books in Spanish and Kaqchikel, in case some people preferred reading in one language over the other. The librarian even had pictures on his computer of other book boxes around the world and knew exactly how he wanted to design it. It would be low cost to make the box and stock it full of books, but the library's budget did not include funding for it. It would also be relatively easy to secure permission to build the book box, only requiring verbal permission from the mayor.

However, I did not help the librarian with his plan. I thought of it as a great idea yet separate from the volunteering that I did in Guatemala. Ideally, I could have used the international volunteer role in this scenario to help bring the book box idea to life. I could have listened to the librarian about his idea and then asked how I could help. I could have committed to his vision by dedicating my time to building the book box. I could have liaised between Guatemala and the United States by asking bookstores in my hometown to donate books in Spanish to the book box and then facilitate the books to be mailed to the library in Guatemala while builders constructed the box. I could have acted as an extra set of helping hands by interviewing contractors, gathering locally made materials for the box, and meeting with the mayor to get permission to put the box in the plaza.

In this instance I did not facilitate the librarian's book box dream because I spent the time trying to accomplish my own volunteering goals. I have learned that as a volunteer, my goals need to match whatever goals that locals have. Since volunteers serve and facilitate the projects that locals want to create, the book box would have been my goal, not a sidetrack from my own. From this situation, I have learned that international volunteering ideally acts as a manifestation of locals' development dreams for their own community. Now that I know how to be the most effective international volunteer, I reached out to the librarian to see if I could help bring his book box goal to fruition in 2018. As he only has time on weekends to take care of the book box, the project remains paused for now.

Locals as Creators

The new international volunteer recognizes that locals are inherently just as capable as volunteers to make their community a better place to live. Gilberto Valladares, a resident of Havana, Cuba, started his own hair salon. His business became successful and as time went on, he opened a museum inside it dedicated to vintage hair cutting products. Gilberto wanted to revitalize the street leading to his salon, known as Hairdresser's Alley. With the help of local historian Eusebio Leal, the two beautified the road by repaving the street, fixing up the fronts of the other houses and businesses and installing hair-themed art installations on walls and on the street. From there, Gilberto began a haircutting school for young people without jobs to gain employment. Many of them have gone on to work as hairdressers, even internationally aboard cruise ships. The revitalization of Hairdresser's Alley attracted tourists who brought business with them. The positive cycle continued as locals started new businesses in the alley that attracted more tourists, which expanded the businesses and provided more jobs. Living standards universally rose for Cubans living and working in Hairdresser's Alley, a testimony to the tangible effect of Gilberto's work in his community.[7]

I saw this transformation in-person when I visited Havana. Hairdresser's Alley became iconic because of the Cuban experts who created it. The Alley cultivated a Cuban haircutting identity, displaying its history and Cuban-made art. Gilberto and Eusebio's creativity directly led to the success of Hairdresser's Alley because the authentically Cuban space and unique hairdresser's theme attracts tourists. Tourists get their hair cut, purchase souvenirs and inject cash into the area, which grows the economy. If international volunteers instead of Gilberto created the space, then it would not have the same injection of Cuban culture that makes it successful. When locals create instead of international volunteers, it makes all the difference for the success of the project.

International volunteering can fail to live up to its potential if well-meaning people create projects that they think will improve lives without involving local opinion. When volunteers do this, they miss an opportunity to see their idea from the locals' perspective(s), and so do not spot potential problems and negative long-term consequences that only locals can see. When a project does not involve local opinion, it downplays the project's ability to be as helpful as possible. In these cases, international volunteering can have less than optimal outcomes.[8] For instance, I know a long-term volunteer in Guatemala who moved there to help Guatemalans learn how to cut hair. She reasons that if she teaches Guatemalans how to cut hair, then they can use those skills to find stable employment as barbers, hair dressers or colorists. She set up a non-profit organization without involving locals in the process and began teaching Guatemalans. However, this well-meaning international volunteering project has problems. These issues mostly stem from the fact that the volunteer has great knowledge of the haircutting industry in America but little knowledge of the hair cutting industry in Guatemala. This causes three main issues in the way the nonprofit tries to function. (Ideally, the volunteer would have consulted Guatemalan hairdressers before starting out.)

First off, the volunteer does not teach classes at the same place nor time each day. She teaches in different places within a geographical region. Due to this setup, some students have to travel far and can miss some classes because of the distance. Additionally, without a consistent meeting time, people miss classes when the classes are held at a time they cannot come. When students cannot take every class, they miss valuable lessons on becoming a hair stylist that they would need in order to become proficient in the skill. Development needs consistency because it enables people to get what they need when they need it.

Secondly, the international volunteer travels to different towns in Guatemala and gives free haircuts to people who live there. She tracks her non-profit's impact by the number of haircuts she and other volunteers give to Guatemalans. However, by giving away free haircuts, Guatemalans employed in the hair cutting industry lose business, and thus income. Effectively, by giving free haircuts, the non-profit works against its goal to help people become haircutters for a salary. Giving free haircuts in various Guatemalan towns can cause additional problems. The haircuts do not occur regularly, so participants cannot rely on them. The main volunteer only lives in Guatemala for a few months at a time with no set haircutting schedule; thus, Guatemalans may only ever get one free haircut. Additionally, the haircuts can be insulting because of the underlying assumption that Guatemalans need the charity of free haircuts because they cannot afford them.[9] However, in reality, this does not ring true. In fact, I never saw anyone in Guatemala who did not have a recent haircut. Only a very small percentage of the population cannot afford haircuts. The free haircuts take money away from Guatemalan hairdressers, which reduces GDP in the name of volunteering. A byproduct of volunteering should be to create or stimulate economic growth.

Lastly, the international volunteer started a fundraiser in the United States, asking people to donate money to purchase starter kits for each student who completed the program. The fundraiser information said that each of the cheapest starter kits available for purchase costs five hundred U.S. dollars. The fundraiser accounted for choosing the cheapest starter kits by saying that they will not last permanently, but that the trainees can get jobs as haircutters and then use the money they earn to purchase long-lasting haircutting kits. However, students do not get a guaranteed job after finishing the program. Many hairdressers work in the informal economy so the amount of money they will make will vary depending on the job they take and how many customers they get. They may even self-employ until the kit breaks. The average Guatemalan made $4,060 a year in 2017, according to World Bank Data.[10] A $4,060 salary would make replacing the kit with even the same $500 one unaffordable, at over one eighth of yearly income.

Similarly, what if trainees start their own businesses and the kits break? They may have to quit cutting hair or get a loan for a new kit. However, most loan options in Guatemala come with high interest rates, especially for people who do not have a credit history.[11] The fundraiser additionally assumes that top-of-the-line kits will be available to purchase in the area where the trainees live and work. This assumption does not hold true because many places in Guatemala do not have shopping malls, but local markets instead. In general, the region faces a problem of lack of access to markets.[12] Not everyone will be able to travel to Guatemala City to purchase a new starter kit, or an improved starter kit, especially since that trip takes the whole day from many rural areas the volunteer worked in.

Even though this person wants to help development in Guatemala, the current methods of working without local feedback and by creating the nonprofit herself can be improved. Imagine how powerful her skills could be if she partnered with locals to assist them instead of going at it alone. Working alone has led to no local involvement, no consistency and no sustainability. In contrast, Cuban hairdressers know how to create successful hairdressers in their home environment. However, a single international volunteer does not know everything she needs to in order to create successful Guatemalan hairdressers. Optimal volunteering happens when locals and volunteers work together because locals provide the expertise and volunteers provide extra sets of helping hands to complete the vision.

The Elephant-Human Relations Aid, a not-for-gain organization, presents an example of how international volunteers help to achieve locals' vision in Namibia. As a depleted population of elephants began to grow, so did their need for water in the desert environment. They had to compete with subsistence farmers, livestock and communities to meet their water needs, causing conflict and destroying property in the process. Elephants have wrecked wells and hand water pumps that townspeople rely on to meet their own water needs. International volunteers at the Elephant-Human Relations Aid work with Namibians and immigrants from surrounding countries, such as South Africa and Mauritius, to fulfill their vision of a harmonious environment between people and elephants. Volunteers help meet the organization's need for physical labor and funds to power the Conflict Prevention Program by working in a short-term style of two weeks and by paying a fee to fund the program. Volunteers spend the first week building walls to prevent elephants from causing property damage around susceptible land. During the second week, volunteers go on an elephant patrol, where they track the elephants and gather data on them in order to help the organization's conservation management efforts. Due to the partnership between Namibians, Africans and international volunteers at the Elephant-Human Relations Aid, these desert elephants that humans once thought to be extinct have now grown to a population of approximately six hundred. Now elephants coexist sharing water with humans and their livestock.[13]

It can be difficult to find examples of locals creating a project or organization where international volunteers assist them in their development vision. This needs to become the new normal for international volunteering. It has not become a norm thus far because some volunteers see international volunteering as separate from the community instead of with the community. As a consequence, some international volunteering has happened in a separate sphere where volunteers come in, do work and leave without much local leadership, opinion and involvement.[14] Volunteering does not need to be an insertion into the community, but rather be at one with the community. This leads to optimal results, increased transparency and local accountability. Volunteers can create a new normal by making a point to get invited into the community instead of going into the community independently. In development, volunteers must structure projects after local needs instead of volunteers' ideas.

Local Leadership

I once saw a webinar hosted by several charitable foundations that specialize in providing green electricity to areas currently without power in Africa. The panelists tended to be policymakers and nonprofit workers based in the United States. The seminar talked about electrifying Africa with green energy, but it mostly focused on the obstacles the foundations face in trying to electrify Africa with green energy sources. All of the webinar speakers knew a lot about green energy electrification, but they did not know and even asked for ideas about how to put their plans into action in Africa.

Throughout the seminar I learned that panelists see some towns as too small to be connected to the traditional grid and that those towns cannot afford a solar panel mini-grid that the foundations want to install as an alternative. The foundations have limited money to install the mini-grids, so they focused the conversation on how impractical they think it would be to light those areas. In fact, they do not have a plan to provide energy access in those towns anytime soon, only an idea of how they would do it if they could secure more donations and financing. They said that project finance acts as their main obstacle to building the mini-grids. From their point of view, to get the amount of money they need to electrify Africa, an international shift toward green mini-grid electricity financing will have to happen—and they do not think it will happen soon. Therefore, they reason, most of unelectrified Africa will stay in the dark until they can get more financing to install the mini-grids. The panelists currently seem wholly dependent on project finance in order to execute their plan to electrify Africa. They have a vague idea of how green energy electrification would work and a thorough knowledge of the project finance obstacles standing in their way, but little knowledge on how to surmount the obstacles to actually begin installing mini-grids.

Fast forward to what actually happens in Africa today. According to *The Economist*, African entrepreneurs have had their own success in electrifying Africa with green energy. The entrepreneurs implement a pay-as-you-go model that installs solar panels owned by the company on the roof of customers' houses and charges them only for the electricity that they use. Customers who utilize solar power stored in a battery at night can stop paying for kerosene lamps and use that money to pay the solar electricity bill instead. That way, towns do not have to pay the prohibitive upfront costs for solar mini-grids, or even for the prohibitive cost of the solar panels or solar lamps that provide their electricity. The solar companies make a profit just from the electricity bills of customers, without customers needing to buy a green energy system up front. In 2016, over 600,000 families had access to this off-grid solar technology.

Similarly, the company M-Kopa provides access to solar electricity as an alternative to connecting to the grid. Customers pay a small deposit in order to get a rooftop solar panel installed at their house, and then pay an even smaller amount daily to keep the lights on. Eventually, these payments will cover the cost of the solar panel so the customer will own it outright. After ownership, customers no longer need to make payments for solar power. This entire process from installation to ownership can take less than a year. As of 2016, M-Kopa provided 325,000 solar panels to customers in Africa.

M-Kopa and other entrepreneurs differ from the approach of the webinar panelists by actively electrifying Africa with green energy. The webinar panelists have some ideas of how they would like to electrify Africa with green energy as outsiders. As local experts, M-Kopa found solutions to the unaffordability of the traditional grid and alternative mini-grids. Most significantly, M-Kopa and entrepreneurs figured out how to implement their solutions. They started small but now many Africans now have access to clean electricity because of them. The M-Kopa approach does not electrify a whole town all at once like a mini-grid would, but it gets people electrified now instead of waiting to figure out the financing indefinitely. And while the webinar panelists see Africans as poor people in need of outside financing and donations to get electricity, M-Kopa and others see Africans as consumers who demand green electricity and strive to meet that demand.

In this way, international volunteers can be most effective when they support instead of lead. The webinar panelists and companies like M-Kopa have the same goal to electrify Africa with green energy. A partnership between them could be beneficial toward achieving the development goal. The panelists can help the locals who already make progress by asking how they can help. Maybe the panelists can use their foundations' financing to expand M-Kopa's business. This would get more Africans green electricity access quickly. The optimal solution would be to combine the ideas of locals with the manpower of philanthropically-minded volunteers under the leadership of the expert locals. In this case, financiers could help the African solar providers by providing loans, logistics help, quality control and advertising.[15]

Imagine the success of a project where locals lead and volunteers assist instead. José Fuster, known internationally as the Picasso of the Caribbean, created Fusterlandia, a community art project in Havana, Cuba. The project transformed Fuster's neighborhood into a mosaic work of art inspired by Barcelona architect Antoni Gaudí. Every outside surface, from houses and yards to walls and bus stops gleam with mosaic tiles that form sculptures and murals, making the neighborhood a living work of art. José Fuster has led the artistic vision of Fusterlandia throughout, leading from his studio inside his house in the neighborhood. José's leadership has enabled his vision to be cohesive in the neighborhood so that the mosaics come to fruition in a manner true to his original vision. His volunteers help make his visions come to life, and keep the art open to the public.

Fuster first solicited his family as volunteers. They helped him install the mosaic tiles at his own home and yard. To this day they continue to watch his studio and mop the slippery tiles when it rains so it does not become a hazard to tourists who visit. Next, he asked his neighbors for permission to use their properties as a canvas as well. His neighbors helped support his project, which mutually benefited all of them. Not only did José Fuster beautify the neighborhood with his art, but he also created a tourist attraction that has profited his neighbors. They now run art shops and convenience stores selling drinks, snacks and artistic souvenirs for tourists who visit to see the Picasso of the Caribbean's masterpiece.

International volunteers have more potential to assist Fusterlandia. Donations and purchases of artwork help fund the continuation of the neighborhood transformation since Fuster expands Fusterlandia as he can pay for it. He wants to add a music center in the neighborhood in the future. International volunteers also have extreme potential as manual labor and tile suppliers for Fusterlandia. This especially helps because it can be difficult to find mosaic tiles within Cuba.[16] Fusterlandia shows why the new international volunteer helps bring locals' visions to life under their leadership instead of leading the projects themselves. In fact, as evidenced with Fusterlandia, international volunteers need local leadership. They know better than international volunteers what obstacles they and their communities face, and through observation and experience, locals know what would work to make the best of a situation more than an outside international volunteer would.

VI

Core Project Strategy

Development versus Relief

Development can be defined as the long-term process in which a community or nation creates and implements practical, beneficial, sustainable, and environmentally–friendly solutions to important and pressing needs. In development, needs identified by locals get broken down into stages and implemented step-by-step. Ideally, over time, as each stakeholder completes each phase of development, communities and countries will feel better off, healthier and more financially stable. Development can be a straightforward action, like bringing electricity to a town by installing solar panels, or it can be something extremely complex, like reforming a governmental system that hinders the growth of the people it governs. Development in any situation leads to the betterment of the people in a way that reflects the culture.

Relief can be defined as emergency aid that helps people survive and rebuild immediately after a natural disaster or humanitarian crisis. Relief can be useful in environmental situations like a famine or drought, in the aftermath of natural disasters and also in humanitarian crises such as genocide and war. International volunteers provide relief by giving basic necessities or other helpful items to people who urgently need them. Emergency aid can include blankets, water, food, medicine, toiletries and even housing. Relief can be helpful after crises because the people who need it cannot procure necessary items without outside help. In sum, relief works temporarily to help people get by in the short term.

To distinguish between the two concepts of development and relief, development functions as a long-term solution that temporary relief cannot provide. Volunteers can decide if they can help using relief or development based on the level of urgency and the events surrounding a situation. Relief may be the necessary tool to use if a horrible catastrophe has occurred, and volunteers will be assisting during or immediately afterward. Development would be an ideal tool in non-emergency situations.

Development also helps after an urgent need for relief has passed. Development can take over for relief to tackle systemic problems after a relief program to reduce the likelihood that people do not need relief in the future. For example, if volunteers assist a few days after an earthquake happens, then they would choose to help using relief. If, however, volunteers want to help a few years after an earthquake, then development would be the best fit for the situation. Similarly, if a famine occurs, distributing emergency food relief would be appropriate to prevent people from starving. Then, after the famine ends, volunteers could transition to a development program that focuses on preventing famines in the future. The transition to development can happen once the danger that caused the need for relief has passed and people can survive without it.

	Development	*Relief*
When to Use	Under Regular Circumstances	During and/or Immediately After a Natural Disaster, Humanitarian Crisis or War
Duration	Long Term	Short Term
Purpose	Economic & Social Growth	Emergency Assistance
Sustainable	Yes	No

Relief can be confused with development because some volunteers, non-profit organizations or Non-Governmental Organizations (NGOs) have implemented a relief initiative when a development program would have been more helpful instead. Some people have believed that emergency assistance will suffice as development because it meets a need. However, it does not meet a need in a long-term, non-dependent, sustainable way, so emergency relief does not suffice as development. Relief and development both have their place. But if volunteers use the wrong methods in the wrong situation, it can have negative ramifications.[1]

An organization called Hope International creates easy to cook meals high in protein and nutrients. They have meal packaging events where people can package meals, which cost twenty cents each. The ease to make, high nutrient content, and low cost make these meals a good option for emergency relief after a natural disaster. These meals also help people in their community who need to visit a food pantry or homeless shelter to feed their families when they fall on hard times.[2] However, the meals can be used as misplaced relief because the people who package the meals, like a business or church, can send the food anywhere they would like. If they choose to send it to a food insecure area instead of a natural disaster area then they would be using relief methods when development would help instead. This misplaced relief puts a band-aid on a food insecure situation that needs a permanent fix. Misplaced relief matters because it creates unsustainability and does not solve the real issue at hand, the food insecurity. Instead, it temporarily pauses the larger issue by sending some boxes of food.[3] The real problem could be something like food insecurity relating to inefficient agriculture production. The new international volunteer could redirect their effort to help solve that issue instead.

Volunteers have also erroneously used relief when they want a quick fix to a complex problem that actually requires development methods. In this way, quick fixes will not adequately address the problems at hand. An organization called Food Aid International has a similar setup to Hope International. It sends meals with high nutrient and protein content for a low cost to people around the world. The About Us page of its website, under the Why We Do It section, states, "The problem is not finding volunteers, or one of logistics, although these are real issues. We have the food solution. The real problem is finding the funding necessary to achieve the goal. We must continue to raise awareness of the issue of world hunger … so that the resources that are available can be focused on what is arguably the most pressing issue of our time: that of STARVATION!"[4] Starvation indeed constitutes a pressing issue of our time but it will not be solved by sending such meals to everyone in the world who needs food. The meals cannot solve starvation because they act only as emergency relief. When using the meals as a replacement for development, instead of in the appropriate relief context, it undermines the complexity and real need for a permanent solution to food insecurity worldwide. Giving people meals cannot solve global hunger because it lacks sustainability.[5]

Hope International has a similar quotation from the About Us page on its website, which reads, "Sometimes a crisis is a powerful thirst which can be quenched as easily as a bottle of water. A crisis could be a lack of funds to send their children to school with adequate supplies, or not having the funds to feed their family."[6] Hope International does a great job helping the kids in its community get school supplies. However, giving someone a bottle of water only works until they get thirsty again. Food and water insecurity exist for a variety of reasons that can be different in every place affected by them. Long-term development really matters because it prioritizes the agency and autonomy of the people experiencing the food or water insecurity. Long-term development takes a large amount of time, resources and effort, but the results work better than the alternative of misplaced relief.[7] In this way, the new international volunteer needs to prioritize permanent development solutions that will make a lasting impact.

The mix-up between development and relief can be changed when the new international volunteer thinks about how their intended methodology fits into the short term, the long term and specifically how it meets a need. If it meets a need in the short term but would create dependency in the long term and not be sustainable, then it gets classified as relief. Would relief be appropriate in the situation due to a natural disaster, environmental problem, or humanitarian crisis? If no, then development would be the best methodology for the international development endeavor. Alternatively, if the project meets a long-term need in a sustainable, permanent way that does not create dependency, then development would be the main method employed by volunteers. If no natural disaster or humanitarian crisis has occurred recently, then development would be employed because the situation requires a long-term and permanent solution. Relief only becomes necessary when providing short-term aid because a destructive event happened where people temporarily lost the ability to meet their needs for survival. In all other cases, volunteers should think in terms of development.

Sustainability

Sustainability means making sure that international volunteers act in a self-sufficient, self-reliant, long-lasting, and environmentally-friendly manner. New international volunteers see sustainability as one of the most important aspects of international volunteering, and they strive for sustainability in every possible way. Sustainability matters because it ensures that the good volunteers do in development truly lasts. Sustainable development does not harm the environment or unduly take away from the planet's natural resources in a destructive way. Volunteers can think about sustainability as both a state of mind and a series of actions to take each time they volunteer.

Volunteers who think sustainably make sure that the development work they do internationally will make the biggest, most positive impact possible. Although international volunteers think of sustainability in terms of the environment, and they are correct to do so, it also means that the project will stand on its own and not cause dependency. Dependency can cause damage because it robs people of agency and does not guarantee the project's permanency. Only self-sustaining projects can be reliable in the long term because they do not count on outside forces to maintain themselves. Self-sustaining projects can adjust their methods to maintain their functionality amongst changing conditions because they have the autonomy to do so.

The new international volunteer acts sustainably by making sure they use environmentally-friendly materials, keep a low carbon footprint and do not harm any of the Earth's natural resources (like trees, air quality and bodies of water). Sustainability prevents negative consequences. For instance, if a project pollutes, then it harms air and water quality, which does not help the host community in the long term. Or, if a project damages natural resources, then it takes away from the many benefits they offer the people who live near them, such as medicinal benefits from plants, and clean air from trees.

Without sustainability, a development project could pollute the earth, which would ultimately hurt humanity. For example, if volunteers did not implement sustainable development practices, then they might build a health clinic but cut down a half-acre of the forest in order to do so. They may even use the trees to build the health clinic with, but the clinic still deforested the land and took away the health benefits of the trees. When struggling forests become deforested, it can reduce biodiversity and lead to extinction of rare animal species. Therefore, the health clinic would not be an example of sustainable development.

Alternatively, if volunteers build a health clinic with a locally available, naturally occurring material, the project will be sustainable, especially if volunteers replant the material used. In this way, sustainable development uses environmentally-friendly methods, such as replanting the same amount of material used during construction and building on land that townspeople already use (if locals think replanting would be beneficial). This sustainable alternative prevents deforesting to build a clinic.

The new international volunteer helps ensure sustainability by communicating with locals to find out what may hurt the environment in that area before implementing any project. In Guatemala, I learned that a group of international volunteers bought reeds to put on the edge of Lake Atitlán, Guatemala (without consulting locals), in order to reduce lake pollution. The reeds, in theory, take in small pollutants to improve the quality of water. The volunteers did not research enough to learn that in order to survive, reeds must be regularly moved closer inland so they do not drown when the water gets too deep. If the reeds drowned, they would not prevent pollution—they would become pollution. Since the volunteers did not solicit the locals' opinions on how to care for the reeds, all the reeds drowned. Not only did they do no good, but they also added pollution to the lake instead of taking it away.

In the same way, the new international volunteer prevents dependency and promotes sustainability by using locally available resources always. When volunteers do not use locally available resources, one of two things could happen. First, locals cannot fix what volunteers built when it breaks, since they do not have replacement supplies. Secondly, locals do not use what volunteers built because they find it incompatible with their way of life. Sustainable development does not occur in either outcome. As these examples show, if volunteers communicate with locals before acting, they would ensure sustainability. NC State Professor Dr. Bob Patterson once told me a story of his travels abroad. One group of volunteers decided to import motors to build wells in Africa. They worked correctly, solving a water issue in the community. However, a year later the group returned to the community to find that the motors did not work any longer. The motors broke and the people living in the community could not find the parts to fix the imported motors, so the well became useless. To be sustainable, the new international volunteer uses only locally available parts to avoid this situation from happening. If parts need to be imported, then the project cannot be sustainable because it will only work until the parts break down. It also creates dependency when locals have to rely on more imports from volunteers to fix it.

Dr. Patterson saw a different group of volunteers who built a well in the center of a village in Africa. The group returned later to find locals bypassing the functioning well on the way to an out-of-town well they made themselves. The new well deprived villagers of a long walk each day to collect water, which doubled as an opportunity to talk to the children about tribal culture and history. The parents decided to go to the old well, even though it took longer to travel to, so they could prioritize their children's education. These examples underscore the need for volunteers to consult locals before beginning a project to find a sustainable solution up front.

The new international volunteer can also promote sustainability through clean energy usage and solutions. In Malawi, for example, William Kamkwamba, a boy at the time, read a book about windmills. His town did not have electricity, so he decided to make a windmill himself to provide electricity for his family. The windmill generates renewable energy and does not pollute. William made the windmill with locally available and replaceable parts that he upcycled from a junkyard. After successfully operating a windmill, William expanded his project over time to give electricity access to people around him. Neighbors could go to the windmill to charge their cell phones, for example. Before electricity, owning a cell phone could be almost impossible when people did not have access to a power source. The benefits of the windmill also grew to include potable water via a pump, adding another resource the town did not have before. During William's childhood, his community experienced famine, so to prevent famine in the future, he built a system for the windmill to water his family's fields. Eventually, not only did the windmill provide clean energy, but it also replaced dirty energy sources such as paraffin lamps that pollute with kerosene. In this way, sustainable energy helps in international volunteering because certain solutions like William's windmills offer an opportunity to access clean and sustainable energy.[8]

Incremental Change

Governments commonly use sweeping change to impose large changes all at once. Oftentimes, however, in daily life, big social and economic changes happen incrementally over a period of time. Large changes can happen by taking several smaller steps over time to lead up to a big result. Incremental change gives people more time to assess how well changes work before implementing more of them. Incremental change can work better than sweeping change when people do not have financial safety nets but would like to create them.

Farmers often try new agricultural methods incrementally, like planting a small area with a new crop to test its yield before planting an entire field of it. Farmers may love big, grand ideas to increase crop yields, in theory, but may not be willing to put them into practice because of the risk it could entail to their livelihoods. Farmers like this can be considered risk averse. Risk averse people avoid taking on a lot of risk at one time in order to protect what they already have.

In international volunteering, if a subsistence farmer (a farmer who only makes enough food to live off of, not enough to sell any leftovers for profit) sees a new cropping technique that would double yields on the same amount of land, they may still not immediately implement it. If it does not work, and the crops do not produce a yield as a result, then the farmer will not have enough food to survive. If, however, the same farmer farmed for profit, had a successful butcher business, and had $10,000 in savings to buy food with if the cropping technique failed, then that farmer would be more likely to try it out. If the technique failed, the farmer would still have a backup savings account to purchase food with, and the butcher business to keep income coming in before the next round of crops matured.

Development often requires big changes, but people cannot afford to make them all at once. Making gradual changes over time can be a solution. If someone has spare money in savings or a second source of income, then they can afford to be innovative. However, if someone barely gets by, then throwing a curveball into how they feed their family may mean malnutrition or starvation if it does not work out. Therefore, volunteers need to think ethically (even more so than normal) with a risk-averse population. If volunteers would like to help a subsistence farmer majorly change their crop techniques, then volunteers need to be sure that the cropping technique is proven, trustworthy, and reliable, such as crop rotation to prevent erosion, which has been in practice for many years. The stakes could not be higher.

In order to help implement a big change, international volunteers can brainstorm low risk solutions with locals that create incremental change over time. Once one risk-averse farmer makes one tiny change to their cropping techniques, and they like the results, then, after a few more small changes help the farmer increase crop yields, volunteers may be able to help the farmer try a major change on a small portion of land. At that point, it might not seem so drastic because the smaller steps lead to the final result more gradually. This can be done in phases. Phases help institute incremental change by measuring progress throughout. This ensures that what has been enacted so far still fits into the overall plan. Each phase in the following diagram represents a time period of small, gradual changes. Each phase can have different aims or can be a natural continuation of the same goal. After each phase volunteers can look back and examine how it went. Did the implementation go according to plan? Does the project remain on track for the next phase? If not, what adjustments need to be made before beginning the next phase? This pause permits the most recent changes to take hold before beginning more incremental change in the next phase. With careful monitoring, the goal will be completed.

Sometimes volunteers can lessen the impact of risk in other ways. In the town of Panajachel, Guatemala, children worked during all hours of the day in order to provide income for their families. However, working deprives children of an education that can increase their earning power as an adult. Some families could not easily make an investment in their child's education since it would entail making a sacrifice of income. The government found a creative solution. Children had to get a license to work, and they could work either in the mornings or in the afternoons but go to school in their off hours. Schools in the area adapted by offering morning and afternoon sessions. If children did not go to school, then they

Progress phases.

could lose their license to work. Children attended school at higher rates to prevent the risk of losing their work license. When children worked and studied, they capitalized on their present and future earning powers. This incremental change makes space for kids to go from full time workers who do not attend school, to part time workers who get an education.[9] If the incremental change continues, then children will be able to move away from working and focus exclusively on school.

Farmers can lessen the impact of risk from incremental change by investing in crop insurance. International volunteers can help farmers who would like to make an incremental change with their cropping techniques by connecting them to reliable crop insurance. Crop insurance may not be a good fit for every farmer because some insurance plans may require farmers to pay a deductible that they cannot afford or there could be holes in coverage.[10] However, in certain cases, paying a deductible could be worth it for a farmer who stands to gain a significant uptick in crop yields by implementing an incremental change technique. Crop insurance can be particularly helpful if a farmer must take out a loan for a later step of the incremental change, such as to buy a pump for new irrigation. Crop insurance could prevent them from defaulting on the loan if the irrigation technique fails. Insurance can be a useful tool in other international volunteering situations as well, such as helping a family purchase home insurance after helping them build a house, for instance. Or it could be insurance on a solar lamp that a person relies on as their only source of electricity. Insurance in all of these situations helps to reduce risk so that people can make positive changes without needing to fear what could happen if they do not turn out as expected.

Diversity, Equity and Inclusion

Diversity, equity and inclusion (DE&I) in international volunteering means that every segment of the population gets involved in the international development project. The new international volunteer takes great efforts to ensure that everyone has a say, participates in and leads the work. International volunteering needs to be a communal affair where everyone hears and implements the others' ideas. This way the outcome benefits everyone, not just the most privileged part of the population. Inclusion encompasses many groups, especially those with a history of being marginalized. This includes racial, ethnic and religious minorities; women; people with disabilities; the elderly; and the LGBTQIA+ community. Any segment of population not welcomed by society or with a history of being marginalized needs to be involved. This could include people not mentioned above, such as people who cannot read or people who live on the outskirts of the community, for instance. The new international volunteer needs to research the community to ensure the project's inclusivity and that everyone's needs will be met.

Inclusion matters greatly in international volunteering. Projects that alienate certain people represent not only unethical volunteering but also ineffective and incomplete volunteer projects. People have different needs based on many factors, such as history, race, sexual orientation, gender, etc., and a non-inclusive project cannot understand those needs in order to meet them. Therefore, everyone will benefit only if women and minorities participate in all parts of the project. Women must be included because a helpful project will not be based on a patriarchal system. A project excluding women would exclude 50 percent of the population from reaping the benefits of the volunteer project. Therefore, any international development project must seek to meet the needs of everyone involved in order to truly help.

Additionally, international development initiatives have the greatest chance of success if minorities and women help design and implement the volunteer project. An academic paper by Endalcachew Bayeh, entitled, The Role of Empowering Women and Achieving Gender Inequality to the Sustainable Development of Ethiopia, concluded from their research that "unless women are empowered and gender equality is achieved so that women can play their role in economic, social, political, and environmental areas, the country will not achieve sustainable development.... The fact that women constitute half the entire population of the country makes empowering them to be an active part of all development initiatives in the country a compelling circumstance."[11] The United Nations agrees with these conclusions and makes women and minority inclusion a key strategy in their poverty reduction work. The UN Development Programme believes that "overcoming the marginalization of minorities has direct benefits for national development processes and the achievement of inclusive growth." To raise awareness and help stakeholders ensure minorities get a seat at the table of development, the United Nations Development Programme created a resource guide and toolkit for Marginalized Minorities in Development Planning. This report points out that historically "the poorest communities in almost any region tend to be minority communities that have been targets of long-standing discrimination, exclusion and sometimes violence." This reality can change. The report goes on to point out that "discrimination and exclusion of national or ethnic, religious and linguistic minorities undermine efforts to achieve poverty reduction.... In contrast, effective participation of minorities enriches decision-making, and helps us plan, implement and monitor sustainable and effective

solutions to development challenges."[12] Development will be most successful if women and minorities become active participants in the process, as
they have every right to be. Every person, regardless of any differentiating
factor, has human rights.

Women and minorities also need to be actively engaged in community planning because the diversity of people and their range of
experience lends to more creative ideas and previously unthought of perspectives. For example, any literacy project in Guatemala must include
indigenous stakeholders and women stakeholders, since indigenous people and women experience lower literacy rates than non-indigenous
men in Guatemala. In all of Guatemala, the average literacy rate for
15+-year-olds equaled 79.103 percent, which is an average between an
84.759 percent rate for men and 74.042 percent for women, according
to thedialogue.org. And it also differs widely among indigenous versus
non-indigenous Guatemalans. In 2011, 29.2 percent more non-indigenous
women ages 15+ years old could read versus indigenous women (81.1 percent versus 51.9 percent) and 14.3 percent more non-indigenous men than
indigenous men (88.9 percent versus 74.6 percent). Non-indigenous men
still tend to be the most likely to be literate in Guatemala, according to
Guatemalan government statistics and thedialogue.org.[13] However, it is
not enough to only include women and minorities in the volunteer project, women and minority host community members need to lead the project. In many societies, women and minorities do not get equal access to
leadership roles as males and the majority do, even though they are just as
capable to lead. New international volunteers promote equity and facilitate these leaders' platform.

The new international volunteer can take several action steps to
ensure that the project fosters an inclusive environment. First, they must
make sure that the project will be inclusive and intersectional in the current stages but also in the future, such as when asking for feedback after
the project to gauge its success. During the pre-project research, the new
international volunteer should research to see if the area has a history of
marginalization of any shape or form there, or if any segment of the population constitutes a minority.

Secondly, volunteers must ensure all people can voice their opinion during the planning phase of the project. To do that, the new international volunteer can make sure they create a safe space where everyone can
express their ideas by listening to people's needs and concerns. In order
to ensure diverse perspectives are heard, people have to feel comfortable
versing them. Some people may not want to talk about their needs in front
of a group of people. For instance, in certain cultures, women may not be
comfortable speaking in front of men or a family may not want to speak

freely in front of their neighbors. Therefore, international volunteers need to reach out individually to community stakeholders and build trust for one-on-one conversations to give everyone a private forum to voice their opinions and concerns.

Thirdly, during the project itself, the local leadership team must include each segment of the population so that they can execute the inclusive vision of the project. This does not mean that only one person of a minority should be on the leadership council. Different people in each population segment have different opinions and needs, so it would be an error to assume one person speaks for a whole group. Additionally, the new international volunteer must speak up if they witness any discrimination and question any exclusive notions, comments or suggestions they hear.

Finally, in order to have a diverse international volunteering project, not only community member representatives, but also the volunteer group, needs to be diverse. This will allow the volunteer group as a whole to relate to more peoples' experiences. If the host community needs assistance finding a solution to an issue, a diverse volunteer team can give more ideas while brainstorming than they would if everyone in the volunteer team has similar life experience.

Equity is another important piece to keep in mind when volunteering inclusively, along with diversity and inclusion. The three concepts of diversity, equity and inclusion work best together. Equity can be defined as fairness plus inclusiveness, but the word carries deeper meaning in a societal context. Equity means being impartial, giving everyone the same opportunities, and not withholding anything at the expense of someone else. Equity applies to race, gender, sexuality and socioeconomic status, to name a few, just as diversity and inclusion do.

With the Covid-19 pandemic, the world witnessed an inequitable vaccine rollout that benefited Western countries at the expense of everyone else. Many people received booster shots when others did not have access to their first shot. The physical and mental toll of lack of access to the Covid-19 vaccines has contributed to more sickness, death and grieving. The inequity has been caused by not sharing vaccine technology information, pricing and purchasing rules, where supply chains are located and the requirements for cooling the vaccine. While solutions to the inequity such as high-income governments donating shots, vaccine manufacturers sharing technology, strengthening cooling infrastructure in countries without it and creating transparent pricing exist, the best solution would be a fair system in which some countries cannot hoard doses at the expense of others and pricing is equal or free among all countries.[14]

Communication

Preparation beforehand helps to prevent challenges in communication in international volunteering. To adequately prepare, the new international volunteer needs to communicate with key locals and partners before arriving. Just like in any relationship, the more communication, the better. The healthiest projects and relationships feature strong and open communication. Therefore, volunteers and project leaders need to communicate with each other in order to be sure that everyone's needs get met. Expectations need to be articulated simply and clearly. This can happen by creating a detailed itinerary and goal sheet for everyone. This not only creates unity, but it also allows people with various perspectives the chance to spot potential problems that project leaders did not yet identify.

Speaking the language of the host community helps ensure clear communication between locals and volunteers. When volunteers speak the language, the project runs more efficiently because the need for an intermediary translator gets negated. Also, volunteers and locals can share their thoughts, suggestions and concerns directly to one another at any time. People in the host community can bounce ideas off one another and the volunteer can understand and respond. Really learning the language gives volunteers the ability to have greater depth of conversations about more technical and nuanced matters when volunteers know the range of vocabulary needed to have those conversations, instead of knowing basic phrases only. Communicating in the language of the host community also helps insuremutual understanding, preventing important details of the project from getting lost in translation. If any miscommunications occur, volunteers who speak the language will know what occurred and how to fix it.

Individuals can utilize several methods to learn a language, but knowing which steps to prioritize depends on how much time the new international volunteer has before going on an international development trip. When the trip will occur in the short term, such as in less than two months, it helps to devote as much time as possible each day to create an immersive language learning environment. Some first steps for those who have an international volunteer trip in the short term can include memorizing common vocabulary words, phrases and questions. This includes memorizing everyday answers to the questions that one can find in a phrasebook. The vocabulary also needs to include trip-specific vocabulary when relevant.

For instance, if the volunteering trip focuses on providing medical services, it would be helpful to learn common medical words. This can be found online by searching for "medical words in relevant language."

Focus on how to pronounce the words so if someone speaks them, volunteers will be able to recognize them and reply in turn. To improve pronunciation and listening skills, volunteers can spend a dedicated amount of time each day with a language learning software that includes a voice component. Or, as an alternative, many people achieve a great amount of fluency by participating in intensive language lessons in a group or private setting. Many language schools offer programs focused on producing students who can speak a new language in a matter of weeks. Volunteers may be able to go to the host community or country a few weeks early to focus on intensive language learning before the project begins.[15]

The ideal outcome of intensive short-term language learning would be to hold a basic conversation and to communicate most daily needs during the international volunteer trip.

The language strategy changes in the medium-term, or when the international volunteer has a trip scheduled for a few months away. In this scenario volunteers will have more time to gain language skills and to participate in immersive activity. I suggest doing all of the activities that people who have a trip in the short term would do, plus the following. Watch news in the new language to learn frequently used vocabulary about commonly discussed events and places. This helps volunteers understand the sonic patterns of the language and what people say when they speak. Similarly, when watching tv shows or movies in the volunteer's native language, put on subtitles in the new language. This helps to absorb as much as possible how the new language relates to the native one. Not only will this help the volunteer pick up on cognates, but it also helps them understand how to phrase sentences in the new languages.

To get a feel for sounds and pronunciation, volunteers can also listen to music in the new language, with the added advantage of learning more about the culture of the host country through music produced there. Similarly, read magazines and newspapers in the new language to learn common vocabulary and sentence structure. This additionally helps readers learn more about culture and current events. Finally, hire a regular tutor specifically to work on any weak or underdeveloped spots in language cognition. In the medium-term volunteers can strive to hold regular conversations, including mildly in-depth ones that express feelings and goals, during the international volunteer project.

The international volunteer who works on learning the host community's language in the long term has the best opportunity for fluency. By taking the steps that short- and medium-term volunteers would take, and the following steps in addition, the new international volunteer will be able to have in-depth conversations and really understand what people in the host community say. Volunteers can take college classes from the beginning to the advanced levels. Postsecondary classes aim for complete comprehension, so volunteers will have a breadth of knowledge. They also ensure that volunteers will emerge with a strong knowledge of reading, writing and speaking. Likewise, it helps to do additional activities outside class as well. For example, read chapter books meant for older children and/or translated versions of favorite books to improve reading levels. Getting a pen pal who communicates in the new language will also help to improve reading comprehension and writing skills.

To improve conversational ability, join a conversation group at a library, community center or university. Conversation groups bring together a dedicated group of people who listen and speak in the new language. Alternatively, do a language exchange with someone. In a language exchange, each person wants to learn the other's native language as a second language and both people speak in the language they want to learn. A language exchange could be between a native English speaker who will speak Spanish and a native Spanish speaker who will speak in English, for example. It fosters mutual improvement when each person corrects the other's incorrect sentences, and it can build friendships as well. Finally, the new international volunteer who has a long time to learn the host community's language can shadow professionals who speak the new language and who do the same scope of work as the volunteer project will, like a dentist who speaks Spanish for a volunteer dentist who will go on a project in the Dominican Republic.

Learning Spanish prior to my study abroad and volunteering trip helped me understand the usefulness of knowing the local languages. In Guatemala, knowing Spanish allowed me to read government websites and statistics about literacy and conduct interviews with locals. Once I landed in Guatemala, it became apparent that in order to travel around, communicate about fares, get directions and live everyday life, knowing Spanish allowed me to function at a higher level than if I had only a basic understanding. I could ask deeper questions in each conversation and receive information about Guatemalans' opinions about literacy. Knowing Spanish gave me the confidence to interview government education officials and learn more about the situation, informing my research and gaining perspectives I would not have gotten elsewhere. My one regret in this situation would be not learning the local indigenous languages.

Research

Sometimes volunteers cannot know what to prepare until they arrive at the project location, but research can give an overview of what goes on in the host community. Volunteers can conduct two types of research—desk research and in-person research. Various methods for both can be found in the following chart.

Desk Research	In-Person Research
Phone/Email	Surveys
Interviews	Questionnaires
Internet Searches	Focus Groups
Academic and News Articles	Brainstorm Sessions
Literature and History Books	Interviews

Desk research encompasses learning important and relevant information about a location or community prior to travel. Volunteers typically do desk research first as it allows them time to prepare. Desk research guides the questions to ask for the in-person research, gives general knowledge of history, culture, current events etc. Phone/Email would be ideal if volunteers need to connect with specific people in the area before arriving there. Interviews take desk research a little further as it helps volunteers drill down to understand a specific topic. An interview could be the first step in a relationship that will be furthered when traveling to the region.

Internet searches aid volunteers in gathering primary research and statistics about a country or region. It will not allow volunteers to get into the weeds, but it will give a good baseline to start asking questions from. Academic and news articles take research one step further when looking for specific research on topics. Academic research offers a solution for the volunteer who wants to focus on a very specific project but has not traveled in the host community. Literature, history and cultural research assists volunteers in learning about the customs and uniqueness of the region.

I did not use phone, email, and interviews to prepare for Guatemala. However, for many people, this component cannot be skipped. I read three books about Guatemalan literature and history, but mostly I used internet searches to plan my literacy project and volunteering experiences. First, I googled general facts about the nation and the indigenous population that lived in the highlands where I would be staying. Then, I searched the Guatemala version, *google.com.gt*, to search terms in Spanish relating to my literacy project. This allowed me to find government data and statistics that did not show up on the U.S. Google page. I also found a breakdown of literacy by town in the region I stayed, using Guatemala's Google page. I used this site to search academic articles on literature after the civil war, shaping the scope of my project, because I decided to make the project about how literacy had improved after the war ended.

The in-person research follows after desk research. In-person research gathers opinions and insights from people directly experiencing conditions that the international volunteer project will address. In-person research connects volunteers with locals who think about the tenets of the project and who have varied opinions about its methods and goals. Arriving to the project site early to do in-person research will help volunteers learn about the host community most directly. Taking time to research in the host community before beginning an international volunteering project ensures that volunteers will use the right development methods and that the host community agrees about the scope of work volunteers will be doing. Doing research in-person also gives volunteers the opportunity to learn insights that they could not know until arriving in-person. In-person interviews could be part of a continued conversation that began with an interview over the phone. Some interviewing methods, such as surveys and questionnaires, facilitate insights from a group of locals. Similarly, focus groups allow volunteers to get a smaller, more specific groups' opinions on a topic. Brainstorm sessions bring locals and volunteers together to work toward the same goal. This approach can yield good results.

In Guatemala I learned many insights once I got there that I did not know from my desk research. For example, people ride standing up in the bed of pickup trucks as a form of public transportation. The modified trucks have metal railings on each side for people to hold on to, like on a metro. I asked riders why they used this form of public transportation because in some other places people cannot ride in the back of a pickup truck due to safety concerns. However, I learned that Guatemalans found the trucks to be a reliable and safe form of transportation partly because trucks cannot go very fast on the roads. They can also navigate very narrow and winding roads easier than buses can. Additionally, trucks stop between smaller towns that buses and boats do not service. The trucks offer other advantages, such as allowing people to bring more things with them and the ability to hop off anywhere along the route. I met farmers who carried their equipment with them on the truck and would whistle when they wanted it to stop at the specific field they would be working at that day.

For my in-person research I conducted several interviews with parents of school-aged children, teachers, principals and government workers. The desk research I did helped me frame the questions for the in-person interviews. I also employed surveys and questionnaires for my research. I gave each person that I met a survey asking them to rank the importance of different factors to achieving literacy. That helped me to see where different sectors had varying opinions. The answers from the surveys allowed me to see the fuller picture of how literacy had improved after the civil war. In brainstorm sessions the librarian and I came up with ideas on how we could get more children into the library.

VII

Donations

Donations

Donations can go hand in hand with volunteering on international development trips. Some volunteers bring donations for the host community with them in their suitcases, including clothes, shoes and medical supplies. Volunteers can alternatively donate money as part of volunteering internationally. Donations can be perceived as either a quick fix to a problem or as a gift that can create more equality between volunteers and the host community. However, in reality, the outcome from donations is more complex and not always that positive.[1]

Sometimes the host community does not need what volunteers donate. I met a girl in college who volunteered in Haiti after the earthquake there in 2010. On a free day she visited the border between Haiti and the Dominican Republic and witnessed a medicine and food exchange between Haitians and Dominicans. Many organizations distributed antibiotics to families in Haiti, and some of those families traded the antibiotics for food at the border. She learned that while Haitians needed medicine, most families needed food more urgently than medicine. Dominicans who came to trade for medicine had more food security than Haitians and could afford to trade food for medicine because they too needed medicine but had their food needs met more readily. This taught her to ask what people need before donating after disaster strikes.

Giving shoes, medical supplies, and clothes can devastate an already potentially fragile job market in the host community. Tom's Shoes gives a pair of shoes to someone for each pair that customers buy. In the early days of Tom's, I bought a pair of canvas shoes. I learned from experience that the shoes get holes in them quickly—in both the soles and sides. I bought a second pair and they wore out just as quickly. It got me thinking: What do the people who get a pair of Tom's Shoes do after they wear out from holes? I only walked around a college campus, and the shoes still wore out quicker than my other pairs of shoes did. Growing up walking barefoot in the country, I knew that bare feet have an easier time when calluses develop, and that wearing shoes allows the calluses to diminish. It hurts more to walk on rocks and gravel once calluses have somewhat abated. I began to ask myself: If I purchase a pair of Tom's Shoes and the firm donates a pair (along with other pairs) to the same area, and a shoemaker goes out of business, what do people do when the shoes become old and worn out? How will they be replaced? With more donations? What happens when the donations run out sometime in the future?

After my experience with Tom's, I began reading articles warning that Tom's harms local shoe markets. When Tom's donates shoes to everyone in an area, no one needs to purchase shoes, and as a consequence, shoe stores in the area can close or shoemakers lose a significant volume of work. Many job markets in developing areas are relatively new and small. These job markets can be fragile because they are not maximized to scale and not established to withstand large shocks, such as bulk shoe inventories being donated from abroad. Vulnerable shoe industries, for example, can be harmed by Tom's. And Tom's do not get made by people who already work in the shoe industry in the area they get donated in. Setting aside the fact that donating shoes does not meet sustainability standards, the Tom's donation model would be much easier on shoe markets and the people employed in the shoe industry if Tom's hired people in the area where shoes would be donated and paid them for their work. In economic terms, when Tom's gives shoes to people in the same area, those people temporarily stop demanding shoes from the local economy. When demand falters, suppliers of shoes cannot sell shoes, and thus lose money or even go out of business. In this way, donations, especially unneeded and unsustainable ones, can hurt the local economy. When the local economy weakens, poverty increases.[2]

A study of Tom's Shoes in El Salvador by Bruce Wydick found that "the overall impact of the shoe donation program appears to be negligible, illustrating the importance of more careful targeting of in-kind donation programs." This occurred because, as summarized by Humanosphere, "some 88% of children in the region owned two or more pairs of shoes or sandals. Most children had shoes and even the poorest families could likely afford at least one pair for each child. People who traveled around barefoot did so out of their own choice, not because of a lack of shoes."[3] The study, summarized by Racked, showed that "the shoes weren't making a noticeable difference in kids' lives, according to Vox. com. 'The bad news is that there is no evidence that the shoes exhibit any kind of life-changing impact, except for potentially making them feel somewhat more reliant on external aid,' professor Bruce Wydick wrote."[4] If Tom's applied donations more thoughtfully or instead supported growing local industry, then the firm could have the desired impact without the negative side effects.

The same applies when volunteers donate medical supplies internationally. Medical supplies can have harmful effects for two reasons. Firstly, medical supplies do not meet sustainability requirements. Locals will only receive medical supplies until volunteers stop sending them, which inevitably will happen, even if only in the long term. Patients will not have enough substitutes when the supplies stop arriving. When medical supplies run out, patients, doctors and hospitals will be in the same situation, or worse, than before. This destructive cycle becomes unhealthy and unsustainable. New international volunteering does not create nor elongate a cycle of dependency.

Secondly, donated medical supplies can harm important local rituals. Professor Bob Patterson once told me that when he visited Africa, locals told him never to give an American toothbrush to the children who lived in the town he researched in. The children learned to brush their teeth using a naturally occurring branch from a tree that cleaned teeth and allowed for good gum health. Children would apparently not use this branch if Americans gave them a shiny new toothbrush from the United States, and their dental health would decline, as the American toothbrush would over time.

Sometimes donations can be improved. Operation Christmas Child asks people in industrialized countries to fill a shoebox filled with nonperishable toiletry items and toys to give to a child in a low-income country. I myself grew up packing a box for Operation Christmas Child each year. As a teenager, I also volunteered at an Operation Christmas Child distribution center one Christmas season, taking out prohibited items from boxes, taping them and praying for the box. However, they can be inappropriate and even offensive. For instance, toys popular in America do not account for cultural differences. Many toys do not mimic the children receiving them, especially dolls depicting white girls as a standard of beauty. Additionally, some items packed in the boxes like gloves and socks do not help at their destination. Operation Christmas Child ships boxes to over one hundred countries with climates that range from cold to rainy to hot, and so the needs for weather-related items differ. Finally, many toys and toiletries sent in the boxes will not be sustainable for the children. Cheap plastic toys break quickly and toothbrushes and toothpaste only last a short while.

The shoeboxes show the children who receive them the cycle of foreign aid, which tends to be unsustainable and unhealthy, while taking away autonomy and agency. It also perpetuates the idea in the children who give the boxes the false idea that they can give things to "less fortunate children" and that those things will help them. Materialism (giving a shoe-box of toys) will not solve complex socioeconomic and geopolitical problems that perpetuate poverty. A box of toiletries will not change the living situation of the kids who receive them. New international volunteers thus take it upon themselves to ensure that they do not engage in these cycles and instead immerse themselves into understanding lack of opportunity, social mobility and economic growth in impoverished places, redirecting donations to maximize positive impact.

Donating items with organizations like Operation Christmas Child can be more effective. First, people can more mindfully consider what they pack in the boxes, searching for sustainable and appropriate items. This short-term solution would be easy to implement although it does not make things permanently better for the children. Some examples include packing a teddy bear instead of plastic dolls as to not perpetuate white women as standards of beauty and because teddy bears tend to last longer than many plastic toys. In fact, wooden puzzles can be more durable than plastic toys in general. Since Operation Christmas Child boxes have gender-specific labeling, people can substitute school supplies instead of gender-specific items so that they can be enjoyed by all. Finally, to make the box as sustainable as possible, consider packing a washcloth instead of toothbrush for toiletry items, or something else meant to last longer than a toothbrush.[5]

The next step involves investing in long-term growth by changing the pattern of donations. It can be more sustainable to switch from donating boxes to donating to educational programs that help children get an education who otherwise could not afford to. Additionally, donors can get involved in a community abroad by asking them how to help. For instance, if a town needed to build a road and needed a pipe for under the road so water would not flood it, then a donation of a pipe would make a huge difference. It would be especially beneficial if locals knew how to repair and replace the pipe with locally available parts if it breaks. Volunteers would also make the greatest impact by purchasing the pipe from a local merchant.

The general rule of thumb with international donations is that one-size donations do not fit all. This means that donations do not need to be given on every volunteer trip, they will not help in every situation, and that volunteers need to take directions from locals on donations. Donations help to solve a short-term constraint, such as in a refugee camp, in a homeless shelter or after a natural disaster. But even then, the donations need to be appropriate. Appropriate donations will not insult locals, be positively received and make a difference to a dire problem.

The new international volunteer ensures that donations will be appropriate and helpful by first communicating with locals before donating. By communicating with locals, volunteers have the opportunity to be respectful by asking what locals need and how volunteers can help meet those needs. In many cases, the host community needs volunteers to donate their time, manpower and logistical skills more than second-hand items from home. But if locals do need items, volunteers can be sure that they will be welcomed and appreciated. The new international volunteer does not hurt local industry. Researching and being a smart consumer ensures that donations like Tom's will not hurt. This also applies before an international volunteer trip when the group contemplates bringing items to donate. In deciding, ask if the donations will be sustainable and not harm the local economy. Some key questions include: What would the outcome be if I donate the items? What might happen if I do not donate the items? Will the donations be sustainable? Do locals want me to donate the items?

When volunteers donate items, they act as suppliers and the host community becomes the consumer of those donations. If volunteer donations would be hurtful, an alternative exists. International volunteers can be the consumers while the host community acts as suppliers. International volunteers who want to give donations do so out of a desire to meet the needs of the community. When donations will not meet those needs, but volunteers still want to help, they can inject cash into the local economy. Injecting cash could look like purchasing souvenirs, supplies, food and the services of guides and translators from the host community. The influx of cash will help people purchase what they need more so than donations planned by volunteers without local feedback would. This consumer-supplier relationship can have a tangible impact in the economic growth of the tourism sector.

In Guatemala, the town of Santiago Atitlán is both a hub for travelers passing through and also a home to various international volunteer projects. Santiago Atitlán gets a significant portion of its GDP from selling handmade souvenirs, and providing services, lodging and food to tourists and international volunteers. For instance, some medical projects base themselves in Santiago Atitlán and travel to surrounding towns during the day. I frequently traveled through Santiago Atitlán from Panajachel by boat and then took a pickup truck back to the town of San Lucas Tolimán, where I lived. After leaving the boat and walking to the pickup trucks, many tourists and international volunteers bought handicrafts made and sold in small booths lining the pathway. But Santiago also houses hotels and meeting spaces, one of which I had a class in, situated by the lake, with waiters serving the group fresh fish ravioli sourced from the lake. The steady demand for souvenirs, services and goods by international volunteers helps provide stable employment for many co-ops, crafters, hoteliers and restaurant workers.

Helping Via Donations

Refugees oftentimes live in some of the most devastating situations on Earth. They can be trapped in a strange land and they have to deal with obstacles to gainful employment and housing, shortages of basic supplies, language barriers and mental trauma from past and current experiences. Even refugee children may not have access to schools to get an education in some refugee camps.[6] When refugees arrive to a place beyond their nation's borders, they get housed in refugee camps by the government that invites them in. This government does not have to give refugees permission to work, so it can be incredibly hard for refugees to make a living to support themselves and their families.[7]

Refugee populations often need aid via donations because they must leave almost all or all of their possessions behind in their home country as they flee to another country. Donations of items that could hurt a local market elsewhere in the world could benefit refugees where no local market exists for these goods. Refugees may rely exclusively on the outside world for clothing, food and medicine. Donations prove useful in combating these basic shortages. Items so basic as blankets and coats during wintertime could really help refugees in refugee camps.

The Burmese army committed mass atrocities against Rohingya Muslims, who have fled to Bangladesh for safety. Over 700,000 people have lived in refugee camps because of this, mostly in makeshift plastic tents. Humans of New York, led by Brandon Stanton, shared stories and pictures of Rohingya refugees. Humans of New York (HONY) takes photos of people and interviews them. They shared a partial transcript of the interview along with a portrait to over twenty million followers on social media at the time. Brandon and team know that the refugees have an urgent need for sturdier and more reliable shelter in the Bangladeshi refugee camps. As a way to meet the need, HONY began a fundraiser asking followers to donate money to fund the cost of bamboo housing for as many refugee families as possible. As monsoon season approached, the bamboo housing helped refugees stay dry and safe. It cost six hundred U.S. dollars to build a house. The fundraiser raised $2,031,180 of a million-dollar goal on Go Fund Me by 29,063 people in thirteen days, which housed 48,361 refugees in 3,224 houses. This exhibits the power of volunteering and contributing to tangibly making the world a better place.[8]

Short-term projects could also make a difference in the lives of refugees, especially if international volunteers can provide a service that they need but live without, like dental care. Holding dental clinics in refugee camps can not only keep children's oral hygiene on track, but also it can help alleviate pain of anyone with a toothache or major mouth problem. If no dentists currently provide services for refugees, then a dental clinic, even in the short term, could help a lot of people live life with less pain and better overall health.

Refugees can use donated goods and services because local markets for goods and services generally do not exist in refugee camps.[9] Refugees can try to create markets in certain instances, however. For instance, South Sudanese refugee Mama Safi lives in a refugee camp in Kakuma, Kenya. Many South Sudanese families sought refuge in Kenya from continual conflict stemming from a civil war in 2013–2015. Mama Safi started a bakery, baking bread for school lunches in the refugee camp, after getting a small startup loan from a local bank. She employs up to ten people on an as needed basis when she receives a large order for bread. By starting her own bakery, Mama Safi created a market for her goods.[10]

The domestic and international homeless community can put donations from international volunteers to good use. Homeless shelters rely on donations of food and toiletries to operate continuously, but they need more than donations to help the homeless community. In this way, homeless individuals can also benefit from services as well. Donations of suits and free haircuts for job interviews, along with job training and resume-building workshops can help homeless people get a job so they can afford to transition back into living in a home. The Wayfarer Foundation, led by actor and director Justin Baldoni, and his wife, actor and entrepreneur Emily Baldoni, takes the lead with volunteering with the homeless community of Los Angeles at an annual event called The Skid Row Carnival of Love. Volunteers at the Carnival donate clothes, food and toiletries to the local homeless population and also provide services such as a spa, medical testing and checkups, children's activities, grooming for pets, and employment services, including job interviews. The larger purpose of the Carnival of Love gives the often-overlooked homeless community an opportunity to have a fun day, with music, dancing, crafts and more. The foundation has tried to build a more continuous relationship with the Skid Row community by pairing a volunteer with a homeless person for a year to help facilitate their needs and provide companionship.[11]

New international volunteers strive to eradicate inequality in all forms, including the inequality of homelessness. If the international volunteering community can influence and educate others to the deep need that homeless people worldwide face, then as donations pour in, shelters can ensure that homeless people everywhere eat enough and have access to the toiletries that every human needs. Many homeless shelters around the world would benefit from volunteers pitching in to build extra showering facilities and rooms to sleep in, so that homeless people would never get turned away from the shelter due to lack of space.

While homeless people have unmet needs that donations can immediately help, the international volunteering community can also help provide long-term solutions to end homelessness around the world. As each place functions differently, various homeless communities face different obstacles to overcoming poverty, finding a place to live and food to eat. Therefore, solutions will need to be custom made for each specific situation.

For example, organizations such as Goodwill create jobs for homeless people in the United States to work in their retail stores. New York City offers information and services for people at risk of losing their homes to prevent homelessness before it happens. The Low Income Housing Institute in Seattle builds tiny houses for homeless people to live in.[12] But homeless individuals need creative solutions on the national level in countries around the world. The international volunteering community could begin to help with this unmet need by innovating to prevent homelessness and end the crisis worldwide, one place and one solution at a time.

Similarly, donations of staple items can help during times of shortage, such as after a natural disaster occurs. People oftentimes urgently need non-perishable food, clothes, toiletries and clean drinking water to survive in the aftermath of a catastrophe. People lose many of these necessities during the disaster and they may be unavailable in the short term, such as if a hurricane contaminated the water supply and people cannot obtain any potable water. Humans need food during famines, where crops do not reach harvest and people become malnourished. For example, Save the Children works in famine areas and conflict zones to provide emergency food to malnourished children. This helps because food can be hard to find during a war and during famine. Save the Children workers set up areas for malnutrition screening and feedings. Children eat a peanut paste formulated with all the nutrition they need to regain weight.[13]

Donations also help hospitals provide medical care after disasters cause supply shortages due to a large influx of injured and sick people. In this way, hospitals can benefit from extra backup generators and medical supplies. Sometimes, an area lacks enough working hospitals and entire field hospitals need to be erected to care for injured people. After the 2010 earthquake in Haiti, for instance, surgeons from the United States set up a field hospital to perform emergency surgery on injured Haitians just across the Haitian-Dominican border. They brought anesthesia with them to use during surgeries because post-disaster Haiti did not have enough.

The anesthesia donation allowed volunteers to perform surgeries in the short term while international disaster relief began to be implemented. Well thought-out donations like this can make a huge difference in the international community. These volunteers saved lives thanks to their skills and their anesthesia.[14]

The important thing to think about when donating items during a crisis or after an international disaster is that if the shortages being temporarily filled by donations are also a chronic problem, then volunteers need to help find a long-term, sustainable solution to replace the donations. Donations can never be sustainable, but rather they help meet a need temporarily, which can work for a time. Donations provide a window in the short term to brainstorm with locals and begin to implement ideas to solve any chronic shortages. Donations of this kind will make a lasting impact and alleviate urgent needs.

In fact, some people believe so strongly in the power of donation that they propose exclusively donating instead of volunteering internationally. In this theory, pioneered by the philosopher Peter Singer, a potential international volunteer would donate all the money they planned to spend while volunteering internationally to existing aid organizations that already send people abroad. Peter Singer would propose that people interested in volunteering internationally should use their time working at a job with the largest salary possible and donating as much of that money as they can to existing aid organizations. The overall idea is that every person has a limited amount of both time and money, so donating, rather than volunteering internationally, would make the most use out of those limited resources.[15]

This may be an effective method when aid organizations are already doing good work in a cause and geographic location people considered volunteering for. By forgoing volunteering, one could prevent a too many cooks in the kitchen situation and participate in more effective altruism. This could also give donors a bigger bang for their buck by invoking the economies of scale method whereby the organization has a streamlined system that is more effective than the potential volunteers would be. Peter Singer created a nonprofit, The Life You Can Save, and wrote a book by the same name, that makes it easy to donate to an effective organization that he identified.

On the other hand, the donation model may not work in all instances and international volunteering oneself could be the better method. For instance, this could be the case if an organization does good work but needs more hands-on assistance from volunteers. Similarly, international volunteering could be particularly effective if there are issues locals would like help with but an organization had not yet helped meet that need. Volunteering could also be most helpful if an existing organization does not use best practices and skilled volunteers could help them course correct.

Donation methods similar to The Life You Can Save can work well side-by-side with international volunteering. For example, after Hurricane Maria ravaged Puerto Rico, connectrelief.com has been matching donors to places across the island that have a specific list of items they need. Volunteers going to Puerto Rico can click on a map of the area they will be volunteering in to see which organizations need supplies. It also gives contact information for donors to schedule a donation directly to the place that has the wish list. This is a better donation model than bringing unsolicited donations because it makes sure that donors will be meeting a true need.[16]

Other Finanancial Strategies

In high-income countries people pour money into vaccines for deadly diseases that threaten the population, such as the flu. But in low-income countries, vaccines for common illnesses prevalently found in those regions do not get sufficient funding. This happens partially because the people who hold the purse strings do not have to fear getting these diseases unless they travel to a region where the disease lurks. People with limited incomes cannot pay the same amount as wealthy people do for vaccines so pharmaceutical companies do not see a profit motive by vaccinating them. This creates a disincentive for pharmaceutical companies to invest heavily in research and development for those vaccines.[17] If we can create an incentive structure or an opportunity to make money by developing vaccines for Neglected Infectious Diseases (NIDs), then the world will be a better place. In addition to vaccines being a human right, when less people die from illness, then the economy where they live has the potential to grow more robustly as more people work and produce GDP.

International volunteers can create awareness and raise money to create an alternate incentive structure where none currently exist. Volunteers can do this with a walk that raises awareness and money. Or people can volunteer with organizations who work on these issues as an alternative way to end NIDs without vaccinations. Former President Jimmy Carter has used his platform to find and implement solutions to one NID called River Blindness using donated medications from the pharmaceutical company Merck instead of creating a vaccine. River Blindness comes from parasites and the pill kills them. This stops the progression of River Blindness in the body of the person who took it and in turn ends the possibility of a contaminated person contaminating others. The Carter Center has helped end River Blindness in the countries of Mexico, Guatemala, Ecuador and Colombia.[18] Additionally, the Carter Center has been a major player to completely end Guinea Worm without the use of a vaccine or medicine, but rather through preventative measures. The Carter Center utilizes its staff and volunteers to spread the word about prevention tactics in areas where Guinea Worm infected people.[19]

A more established type of finance, microfinance, has a track record of benefiting host communities. Microfinance can change the lives of individuals and families in an effective manner because it allows people to move forward financially. Microfinance creates small pockets of economic change that, over time, fosters large-scale benefits. Microfinance helps a family, co-op, or individual take out a loan for as little as a dollar to begin a business with. Microfinance features low interest rates compared to other available debt financing methods, so people can repay the loan quickly, enabling them to swiftly turn a profit. It sets entrepreneurs on the path to economic freedom. Access to microloans can empower individuals and communities as more capital will become available for people to invest in education for their kids, food for their families and other needs.

The international volunteering community has the potential to be helpers in the microfinance field by donating to microfinance organizations or by implementing microfinance programs in their projects when applicable. Volunteers can donate money to organizations such as Kiva to fund an approved microloan, which generally gets repaid to lenders. After repayment, the lenders can choose to reinvest the money into another microloan. Kiva provides microloans to individuals and small groups of people to help them grow their businesses or for community investment projects. Kiva has a 96.4 percent loan repayment rate. The loans impact growing businesses in eighty-four countries around the world.[20] For example, Lourdes took out a $975 loan to grow her snacks business in Paraguay. The old snack shop had been robbed four times. She used the microloan to expand her business, which grew her profit. In turn, more profit enabled her to rent a snack shop with better security that also had a place attached for her family to live in. This improved her quality of life and peace of mind.[21]

Microfinance becomes a particularly important financial strategy in international development because it eliminates several barriers that prevent people from obtaining a traditional bank loan. For instance, most banks will not lend to people without a credit history or national ID card. However, in many places around the world, people do not have the opportunity to create and build a credit history because of a cash-based economy or an economy where people mostly work in an informal sector. To get a traditional loan, an individual must compile certain documents, which they do not always have and cannot always get. Even if they do, someone still has to lend them their first loan, which banks may not do because of the lack of credit history. This unhelpful cycle leaves people without the finance they need to grow their business or improve their quality of life, such as with a house loan. Even if a bank would overlook someone's lack of credit history, the loans that banks offer can fail to meet the needs of potential borrowers. For instance, brick and mortar banks generally will not lend in small amounts, which many small businesses need. They also can charge prohibitively high interest rates. This prevents people from getting a loan if the monthly payments tend to be unrealistically high.[22]

Microfinance effectively works around these barriers by offering flexible and nontraditional loans. For instance, microloan lenders tend to offer loans in small denominations, which meets the needs of many borrowers and also reduces the risk to the lender that they will lose a large amount of money if that person defaults. These small loans can help borrowers build their business by providing money upfront to purchase a previously unaffordable item. This can also help start new businesses when the microloan money pays for the startup costs of the business, like purchasing an oven for a bakery. The oven symbolizes a barrier to entry into the market that a microloan eliminates. Microloans can also be helpful when an individual or business previously needed to pick and choose between which essential goods to buy because they did not have much cash.

Microfinance can be beneficial in international volunteering because traditional banks stagnate potential economic growth in host communities by refusing to lend to people who do not meet the guidelines under a traditional loan risk profile. Banks can see those loans as risk they do not want to take, but microfinance organizations like Kiva see that if someone gets loaned x amount of money, then they will make y profits from that investment, and then y profits will magnify to help the community in z beneficial ways. The people that microloan organizations lend to tend to be nontraditional entrepreneurs with tremendous potential for success. Kiva knows that no traditional method of measuring potential default will work for untraditional entrepreneurs trying to grow in untraditional markets. One of the best ways to identify microloan creditworthiness can be to estimate the revenue generation of the borrower after loan disbursal. Kiva does not get a 96.4 percent success rate of repayment in $1.75 billion of loans from 4.4 million borrowers without tapping into a positive new way of loaning to people in places where international volunteers work.[23] In this way, the new international volunteer recognizes that microfinance positively impacts the host community. Economic growth begets more economic growth for the community and then the larger area as a whole. International volunteers can invest in microloans and apply them, when possible, to their community projects, as part of a strategy of a rising tide lifting all boats.

Additionally, a group of volunteers can pool funds together to donate to something specific, such as an organization or a project. Many people already do this regularly, like with special offerings designated to a development cause at a church, synagogue, mosque or temple. However, donations of this type can be ineffective in their current state. For instance, in parts of Africa, people do not have access to potable drinking water. Women can travel long distances each day to carry water from a local water source to their homes, where it then must be purified before household use. The containers filled with water are heavy and the walk to the water source is not always safe.

These obstacles to fresh water have compelled many international volunteer groups to donate money for wells. However, these donations do not always help in the way donors expected. For instance, in 2009 a report found that 50,000 well boreholes in Africa did not function and that international donors and aid organizations funded most of them. The report found instances of contaminated water supply, non-functioning pumps and unsustainable and improperly drilled boreholes. Donors funded the wells, drilled them and left without communicating with the local community about their obstacles to maintaining them. Many times, the organizations did not even properly drill the wells. Additionally, some communities had no way to fix the hand pumps if they broke. Other wells did not have a long-lasting water supply and subsequently ran dry.[24]

Pooling funds can be inefficient when people do not sufficiently look into the money's intended purpose. Sometimes the money goes to an intermediary who created the idea, instead of coming directly from a community or a renowned international organization. If the plan does not originate from one of these sources it can end up not maximizing the potential of the donation.[25] To solve this problem, the new international volunteer researches the specific project or organization to make sure it would be beneficial and legitimate. This due diligence can be done by reading about the project or organization from several outside and trustworthy sources. In this case, due diligence means verifying information about the project and organization by asking questions about the details of the project.

When I think of donations in international volunteering, I look back to the clinic run by volunteers that I attended as a patient in Guatemala. I especially think about how their donations of medicine cost the nearby pharmacy a significant amount of business, and how the clothes donations were unnecessary for Guatemalans who simply need an alternative healthcare option. The donations at the clinic can be considered non-essential donations. What if an alternative existed to medicine and clothing donations that helped the clinic with more urgent and essential needs? As I see it, two alternatives would work. Since church members provide the donations, what if the volunteers asked them instead to donate money to fund a salary for full time Guatemalan doctors? Guatemalan doctors know prevalent illnesses in the area better than volunteer doctors do. They also can communicate directly with patients, eliminating the need for translators. Or volunteers could ask donors for money to purchase chairs to make a waiting room at the clinic. That would be more effective by supplying the clinic with the funds it needs to meet its most urgent needs. If the church members have used clothing to give but not money, they could organize a yard sale at home to sell the clothes and donate the profits toward the waiting room costs and doctor salaries instead. This purposeful act could ensure that resources go toward what Guatemalans need the most.

Part 3

*What Volunteers
Need to Know About
International Volunteering*

VIII

Health

Illness Prevention

Many people who volunteer internationally do not get sick. However, some people do get sick while volunteering internationally. A lot of times getting sick abroad can be similar to getting sick at home, and resting and medication will heal the body. But, in some cases, getting sick while volunteering internationally can be more severe and take more recovery time than normal. The recovery time can be long when volunteers get parasites from water or bacteria like E. coli.[1] To avoid getting sick while volunteering internationally, focus on preventing exposure to illness.

Previous volunteers and travelers found tried and true ways to minimize exposure to contaminants while volunteering abroad. First, be diligent about avoiding sources of food and water that could be possible areas of contamination. Examples include food made with non-potable water or food that has been left out for hours after being cooked. Secondly, do not drink non-potable water. Even if non-potable water looks clear, it still can contain invisible single celled parasites. Therefore, do not drink anything that has ice in it, because the cleanliness of the ice cannot be guaranteed. Drinking bottled potable water offers advantages over filtered potable water, because filtered non-potable water can lose purification over time if the filter has not been replaced often enough. Boiling water needs to be boiled for at least fifteen minutes to kill all contaminants. Additionally, volunteers can purchase a water bottle that will kill all water impurities with UV light at camping stores. Locally bottled water can also be iffy in certain instances. Some water bottles contain locally filtered water instead of purified water cleaned in a plant. Locally filtered standards can be less stringent, which can cause stomach issues for volunteers.[2] Always choose recognizable name brand water bottles, when possible, for quality assurance. According to my physician, sometimes soda can be a safer alternative than locally filtered water because big name soda companies tend to operate regionally and have a large plant to treat the water that becomes the basis for soda.

Volunteers should keep their mouth closed at all times while taking a shower and washing their face in order to not get non-potable water in the mouth accidentally. It can be difficult to remember to keep one's mouth closed in the shower at all times though. In order to avoid getting non-potable water in the nose and mouth during a shower, volunteers can protect themselves even more with a travel hack. When showering in unpotable water, volunteers can try to not put the water directly on their face while still keeping their mouth closed. When shampooing their hair, volunteers can tilt their face back so the water only gets on their hair. If any water accidentally does get on their face anyway, volunteers can immediately wipe it off with a towel. To clean their face after showering, volunteers can wash their face in the sink using water from a liter-sized bottle of drinking water instead of from the tap. That way, if any water gets in the nose or mouth, it will be potable water that does not cause parasites. After washing their face with the liter of bottled water, volunteers can place the water bottle directly in the sink. That way, they have to move it in order to brush their teeth or wash their face. This helps volunteers to not forget to use safe water for teeth brushing and face washing. If they try to turn on the non-potable tap water to brush their teeth later on, they will be stopped from doing so when seeing the water bottle in the sink.

The Centers for Disease Control and Prevention offers tips to prevent getting sick from foodborne illness while traveling. Some suggestions include avoiding salads and unpeeled vegetables. When eating food, make sure the cook prepares it with potable water instead of tap water (like when cleaning peeled vegetables and pasta rinsed off after cooking). Never eat at a buffet or from a street vendor because food that has been sitting out can become tepid instead of hot, allowing bacteria to grow. Only room temperature food, such as bread or cookies, will be safe to eat after sitting out for more than an hour. Other foods should only be eaten if hot to the touch. Sometimes the only food available does not meet the requirements for food safety and can pose a health risk. Therefore, it can be helpful to bring along prepackaged food such as protein bars, jerky, chips, crackers or cookies for a snack if no suitable food options present themselves at mealtime.[3]

Food and waterborne sickness can be avoided in restaurants with a history of inadequate sanitation practices. Before eating at a restaurant, international volunteers can check Google, Yelp and Travel Advisor reviews to see if previous travelers got sick after eating there. These reviews can usually be filtered by lowest first, so volunteers can see if low reviews are due to slow service or something more dire. If someone has gotten sick from the restaurant, then volunteers can avoid eating there to mitigate their risk of illness. This search can be a helpful alternative in countries that do not require mandatory restaurant inspections with ratings posted on the door. This, however, does not protect volunteers against getting sick at a restaurant that recently lowered their food safety standards, because no one has previously gotten sick and left that information on a review. But in most cases, restaurants maintain their quality over time, so volunteers can eat there safely.

Volunteers need to do location-specific research to see if they need to make any special health considerations or prepare to prevent illness. Doctors and the Centers for Disease Control's website have information volunteers need. This includes which vaccines to get, how to prevent bug bites and to brush teeth with potable water, to name a few.[4] Although most volunteers will avoid illness while volunteering internationally, volunteers with pre-existing conditions need to do additional research and ask their doctor before traveling to the area as a volunteer. People with certain medical histories can be more prone to getting sick from food and water-based bacteria while volunteering internationally.[5]

Volunteers can also ask previous participants if they got sick or know anyone who got sick while volunteering. If the project does not have previous participants, volunteers can reach out to people who traveled to the area for vacation or volunteering instead. Some good questions to ask include: What illness did they get? How did they get treated (medicine, pain relief etc.)? How long did it take them to recuperate? Looking back, could they have done anything differently to avoid getting sick? This helps volunteers make informed decisions. If one area would be a bad choice to volunteer at for health reasons, then there will be other places where volunteers will be less likely to experience negative health effects. Large cities, for example, can have better quality water and restaurants with good sanitation practices that have been reviewed by other travelers on sites such as Yelp or Trip Advisor. It can be better to volunteer somewhere that will not be a risk to health than volunteer and get sick. Sickness reduces volunteers' usefulness and efficiency. Everyone needs to be at their best to have the most positive impact while volunteering internationally.

Once volunteers have chosen a place to volunteer that should not cause harm to their health, they can plan for international medical care. The type of healthcare available at home may be different than abroad. To make a healthcare plan, research the medical care options available in the town hosting volunteers. For instance, in one Guatemalan town where I lived, sick people could go to a free volunteer-run clinic, the hospital, or a private doctor. Once volunteers know the options, they can choose which one they would prefer if they happen to get sick. If possible, ask the locals who the best doctor in town is, and meet with the doctor at the beginning of the trip to evaluate what kind of medical assistance volunteers would be receiving from them. If volunteers do not like their options, or if the area does not have a healthcare system, consider bringing a medical professional as a part of the volunteer team who could treat any illnesses contracted by volunteers.

Additionally, each individual volunteer needs to get traveler's insurance. This is a must, even for the healthiest volunteers. An accident would be unlikely, but they do happen, and if they do, it would be better to have traveler's insurance. The adage "It is better to have it and not need it, than to need it and not have it" applies to traveler's insurance. Before purchasing traveler's insurance, know what it covers. It may be different than domestic health insurance. For instance, the traveler's insurance I purchased for Guatemala required me to pay all the medical costs in cash up front and to bring receipts back to the United States to get reimbursement after my return home. Also, domestic health insurance may not cover international health expenses. For many travel insurance companies, volunteers need to disclose which country they will travel to, the dates, and their date of birth in order to receive coverage. Confirm that the policy will cover health, flight, hotel and luggage issues at a minimum.

I am not an expert in insurance, but from my research and experience, I will say that quality differs by company. Some international volunteering trips require participants get travel insurance, and each organization may have different requirements and preferred vendors. It can help to ask questions about which types of travel insurance a volunteer could need, and recommended coverage for each category.

For a trip to Peru, I purchased a travel insurance policy from World Nomads, a popular choice recommended by many travel influencers, and did not have good luck. I was in Cusco and found out that the airline that was supposed to take me back to Lima went bankrupt and would no longer be flying any planes. World Nomads did not cover all the costs because the new flight departed a few hours before the scheduled time of the original flight. I tried to explain that the airline went out of business but the claim was still denied.

On the other hand, I purchased trip insurance from Expedia and got reimbursed quickly for a different trip. The flight and hotel protection would not be enough to cover international volunteers, however, who should consider trip protection, health insurance, death, dismemberment, and repatriation benefits.

The travel insurance industry has adapted to the needs of volunteers during the pandemic. Forbes recommends purchasing "cancel for any reason" coverage in case countries shut their borders once a trip has been planned or if a volunteer contracts Covid-19. It has a "Best Covid-19 Travel

Insurance Plans" tool, in addition to a "Compare Travel Insurance" tool.[6] To avoid any Covid-19 related delays, be sure to research the vaccination, health insurance, negative Covid test and quarantine requirements for the country you will volunteer in. These requirements can change frequently, so be sure to keep checking in the weeks and days prior to departure. In case of a positive test for Covid-19 or if a mandatory quarantine becomes necessary, be sure to save all documents, including receipts from doctors' offices and pharmacies, documents from the government, along with test results to submit to insurance.

Finally, volunteers need to keep a copy of their traveler's insurance information with other important documents, such as passport and ID, and to have all of those documents readily available. As a backup, volunteers can give a family member or friend a copy of the traveler's insurance, along with a copy of the passport information page and travel itinerary.

If all precautions fail, and a volunteer experiences recurring health issues after volunteering abroad, I recommend scheduling a visit with a doctor upon arriving back home. Along with a full blood workup, it will be helpful to get checked for parasites and other maladies if the volunteer experienced stomach problems while volunteering abroad. Ask a physician or dietician for a full GI Map test instead of a microscope parasite test, because a microscope test can miss many single-celled (amoeba) parasites. Additionally, a microscope test cannot determine bacterial dysbiosis, an imbalance of good and bad gut bacteria, that can also cause GI issues.

It took nine years, a microscope parasite test, a colonoscopy and endoscopy, a CT scan, an ultrasound, a restricted diet, and continually worsening GI symptoms to get the correct GI Map testing to determine that the amoebas I contracted in Guatemala were still present all those years later. I saw many of the best specialists but none of them did the correct testing. I found Team HAN, composed of Hannah Aylward, HHC, and Brooke Gacek, RDN, on Instagram (@hannahaylwardhhc) and they helped me fix the amoebas and the gut issues that came with having them for so many years. Brooke recommended an antimicrobial approach, which is less damaging to the overall gut than antibiotics. Seeing a natural doctor or dietician who has a lot of experience with gut illnesses can sort out issues better than an internist or gastroenterologist, at least in my experience.

Covid-19 Prevention

It is important for both volunteers and the host community to not catch Covid-19 and other airborne illnesses like the flu. With the travel inherently involved in international volunteering, volunteers could catch an illness on the way. However, there are proven risk-mitigation strategies volunteers can take to minimize the possibility. Covid-19 vaccinations and boosters will prevent Covid-19 in some cases and reduce the severity of symptoms in others.[7] This holds true for other vaccines such as the flu.[8] Remember to check for the required and recommended vaccinations on the Centers for Disease Control and Prevention's (CDC) website as far out as possible before the trip in case some vaccines need multiple doses on different dates.

Before traveling, check the country's requirements for pre-trip Covid-19 testing. Some countries require a specific type of test and it must be administered in a certain time frame before the day of departure. It may also be a requirement that volunteers get a negative test once arriving as well, or several over the course of the trip. Have a plan in place of where to get the required testing and when, so the process will go smoothly and not add stress to the travel experience.

On the plane itself, be sure to sanitize the seat and tray table and hand sanitize often. Wear a mask securely (over the nose and mouth) while traveling to reduce the risk of contracting Covid-19 and other airborne illnesses. Volunteers can reduce risk indoors by wearing high quality masks, and not just on the plane and in the airport, but during the volunteer work and in the host community as well. Keep in mind that mask wearing not only protects the person wearing it, but also those around as well, including immunocompromised people who are at a greater risk of developing severe illness. The Mayo Clinic states that the most effective masks are N95, followed by KN95, surgical masks, then cloth masks.[9]

After arriving, it may be required that volunteers quarantine. It may be a quarantine where the government regulates where and for how long, or it could be an honor system where volunteers need to self-isolate at their hotel for a certain period. Be sure to research this requirement and to ensure nothing changes in the days leading up to departure. Once again, have a plan of where quarantine will take place, what the requirements are, for how long and other logistics, such as how will food be brought to the quarantine location.

To ensure that no one in the host community gets Covid-19 or other airborne illnesses from volunteers, consider an additional quarantine if the first quarantine will take place in a different location. For instance, if the required quarantine takes place near the airport, it could be a helpful preventative measure to do another quarantine after traveling to the host community. Consult the CDC's and the host government's quarantine suggestions to get the most up to date information on quarantine time frames.

Once the volunteer work begins, screen volunteers daily for symptoms by doing a temperature check and a symptom questionnaire. It can also help to bring Covid-19 rapid tests on the trip to do regular testing as well. While volunteering, it is safer to work outside than inside.[10] If that is not an option, try to increase air circulation by opening windows and running fans. Consider HEPA air purifiers and regularly sanitize surfaces in the work space as well. Research on social distancing is mixed, in that it can be helpful but that six feet might not be the ideal distance between people. It depends on many factors, such as the quality of air circulation, how many people are present and whether volunteering occurs inside or outside.[11]

The Role of Food in Culture

One of the best parts of volunteering internationally includes experiencing new cuisine. Sometimes, however, volunteers get offered food that can be unsafe for them to eat or they would feel uncomfortable eating. These situations, just like all cross-cultural differences, can be tricky to navigate. Refusing food can be a delicate situation, especially since food goes hand and hand with culture. Sometimes giving someone food shows appreciation and acts as an offer of friendship. Food can be used to comfort and show love. Therefore, the new international volunteer never wishes to offend or insult locals by refusing food, especially since the food can carry emotional connotations with it. Everyone has different ways of accepting food that may be unsafe to eat. I have heard people say to accept nothing at all. On the other hand, I have been advised to never refuse food from anyone while abroad because it can hinder trust building and be considered an insult. Then if volunteers get sick as a consequence, have a good doctor waiting at home.

However, many options lie in the middle of the spectrum. Each volunteer can find their own path or creative solution to balance health and local trust. For instance, one student in Guatemala would ask her host mom to go with her to neighbors' houses when she needed to conduct interviews, knowing that the neighbors would serve them coffee, most likely made with non-potable water. When the neighbor would leave the room momentarily, the student would switch coffee cups to trade her full coffee cup for the empty one after her host mom drank it all. The host mom's body had adapted to the water over time and it would not make her sick. This avoided any hurt feelings. I generally took a different route. Depending on my situation, I would tell locals who offered me food or coffee that I do not drink coffee (I actually do not drink coffee), or that I felt sick (because I did), or had already eaten (which happened a lot). I never lied, and I found people to be generally receptive to my responses after I assured the host that I would let them know as soon as I became hungry again or felt better. This seemed to be a culturally acceptable response in Guatemala, but it might not be everywhere. Alternatively, volunteers could ask to take food with them to go instead, as long as it would be culturally acceptable to do so. Since giving food is a symbol of kindness, and volunteering also can be a symbol of kindness, then volunteers need to make every effort to complete the gesture of kindness by taking the food that members of the host community offer them. By taking the food to go, the gesture of kindness will be completed and volunteers can privately decide if they would like to eat it.

Packing for Health

A personalized medical kit needs to be included in the list of items to pack. A medical kit deserves the room it takes up in a suitcase. The importance of a personalized medical kit for each volunteer cannot be overstated. Without one, volunteers may have to pay extra money to purchase medical supplies locally and may not get the exact product they hope to buy. I brought over-the-counter pain pills with me to Guatemala, but other than that I did not bring much in the way of a medical kit. This did not help me at all when I tripped and scraped all the skin off two toes and punctured a toenail. I had to go to every pharmacy in town with a bloody foot to buy Neosporin and some gauze and tape for it. As it turned out, not a single local pharmacy carried Neosporin. I eventually found a cream meant to calm the sting of rashes. My host mom said it would work for the purposes of keeping the wound clean, but Neosporin would have helped it heal faster. Neosporin specifically helps heal scrapes and provides pain relief, both of which I needed. The rash cream did not help with either pain relief or healing the scrapes. I ended up having to wait to use Neosporin to heal the scrapes after I returned home.

I wished I had brought a personalized medical kit with me many times in Guatemala. The first night I arrived I needed some Mucinex for congestion. When I packed for Guatemala, I assumed that I would probably not need Mucinex, and that if I did, then I could just get some when I needed it. This ended up not being the case. The pharmacies near the hotel in Guatemala City only had cough syrup with the same active ingredient as Mucinex. I bought it, and it worked pretty well, but next time I will save myself the money and hassle by bringing some Mucinex pills from home, just in case.

Because of these incidents, I vowed to always keep a basic medical kit with me when I volunteer and travel internationally. I now carry a customized medical kit that includes pain medicine, Band-Aids, gauze and tape, cough medicine, cold medicine and of course, Neosporin and Mucinex. Each volunteer should bring universally needed items in their medical kit, like Band-Aids and pain pills. That way, if anyone on the volunteer team needs to use the medical kit, they will likely find what they need. Additionally, a personalized medical kit will include medicines that each volunteer may need based on their preferences and medical history. I keep Mucinex with me because I have allergies. Someone prone to headaches may want to bring Excedrin or their preferred headache medicine, for example.

The final item in a personalized medical kit would be a volunteer's regular prescription medications. If the international volunteer project lasts for a duration of a month or more, or if the volunteer will run out of a prescription during the project, the volunteer's health insurance company can help. Usually, after contacting the insurance company and telling the representatives the beginning and end dates of the international volunteer project, the representative can put a waiver into the system that will allow an early refill of the prescriptions needed. If the volunteer project will happen in the medium to long term, then the insurance company can also put a waiver into the system that will allow volunteers to get all the medicine they will need for the entire duration of the trip before it begins. Sometimes, depending on the insurance company, volunteers can get all the medicine beforehand from their normal pharmacy once the waivers get approved. However, other insurance companies will want to mail volunteers their prescriptions. In order to make sure all medicine will arrive on time, the initial call to the health insurance company needs to be placed ideally at least six weeks before volunteering abroad. It takes time to get the necessary permissions and waivers from the insurance company.

The following list is the foundation of a personalized medical kit. This list incorporates the non-personalized items that every volunteer should bring with them. Any personalized items can be added to this list.

Medical Kit

- Hand Sanitizer
- Band-Aids
- Neosporin
- Cough Syrup, Cough Drops and/or Mucinex
- Pain Medication of Choice
- Menstrual Supplies
- Non-Scented Toilet Paper

- Tissues
- Prescription Medications
- Dramamine
- Traveler's Insurance Information

Dramamine prevents seasickness, so it may not be necessary to bring, depending on the volunteer trip. I recommend bringing non-scented toilet paper. Tissue packs can also be used in place of non-scented toilet paper rolls on the go, or for convenience if anyone gets a cold.

Culture Shock

Culture shock can be defined as a mental and physical health sensation that international volunteers may experience during the course of a development project. Culture shock often creates emotional sensations such as the longing for something familiar, like an experience from home, an aching for comfort and feelings of being overwhelmed. It can also lead to physical symptoms such as feeling tired and sleeping a lot or the opposite—not sleeping much at all. Culture shock manifests differently in each person, both physically and emotionally. It tends to hit different people at different times during international volunteering projects. In my experience, many people who volunteer on short-term trips of two weeks or less tend to avoid most feelings of culture shock. The excitement of exploring a new place, helping others, meeting new people and doing their part to help a project come together can ward off culture shock until a short-term trip ends. Culture shock tends to hit volunteers on long-term trips after the initial excitement has worn down and a sense of normalcy and routine sets in.

I have found a few ways to successfully end feelings of culture shock. Sometimes culture shock still comes and goes, so these methods may have to be utilized more than once and in different ways. International volunteers can feel particularly vulnerable to culture shock in the evenings, because at the end of the day, volunteers can feel tired, feel lonely, and miss home. To avoid culture shock in the evenings, volunteers can keep busy and make plans with their homestay family or other volunteers and community members each evening. This can help keep their mind off of the feelings that lead to culture shock. It also helps volunteers make the most of their experience abroad. Overall, socializing can significantly prevent culture shock because it leaves no time to miss home. In fact, students I know who studied abroad in a group setting experienced less culture shock than those who studied abroad alone or as one of a few students who stayed in the same town. Therefore, volunteering in a group or staying in a homestay with at least one other volunteer may be a non-negotiable aspect to consider before committing to an international development project.

Socializing in a homestay environment not only helps with culture shock but it can also be fun. In the evenings in Guatemala when culture shock began to sink in, I would watch *The Lion King* in Spanish with my homestay brothers. As we grew closer, they sang the songs in Spanish while I sang them in English, much to their delight. We also practiced our best lion roars together. I grew up watching *The Lion King*, and so watching it in Spanish so often in Guatemala gave me that little slice of home that I missed, while simultaneously allowing me to experience it in a new and wonderful way. In the afternoons I would play tag with my homestay brothers, sit and talk with my homestay mom on the porch, or go watch my host dad play soccer. I basically integrated myself into the family as much as possible. In retrospect, these became my favorite memories from all my time in Guatemala. I feel very lucky to have shared such wonderful times with such great people while I studied and volunteered abroad.

For me it also helped to limit calls and messages to family and friends back home to a specific and short amount of time each day. Doing so allowed me to stop dwelling on what I missed at home and to instead spend more time building relationships in Guatemala. International volunteers need to deeply connect in meaningful relationships with locals, and not just because it helps stave off culture shock. In Guatemala, Teresa (name changed for privacy) became my best friend. At lunchtime she and I would go to the market to bring my host dad his lunch, and on the way there, we would talk about music, celebrities, and what life looked like for each of us. She also took me to the market to buy a traditional Mayan outfit, just like she wore each day, and showed me how to wear it properly. We really bonded in the time we spent together, and I think about her and my host family each and every day, even though it has been a few years since I last saw them.

Additionally, volunteers can help ease culture shock once it has set in by getting really comfortable. Make a point to take extra time, as a form of self-care, to create as comfortable and cozy an environment as possible. If culture shock happens, volunteers can try to make it as positive an experience as it can be. Adding an element of comfort can allow the culture shock to pass more smoothly and pleasantly. Being comfortable may look like packing a travel blanket and a pair of cozy socks to use while relaxing or to bring an extra-comfortable tee shirt from home to wear while volunteering. These little material comforts can make a big difference in combating culture shock.

Similarly, reverse culture shock can happen to any international volunteer, regardless of how long they spent volunteering abroad. Reverse culture shock usually manifests as feelings of frustration and alienation. These feelings can be brought on because volunteering internationally can feel very life changing. A gap needs to be filled between a volunteer's new mindset, or outlook on life, and the return to normal activities at home. It takes time to navigate between the international volunteer's old self that left home and the new self that comes back after volunteering. Reverse culture shock often occurs during that transition time. Keep in mind that no matter how much things have changed within the mind of a volunteer, the surroundings at home will remain mostly the same. It can take time for family and friends to understand that volunteers have changed so much because of the profound experience of volunteering internationally.

When international volunteers experience a new perspective on the world it causes change that leads to a reevaluation of life goals and priorities after the trip ends. After taking time for reflection during reverse culture shock, international volunteers will have to redefine what normal looks like to them. This can be accomplished by asking questions such as: What does this experience lead me to want to do next? Do I want to make any changes in my daily life? The answers will help volunteers find a new normal. This new normal may include changes to routines, hobbies, possibly a college major or career, and even one's priorities and sense of purpose. For me, I realized during reverse culture shock that to move forward with my life, I had to find a new normal. This manifested in many ways over time, from the way I spent my time to my career goals (including writing this book!). It set my life on a new trajectory.

During the process of redefining what normal means after volunteering internationally, some methods can ease reverse culture shock. Most of them revolve around relaxation, fun and focusing on self-care. When reverse culture shock hits, first try to connect with other people who have volunteered abroad. This can include befriending not just fellow volunteers, but anyone else who lived or studied abroad. Keeping in touch with the volunteer group and with other people who had experiences internationally creates a comradery who can support and understand each other. It can be very helpful to spend time doing fun things with this group after arriving back home. It also may be beneficial to see a therapist, as it does with any major life change or meaningful experience. Therapists can assist volunteers and give advice on how to move forward. They can also suggest ways to mentally and physically destress after returning home.

IX

Safety

Understanding Safety Risks

Volunteers must decide if they feel comfortable with safety risks before committing to an international development trip. Volunteers make this choice by knowing all the available safety information up front, such as any risk of crime from recent patterns. The Department of State website provides country-specific safety information that will give volunteers a detailed depiction of what, if any, safety risks volunteers can expect to encounter. On this website, volunteers can click on a country and the government gives detailed information on the types of dangerous events that have happened to Americans recently in that country. Additionally, each country's webpage details what U.S. officials cannot do in each country.[1] Sometimes U.S. government employees have travel and transportation restrictions due to safety that prevents them from doing certain things. For instance, in some countries, U.S. government employees may not travel by bus or by taxi, or cannot visit entire states or regions whatsoever. A good general rule of thumb for international volunteers would be that if U.S. government employees do not travel by taxi or do not go to a certain region, then volunteers should not travel that way as well. The State Department also posts travel warnings for countries and for states within countries, which volunteers should read carefully before volunteering. If volunteers will be working in an area under a travel warning, this information lets them know what to expect and if they need to do anything extra to prepare.

The Peace Corps acts as another source of safety information. If the Peace Corps deems an area too dangerous, Peace Corps volunteers will not be allowed to continue working there. Peace Corps volunteers will sometimes be restricted from specific countries due to violence against volunteers. In fact, the Peace Corps did not place new volunteers in Guatemala when I spent the summer there. The Peace Corps considered the countries of El Salvador, Guatemala and Honduras, collectively known as the

Northern Triangle, too violent for volunteers.[2] International volunteers may wish to avoid volunteering where the Peace Corps will not send volunteers due to safety.

As a caveat, this section does not mean to dissuade volunteers from doing a project. It tries to make sure all international volunteers choose a location where they will be comfortable. Knowing all the relevant safety facts up front encourages volunteers to make informed decisions. This allows volunteers to prepare beforehand so they can focus on volunteering instead of safety disruptions. In fact, I did not pay attention to safety risks before I decided to go to Guatemala, and simply trusted advocates for the program when they said I would be safe. Sometimes I was safe, but other times I was not. It caused me stress and took away time from what I was there to do.

Therefore, it helps to choose a good program from the beginning, where leaders will advocate for volunteers' safety and health and be up front. The right project leaders will choose the welfare of the volunteers over any personal interest, such as keeping the program alive from one year to the next. International volunteers deserve to have honest and upfront answers from project leaders about previous safety incidents, if any, to make the best decisions for them. Even if the program seems like a good fit, it may still be beneficial for volunteers to conduct research about safety risks in the project area as due diligence. That way every volunteer can have peace of mind and know what to expect before volunteering. When asking previous participants health questions, potential volunteers can also ask if they know if any safety incidents occurred or if they felt unsafe for any reason during the trip. If so, find out what caused them to feel unsafe.

Preventing Safety Incidences

To effectively prevent safety incidents abroad, volunteers can ask trusted locals what to do and what to avoid in order to stay safe. Locals know best when it comes to the types of crimes that occur in their hometown. Locals generally have basic rules in place to prevent bad things from happening to them, like we all do at home. This may include using a home security system or not walking alone late at night. After my purse got slashed with a knife at a festival, a local showed me that women hide their money in their shirt, instead of wearing a purse, and I began to follow suit. This effectively protected my money for the duration of the trip. And she taught me that if people do not carry a purse, it looks like they have fewer valuables, which decreases the risk of pickpocketing or robberies. When in doubt, and two locals give conflicting information about safety, follow the advice of the local who has the more stringent safety rule, or get a third opinion.

Another local taught me a second valuable safety tip. To stay safe and not get lost, memorize directions from the location of the homestay to the volunteering site or any other place volunteers need to go. This includes memorizing how to get back as well. Mapping out and memorizing a route can help volunteers feel focused and safer by knowing their location and how to arrive at their destination at every point on the journey.

Lastly, make note if an area lacks emergency services, like not having a 911 to call to request an ambulance service or police assistance. This allows volunteers to make contingency plans in case of emergency. These plans can include alternatives for safety, medical and fire if 911 and ambulances, police and/or firefighters do not service the area. Project leaders need to oversee the creation of contingency plans and the volunteer group as a whole can agree or amend them if needed. In reality, emergencies probably will not occur, but the same adage, "Better to have it and not need it, than to need it and not have it," that applies to packing a personalized medical kit also applies to creating emergency contingency plans.

Packing Tips

Keeping valuables safe means having the right gear. Almost every major retail store carries TSA-approved locks that TSA can open to inspect baggage and then relock. A company called Pacsafe makes anti-theft backpacks with features that make it difficult for anyone to open a zipper or to slash the bag with a knife. Volunteers can also keep valuables hidden on one's person in many ways. Stores such as REI and the Container Store carry travel safety items that can be useful to international volunteers. For instance, a passport pouch can be hung around the neck like a necklace. This has its pros and cons. Pros include being easy to wear and easily accessible, but it can sometimes get heavy, and it can be visible under some shirts. It works best when hidden underneath loose fitting shirts. An alternative would be a hidden undercover pouch. This cannot hold a passport, but can hold money and keys while remaining unnoticeable. Leg garters will hold both passports and money, while still giving the wearer easy access. Money belts function similarly to leg garters but they cannot be easily accessed quickly.

Two new anti-theft technologies have hit the market that I have not yet tried. The first looks like a scarf but has a hidden compartment in it to store a passport and money, and the second has a similar hidden compartment but in a tank top or jacket instead. But, no matter how volunteers carry their valuables, they need to carry debit and credit cards and their passport in an RFID-blocking wallet or case. This prevents thieves from obtaining sensitive information stored electronically in cards and passports. Many passport holders and even anti-theft backpacks come with RFID blockers already included. A simple check of the product labeling can tell if it will bring that added protection. Learning about what not to bring, including the bags themselves, helps volunteers pack for safety. Volunteers should only bring bags or suitcases that they can easily carry over rough terrain without discomfort. In fact, usually carrying a duffle bag rather than a rolling suitcase on uneven roads and sidewalks can make life easier. Volunteers should also not bring purses because they can be a target for robbery. Volunteers should carry the items that would normally go into a purse, such as money and ID, hidden on one's person.

International volunteers need to bring foreign currency with them to the project. Ordering foreign currency from a bank before the trip saves time and will allow the beginning of the trip to go smoothly. Currency exchange at the airport is generally possible as well, depending on the currency and the hours it is open, but I recommend taking care of it at the bank. It may not be safe to exchange currency at the airport because people can see the amount of cash exchanged. This could open volunteers up to becoming a robbery target. It may be difficult for volunteers to find a place to exchange currency outside of the airport, depending on the host community's location. Volunteers should still already have foreign currency before leaving the airport in case they need to buy something outside of the airport. Buying currency from a domestic bank will usually save volunteers money as well. The exchange rate and fees tend to be higher at airports. Keep in mind that a local bank may have to order the foreign currency, which could take approximately a week to arrive.

Usually, outside of the airport, volunteers can purchase foreign currency by doing a currency exchange from dollars (in cash) to cash in the foreign currency. In most countries, this can be done at a bank or at a shop that exchanges currency. Some of these shops will charge a commission to exchange currency on top of the exchange rate. Volunteers need to do their research about which avenues they can utilize to exchange currency in the host country because the rules differ. For instance, in Valencia, Spain, I could not exchange currency at a Spanish bank because I did not have a bank account with the bank. Instead, I had to go to a currency shop and pay a commission to exchange cash dollars for euros. In Guatemala, I could exchange money at any bank with my passport, and I could use my debit card to get out Guatemalan Quetzals at any ATM.

Some banks in the United States may charge a foreign transaction fee and an ATM fee each time a volunteer uses a debit or credit card at a store, restaurant or ATM abroad. Volunteers will need to call their bank to find out what fees will be applicable while volunteering internationally. Certain banks and credit unions do not charge fees. However, in addition to banks, many businesses in the host country may charge a fee if volunteers pay for their items with a dollar denominated debit or credit card. Usually, businesses and restaurants will have signs posted saying how much the fee is, if they have one, near the front door or just inside.

Planning a personal volunteering budget helps avoid bank fees. To do this, a volunteer can estimate how much they will spend on the trip. Then, they can decide how often they would like to use cash versus how often they would like to use their debit or credit card. For instance, I usually pay for souvenirs and activity entrance fees with cash, but pay for any restaurant with a card. I also usually convert 10 percent more cash into foreign currency than I budgeted for so that I will have it if I need it. Carrying both cash and a card in case something happens, like if a restaurant only takes cash or if a debit card gets lost, will always be the safest approach when traveling. Many debit and credit card issues can be avoided by doing some planning before the trip. Volunteers need to call their banks before traveling and tell them where they will be volunteering at and for how long. This prevents the bank from automatically cancelling the card for suspicious activity. Chip cards work best for volunteers because some venues will no longer accept cards without a chip. Lastly, check to be sure that the debit and credit cards will not expire during or immediately after volunteering. This goes for passports as well. Taking these steps will avoid a lot of hassle so that volunteers can focus all their energy on implementing a successful international development project.

Once the correct bags and anti-theft devices have been selected and foreign currency has been exchanged, the volunteer will need to determine what to pack. When deciding what to pack volunteers can ask themselves: Will this item make sense when accounting for both culture and climate? Some clothes will not be culturally appropriate to wear while volunteering abroad. For example, in Guatemala, locals wore tee shirts and maxi skirts or loose-fitting jeans, but not shorts. Alternatively, in Spain, people go out in public dressed up more than in the United States. And when accounting for the climate, research will show that if visiting France in January, it will be quite cold. Or, if traveling to Guatemala in June, it will rain every day.

The following shows a sample packing list for international volunteering. It includes standard toiletries except for the addition of body wipes and baby powder. On some international volunteering trips, volunteers will not be able to shower as much as they would like to. The body wipes can help volunteers to feel clean in between showers and a little bit of baby powder can absorb grease in hair.

Sample Packing List

Toiletries	Money / Safety Items	Clothes	Research Materials
Shampoo	Money Belt	Loungewear Set	Laptop
Conditioner	Debit Card	Plenty of Socks	Phone
Toothbrush	$20 of U.S. Dollars	Plenty of Underwear	Chargers
Body Wipes	$100 of Foreign Currency	Tennis Shoes	Adaptor
Bar Soap	Passport	Waterproof Shoes	Surge Protector
Towel	Driver's License or ID	Hiking Boots	Pens
Sunscreen	Safety Pouch	Flip Flops	Notebook
Bug Spray	Leg Garter	Bathing Suit	Helpful Books
Deodorant	Sandwich Bags	Jacket	Travel Guide
Baby Powder or Dry Shampoo	Health Insurance Information	Shirts	Map
Medical Kit	Backup Copy of Passport & ID	Pants and/or Shorts	

In the money and safety items, a few things are important to note. Remember that a passport should be valid for at least six months from the date of departure. All volunteers should keep a scanned copy of their passport and ID with them. It can be helpful to give a copy to a family member or friend as well. This helps speed up the passport replacement process with the embassy if a passport gets lost, damaged, or stolen. The volunteer's passport should be kept in a sandwich sized plastic bag while wearing it in a leg garter, neck pouch or money belt so that it does not get damaged if it rains or if volunteers sweat. The anti-theft items hide passports, but they will not protect from water and sweat unless they are waterproof.

Not everything in the clothing section will be applicable. Not every volunteer trip will involve swimming, so a bathing suit might not be needed. Alternatively, some volunteer trips will take place in hot environments, so a jacket will not be needed. If the individual needs a jacket, volunteers can bring either a light or a heavy jacket, depending on the climate. Volunteers in tropical climates may not need a jacket, but might wish to bring a waterproof rain jacket and an umbrella for their comfort. Volunteers in cold environments will also not need to bring flip flops. Regardless of climate, some volunteers will not need to bring hiking boots because the terrain will not be rough or hiking will not be a free time activity. However, every volunteer needs to bring waterproof shoes and a pair of closed toe shoes, like tennis shoes for working and walking. Volunteers may still wish to bring a pair of shorts to wear as a set of lounge wear if they have the opportunity to relax alone in their room.

X

Choosing the Right Trip

Considerations When Choosing a Project

Volunteers can consider several factors in order to find the best project to commit to. Ultimately, they all come down to one thing— compatibility. The international volunteer's needs, desires, interests and skills should fit the requirements of the chosen project like a glove, for two reasons. First, a good match ensures that the volunteer will enjoy the work so they can put their best foot forward during the project. Secondly, the volunteer's skills should match the needs of the project in order to make sure that the project will be successful. It can hinder the volunteer project when volunteers do not have the appropriate qualifications. To avoid this, for example, Engineers Without Borders categorizes their projects based on the skill levels of volunteers. Some projects match the skill level of current engineering students, others for engineers who have graduated but have less than two years of work experience, still others for professionals with two to nine years' work experience and highly-skilled engineers with ten or more years of engineering experience.[1]

This especially pertains to educational and medical trips. No one wants their children's teachers or their family's healthcare providers to be underqualified. Underqualified volunteers, especially in these types of projects, can create consequences for the people they seek to help. It would be unethical for volunteers to participate in a trip in which they cannot meet the required qualifications. Not only do a volunteer's professional skills need to be compatible to the international project of their choosing, but their professional skills need to be up to date and customized to the needs of the project as well. Doctors may be qualified to assist at a medical clinic in their home country, but not internationally, unless they spend time making sure they know illnesses specific to the host community. Doctors and medical professionals will then be able to recognize unfamiliar symptoms and give accurate diagnoses.

In this way, in the international volunteering field, it can be especially helpful for medical professionals to research and educate themselves on common ailments in the specific location where they will be volunteering. A doctor from Canada who wants to volunteer in Oaxaca, for instance, should find out what the medical system looks like and what ailments affect that region, along with statistics about health in the community. This will allow the doctor to put their skills to use in the most effective way possible.

Volunteers also need to have sufficient language skills for the project in order to be most effective at their role. If a volunteer wants to choose a project in a Spanish-speaking country but does not speak Spanish, then the volunteer can take time to improve their Spanish before committing to the trip. Volunteers need to have the language skills to match the professional skills they will utilize on the project.

Additionally, personal compatibility factors matter as well when selecting an international volunteering project. These mainly include considerations such as safety and health needs at a given volunteering location. To find personal compatibility alignment with a project, volunteers can compile a short list of non-negotiable criteria. Some of these non-negotiable criteria could include living arrangements (such as staying with a homestay family), medical accommodation (i.e., access to a refrigerator to store medication) and safety precautions (like volunteering in a group setting). Volunteer interest remains the last match volunteers need to make when finding their next international volunteering trip. Every volunteer needs to find their project interesting.

One unconventional way to determine project/volunteer compatibility entails seeing if a volunteer's skills meet an unidentified need in an international volunteering project. Potential volunteers can examine their skills and identify a match between those skills and an unmet need in the project or host community. A lot of volunteer organizations can be understaffed, underfunded and/or in need of expansion. By identifying a gap that needs filling and then closing it with their volunteer work, international volunteers can make their own match between a project and their skills.

Red Flags

In an ideal world, every international volunteer project would be enriching for the host community and volunteers. However, when this does not occur, volunteers can pick up some warning signs from not-so-great projects. These red flags can involve misdirection, incomplete information and bad reviews from former project participants. But they can also be any negative signs that potential volunteers pick up on. This includes if the project methods will likely cause problems for the host community, such as if the project uses wrong tactics, like confusing relief with development, and if the project is harmful to the environment and unsustainable.

Potential volunteers need to pay attention to negative things previous volunteers say about the trip. An offhand comment about bad things that happened or things volunteers did not like can be evidence of a bad project. To find any red flags, potential volunteers can also ask direct questions to former volunteers, such as: Did anything bad happen on the trip? Did the host community like the project and the volunteers? What did you not like? Would you not recommend the trip for any reason? Any negative comment or unenthusiastic recommendation can be warning signs. Potential volunteers can ask follow-up questions to gather more details about what prompted any negative responses. The answers to those questions allow the volunteer to decide if the project meets their expectations or not. This is because former volunteers act as a litmus test for the quality of an international project.

Red flags in pre-trip informational sessions and recruitment meetings may be noticeable. A withholding leader may give conflicting or incomplete information to interested volunteers. A potentially bad leader will not give direct and complete answers to any and all questions posed by would-be volunteers. A bad project leader may also try to pressure people into signing up immediately and act as if the volunteer will not find another similar trip. Avoid these leaders. Leaders can try to rope people into a bad trip by imbuing a false sense of urgency that payment needs to be given immediately to secure a spot on the trip. To counter this red flag, always take time to think about the pros and cons of the project after the interest meetings. Do not commit directly after an informational session. This gives potential volunteers some time to determine if they noticed any red flags from the informational session.

Volunteers need to ask certain questions of project leaders in informational sessions before committing to an international project. These questions include: Have crimes been committed against volunteers on any previous trip? Have any safety incidences occurred? Have any volunteers ever had any health problems during or after a trip? Have locals been positively affected in a tangible way because of previous volunteers' actions? Compare the project leader's answers to previous volunteers' answers to these questions to make sure they match. A red flag would be major discrepancies between previous volunteers' and the project leader's responses.

Once potential volunteers take time to examine any red flags then they can decide if the project fits their needs. It may be helpful to go through the red flags process with a few projects at a time in order to end up with a solid project. Alternatively, if one project needs to be avoided due to red flags, volunteers can pick from other scrutinized options. By thoroughly vetting multiple prospective projects, volunteers will end up on a project that embodies the high quality, safe, and transparent nature they are looking for.

Finding a Project

Volunteers can find international projects advertised in their home communities. Some trips advertise via flyers at community centers and at college student centers. Universities that offer alternative break international volunteering trips usually have information available through the Study Abroad Office. Also, if volunteers like a certain non-profit organization, they can check with that non-profit's office to see if they schedule international volunteer trips. If not, similarly focused non-profits may offer trips. These organizations can be found through a general internet search like "Climate Change Non-Profit" or "International Volunteering Climate Change." Potential volunteers can even search for organizations in a specific country who work in a specific topic, i.e., Peru gender equality organizations. Search their websites to get to know their methods, impact and goals along with what volunteering needs they have.

Volunteers can find trips that match a volunteer's interests and schedule online. The internet also allows volunteers to quickly find reviews of the projects and organization that offers them. However, it may still be hard to determine the quality of a project found online. It can be difficult to properly vet online projects offered by organizations volunteers have not heard of before. For instance, some projects offered through companies online may not utilize proper development methods, or scam volunteers through false advertisements.[2] If a volunteer finds an opportunity posted on an unknown website without overall positive testimonials and reviews on independent, separate websites then the quality can be bad for volunteers and for locals.

Even new projects from the best organizations will not have reviews and testimonials online. In this case it can be difficult to determine the quality of a new project unless volunteers personally feel satisfied with the leader and trust them. If a wonderful team leader needs people to help start a volunteer project with a reputable organization, then this may pass initial red flag scrutiny. Initial scrutiny in this case means evaluating the reliability of the organization, the quality of the leaders, location and safety. However, volunteers will have to find out the details of the new project in order for it to pass the red flag test.

The next step in the process would be for volunteers to contact potential organizations online. Almost every organization's website will have a contact form, email address or Facebook page where potential volunteers can send a message. Reaching out establishes a line of communication and an opportunity to introduce oneself to the organization. The introduction should include the volunteer(s) name(s), purpose for reaching out, dates available to volunteer and any relevant skills volunteers have that the organization could be interested in. It should also include some open-ended questions to determine if the organization's needs match the volunteer's skill set and availability. This ensures that both parties feel on the same page about the scope of the volunteering work. If the organization replies saying that the volunteer work they need help with would not be sustainable or does not meet requirements for sound development methods, then the volunteer can thank the organization and search for an alternative that will. This early communication helps volunteers and the organization know what to expect before the first day of volunteering, especially if they cannot meet in person beforehand. An example of an introductory email would go something like this:

Dear [Organization Name],

My name is _____ and I saw on your website that you need volunteers to help do _____. I have [relevant skills/experience] and will be in [organization's location city] from [start date] to [end date]. Would it be helpful for you if I volunteered? What tasks would you need me to do? Thank you.

Sincerely,

[Volunteer(s) name(s)]

This email may need to be translated into the host community's language, depending on the specifics of the organization.

Short-Term Trips

For the purposes of this book, a short-term international development volunteering trip references projects that last for two weeks or less. Usually, for short-term development trips, volunteers begin work immediately, completely bypassing the planning stage altogether. However, the trips tend to be structured with at least one pre-travel informational session to orient volunteers to the goals of the trip, the place they will be volunteering and the work they will be doing. Some project leaders will ask volunteers to read a book or two, so volunteers can familiarize themselves with historical facts or learn about the culture in the volunteering location. Then, volunteers meet up as a group and travel to the volunteer site. Each day, volunteers work, usually at the same place each day, or sometimes volunteers move around to assist in different locations. Volunteers pause for lunch, which usually consists of local cuisine, so that volunteers can experience the gastronomy of the host culture. Work tends to end at dinnertime, and after dinner volunteers usually meet to recap the day and distribute any necessary information for tomorrow. Some volunteer groups stay in hotels, while others place volunteers in homestay families.

Short-term international volunteering trips usually have goals in proportion to the time volunteers can devote to them, but sometimes short-term trips have goals that would be disproportionally large compared to the time volunteers have to accomplish them. To achieve lofty goals, sometimes volunteer organizations recruit a massive number of volunteers, such as on the show from the 2000s, *Extreme Makeover: Home Edition*. In this tv show, an entire community would volunteer non-stop for a week at a time to build a deserving family a new house. The goal of building a house in one week could be accomplished because of the sheer amount of people who helped build it around the clock.[3] Sometimes, though, volunteer organizations create an oversized goal without sufficient volunteers to see it through to completion. When this happens, project leaders have two options: they can either cut corners to complete the goal or they can do as much as they can in the time allotted but not finish the desired task.[4]

Neither option would be a good one. International volunteer projects exist to help develop an unequal world. When volunteers cut corners, stagnation or ruin can occur.[5] Many short-term projects have a physically-centered goal that can be completed in a short timeframe, yet have a lasting and tangible impact on development. Sustainable and quality development cannot happen if volunteers cut corners. When a team cuts corners, consequences can cause problems. For example, if a volunteer team cuts corners on building a room onto an overcrowded school, then children and teachers' safety becomes at risk. Additionally, the building will not be reliable in the long term, although schools need to be dependable in the long term. Eventually, a poorly built building will need structural repairs, which hinders its usefulness at best, and becomes an unusable safety hazard at worst. If a short-term service project helps a certain number of people but falls short of its goal and cuts corners, then the quality would still be insufficient. For instance, if a dental clinic met its aim to clean two hundred people's teeth in a week's time but rushed the cleanings, then the quality would not be sufficient for good oral health. Rushed for time, volunteers could give inadequate cleanings and overlook dental problems that need to be addressed. In this way, cutting corners to meet a goal on a short-term international development project has serious consequences for real people.

Correspondingly, if an international development project fails to meet its overly ambitious goal due to time constraints the after-effects can be just as grave.[6] If volunteers leave a project incomplete, then it does not help the people who need it. For example, if volunteers build a classroom but do not have time to finish a wall or the roof, children cannot use it. Or, if a dental clinic service-based trip did not cut corners but instead fell short of its goal to clean two hundred people's mouths, then those not served would not receive necessary dental care. This could have consequences almost immediately for people with urgent mouth problems, or in the long run if children did not get their teeth cleaned, thus deteriorating their oral health over time.

The quality and advisability of creating or attending short-term international volunteer trips thus often depends on the realistic nature of its goals, which need to be evaluated on a case-by-case basis. The goals of a short-term trip can be determined to be beneficial based on how sustainable and permanent the assistance will be and how much they make sense in the time that volunteers have. The best-case scenario in a short-term development project would be that it creates development quickly as the goal of the trip comes to fruition. If a need can be met quickly, then a short-term volunteer trip can be a good avenue to achieve development. If, for example, a town wants to stimulate the local economy through a large influx of cash, they may create a yearly event, such as a weeklong food festival, to attract foreigners staying in hotel resorts nearby. Volunteers could help translate, sell tickets at booths, pass out pamphlets and help with marketing. When the festival ends, volunteers would know they helped raise money for the town and achieved the goal.

Short-term volunteering can be helpful when providing relief for locals who already volunteer in their community. To be beneficial, the short-term volunteering would need to be done with an already established nonprofit organization that seeks short-term volunteers. This way, the day-to-day operations remain covered by the existing local volunteer force and short-term volunteers act as an added bonus to the daily operations. The work itself could be working on a wish list of tasks that can help the organization go above and beyond. Or short-term volunteers could cover routine work like sitting at a welcome desk, freeing a local to do more advanced work that they otherwise would not have time to do. Similarly, the scope of work must be either non-skilled that anyone could do or involve tasks that volunteers already know how to do well. Therefore, locals would not need to spend the limited time training short-term volunteers. Training can take away from the daily, ongoing tasks of local volunteers who run the non-profit.

Even if an organization does not have short-term volunteers all the time, and thus short-term labor does not generate a continuous, sustainable source of help they can rely on, many organizations like having short-term international volunteers anyway. In fact, this advantage can help so much that some international nonprofits recruit short-term volunteers all year round. As an exception, short-term volunteering could not be helpful to an international organization if the work requires continuity from several short-term volunteers over a period of time, like a building project or working at a medical clinic, because a future short-term volunteer workforce cannot be guaranteed.

Short-term international volunteering can be beneficial when volunteers go back to the same host community year after year. In this way, repetitive short-term volunteering can build strong relationships between host community members and volunteers throughout the years. The bond between leaders can strengthen as volunteer leaders offer continued support. Volunteers can communicate regularly with the host community after each trip to make sure past projects still function as desired and troubleshoot any problems as needed. A benefit of working with the same host community year after year means that the group can prepare as the community's needs evolve over time.

On the other hand, sometimes the short-term volunteer model acts as a hindrance to development because of its limiting structure. Short-term international development projects can act as a band-aid to a bigger problem, because the limited time frame forces volunteers to implement quick solutions to solve issues that have persisted for years. When this occurs, short-term projects create the illusion that development is over-simple. Oftentimes, development problems cannot be solved in the short term by small volunteer teams.[7] For instance, a short-term traveling health clinic seems like it solves problems because volunteers help sick people heal. However, the bigger development issue encompasses a lack of a comprehensive health care for the region. In sustainable and long-lasting development, even the highest quality short-term volunteer-run health clinic will not satiate the need for permanent health care. That would require more than short-term volunteers could give, such as funding, physical structures and recruitment of qualified local medical professionals.[8]

Voluntourism

Voluntourism can be defined as a trip that combines volunteering abroad with touring an area in a manner similar to a vacation. Voluntourism includes both a vacation and a way to do a volunteer project at the same time. Voluntourism can be classified as a leisure-based subset of short-term international volunteer trips. Voluntourism tends to not be as effective as short-term trips, however, because they focus on the pleasurable experience of the volunteer instead of the needs of the host community.[9] Development and volunteering can be fun, but voluntourism typically markets how much fun volunteers will have as a selling point, thereby focusing on fun more so than on development. Typically, international development volunteering focuses on giving, not receiving, but voluntourism aims to combine giving and receiving. Voluntourists give their time volunteering and also receive the enjoyment that comes with a vacation abroad.

Non-profit organizations, religious groups, community organizations or universities usually run short-term volunteer trips. However, voluntourism tends to be run by for-profit companies. Most often voluntourism companies market projects like a vacation. One of the vacation's highlights would be the volunteering, whereas short-term trips market the project and its benefits for the host community. Voluntourism marketing generally lacks comprehensive information on what the positive effects of volunteering will be for the host community. Instead, voluntourism advertisements profligate what the positive effects will be for the international volunteering vacationers.[10] Usually this means touting the internal benefits, like the good feelings that come with giving back, the interesting people who voluntourists will meet, the great souvenirs voluntourists will have a chance to purchase and the photo-op opportunities that will remind them of fond memories spent abroad.

Even cruise excursions entered into the voluntourism business. Carnival Cruise Line offers excursions for vacationers at some ports of call, such as at La Romana in the Dominican Republic. While cruisers can choose traditional water sports excursions, some pick excursions with a voluntourism element. In La Romana, when touring rural areas, excursion participants can visit an NGO that develops art skills in children.[11] In the Amber Cove port of the Dominican Republic, cruisers can pay to become voluntourists for a few hours by planting chocolate plants and packaging chocolate made at a chocolate farm and factory run by women.[12] Or they can instead visit an orphanage before touring a church, a cassava bread farm and eating lunch at a restaurant.[13]

Since voluntourism does not focus on the quality or sustainability of the development work voluntourists partake in, it can be difficult to understand how to quantify voluntourism success. How can the international volunteering industry define success when voluntourism focuses on the volunteer's experience? In almost all cases, no real development success occurs with the voluntourism focus. However, the for-profit companies that market voluntourism as a vacation have goals for what they consider a successful trip. The companies want to tap into as much revenue as the voluntourism market will provide and also bring in new customers.[14] They can do this by setting a goal to provide high quality vacations that will have customers coming back and also referring their friends.

But this does not embody the purpose of international volunteering at all. Confusing a vacation-oriented experience with actual volunteering can hurt the host community. Mimicking volunteering can be problematic because voluntourists who do not know the importance of sustainable and high-quality international development methods can leave the trip thinking they made an improvement to the world. This underscores the actual effort, planning and research necessary to enact good development practices. Voluntourists can sometimes not be aware of the distinction between helpful development methods, because even unhelpful voluntourist activities can leave them walking away feeling positive due to the internal benefits it provides.[15]

Voluntourism can have negative effects because it does not focus on working hard. If volunteers think they work too hard then the trip loses the vacation vibe. Since many people go on vacations for deep relaxation, working vigorously as volunteers can be unsatisfying to customers. Unsatisfied customers decrease revenue, so host companies do not want voluntourists to work too rigorously. This paradox of vacation versus volunteering means that sometimes voluntourists can lose sight of the fact that international volunteering should be about how the work volunteers do can help the host community sustainably and for the long-haul.

Voluntourism hurts the host community because voluntourism companies tend to take different groups of voluntourists to the same location each week to work on the same project. Although the project and the location remain consistent, since the volunteers differ each week, the projects lack stability due to the influx and outflow of volunteers so frequently.[16] When an international volunteer project does not have consistency, then each time new workers arrive they lose time getting acclimated to the needs of the project. When orientation at the beginning of each week takes too much time, volunteers do not spend their time most efficiently. Progress toward goals suffer when projects take a few steps forward then a few steps back over and over when new workers begin volunteering on a voluntourism project.

On voluntourism projects, not only does less progress get made each week because of a revolving volunteer force, sometimes nothing new gets done at all. Since new volunteers repeat what previous volunteers did the week prior, progress toward a development goal can stagnate or falter as the same work reoccurs many times over.[17] If a voluntourism project had a revolving volunteer force but those volunteers worked in a long-term capacity, then more could be done. Voluntourists would have enough time to settle in and help achieve milestones on the way to the development goal's completion. However, since voluntourism projects occur in the short term and leaders rotate in new volunteers so frequently, total lack of productivity can be a major issue.

The stagnation of productivity can be especially problematic when the voluntourism project teaches children. Some voluntourists go on trips to work at orphanages and schools. When voluntourists act as children's teachers, and new teachers come to teach each week, children can experience repeated lessons and not receive the comprehensive knowledge they need. Complete learning happens over time with the same teachers. Many voluntourists teach English lessons without knowledge of what the children already learned prior to their arrival. These same volunteers leave before the gap in education can be corrected, causing a continuous problem that keeps children from fulfilling their full potential.[18]

Voluntourists can additionally be unqualified for the work that they do. Many voluntourism projects do not require individuals to possess any specific or advanced skills to participate. This can be a problem when the project has technical elements, such as teaching English. Although voluntourists presumably have a command of the English language and grammar, teaching itself requires specialized knowledge. When voluntourists teach English without proper qualification, students can suffer. However, if the voluntourism industry set standards that projects such as teaching English need qualified volunteers, then the problem could be remedied and voluntourism would be more apt to create positive outcomes. Teaching English also can take away jobs from locals. It would be much better for the school children and for the local economy if a trained local taught English instead. Not only would a local English teacher be consistent and qualified, but employing locals remains better for economic development in the host community.

Voluntourism does offer a few benefits. Voluntourism can be ideal for environmental cleanup or post-disaster relief. Voluntourism projects can be initiated quickly after a natural disaster so that people who see the aftermath on the news can help. Rotating workers can be an asset when a relief situation requires all hands on deck. Voluntourism can also be an advantage after the initial surge of volunteers and donations fade post-disaster, but cleanup work still needs to be completed. Since voluntourism companies tend to take new volunteers to the same place to do the same work each week, the new volunteers can keep assisting once most of the world has stopped. However, post-disaster voluntourism minimizes the vacation aspect since infrastructure gets destroyed in a natural disaster. The voluntourism would be more akin to a short-term trip. Short-term projects often do not include repeated trips to the same area to do the same volunteer work week after week, so voluntourism can be an advantage in this case.

Secondly, the tourism part of voluntourism can be beneficial for development. As tourists, voluntourism participants buy food, lodging, activities and souvenirs in the host community. When tourism money goes into the hands of members of the host community, that can be beneficial because the money tends to get distributed around the community. This helps grow the local economy, especially for artisans and the local tourism sector. And if voluntourists advertise the host community as an ideal tourism destination to their friends and family, the industry can grow and employ more locals, thus increasing local GDP.

Vacations and volunteering internationally seem essentially incompatible because they have such opposing objectives. It can be difficult to properly volunteer and vacation together in such a short amount of time. The questionable quality of development that voluntourists undertake leads to the importance of all voluntourists understanding the real-life impact that positive and negative international volunteering has on host communities. In this way, voluntourism does not need to cause negative consequences. If voluntourists look to optimize the outcome of their participation and limit vacation time to designated free periods, then the project will have a better chance of focusing on the needs of the community while also working within the time frame that volunteers have.

Voluntourism Solutions and Alternatives

Sometimes with short-term trips and voluntourism, the paradox of limited time to volunteer can be insurmountable. In this case, would-be international volunteers have a few alternatives. When volunteers would be too short on time, volunteering locally can be much more beneficial than attempting to squeeze in an international volunteering project. Volunteering locally in a short-term capacity can be very successful because locals have such a good knowledge of community needs. Local volunteers can identify quick, sustainable projects and execute them without having to lose time traveling or performing detailed pre-project research. For example, volunteers could work on community beautification and improvement projects. Options include adopting a road to pick up trash periodically, building a picnic bench in a park, building benches at a nursing home, serving meals at a homeless shelter or making gift baskets for children in the hospital. All of these options would allow volunteers to make a real impact on their community by using good development practices, yet do so in the time frame that short-term international volunteering trips utilize.

Some volunteers feel drawn to participating in short-term international volunteering to experience life outside of their home country and to understand poverty firsthand. Voluntourists and short-term volunteers also want to help people, so going on a volunteering trip internationally can feel like two birds, one stone kind of opportunity. However, for the sake of quality development, voluntourists can consider making a separate international trip to experience a different way of life before volunteering internationally. Volunteers and voluntourists could make two trips, the first to visit the host community as a traveler to experience the culture and history. Then, volunteers could return to the host community to volunteer. This method would allow quality volunteering work to be the undivided focus of the second trip.

This alternative travel method allows volunteers to be more active in the planning process after the first trip. After experiencing life in the host community, volunteers can more readily identify projects to collaborate with locals on because they understand the needs of the host community more fully. Taking two trips with different purposes also enables volunteers to build stronger connections with locals, which ultimately aids the development process. Various organizations, such as Witness for Peace, offer international trips for the sole purpose of understanding issues that locals face in overcoming obstacles specific to their region. Certain trips focus on learning about immigration in Mexico and consequences of Plan Colombia in Colombia.[19]

Lastly, if volunteers and voluntourists find themselves in the midst of a project and they notice unintended consequences, a few methods can remedy it. First, volunteers should talk to the project leader about it, demonstrating why the project element in question can lead to negative outcomes. Usually, using a different, proven development method can halt and reverse unintended consequences. To ensure that volunteers and project leaders understand the risks, new international volunteers can spend time before and during the trip educating fellow volunteers on proper development methods if needed. Finally, project leaders can match individual volunteers with opportunities that put their skills to the best use in order to minimize the risk of mistakes occurring during the international development project.

Troubleshooting

Despite all precautions, very occasionally, things do not go as planned when working with a vetted organization. The project matching process generally eliminates nonprofits that display red flags, but it does not prevent red flags from showing up during the beginning of volunteer work. With almost every organization, the mantra "What you see is what you get" holds true. If the workers volunteers converse with online act ethically, then they tend to run their organization to that same standard. This especially holds true if volunteers have the opportunity to meet people in an organization in person before volunteering. Especially in short-term volunteering scenarios, however, many international volunteers do not get the chance to meet people from the organization and see their work in person until the first day they begin volunteering. If a red flag presents itself, or volunteering goes wrong, then volunteers first need to think through some possible reasons why it could be occurring. The volunteer work, the actions of the organization's workers and the organization itself could not be what it appeared to be. Or it could be something smaller, such as the organization changing the scope of the volunteer work. Conversely, the organization could have bad intentions, display unethical behavior or make volunteers feel uncomfortable.

Some ways to recognize in-person red flags once volunteer work has begun includes observing misleading or contradictory statements by organization members or noticing them saying different things to different people. Signs could be smaller, such as keeping volunteers unnecessarily in the dark and not giving direct answers to their questions. Or, on the other hand, the red flags could be more obvious, such as blatantly using non-optimal development methods that the organization had appeared to not condone and conducting their business unethically outright. Or the reality of the organization's day to day operations could not match their website's description, news articles about them, what volunteer testimonials say and what they post on social media accounts, etc.

Volunteers facing one of these situations do have options. The first would be to give it time, especially for a milder situation like changing the scope of the volunteer work after arrival. If volunteers roll with the unexpected (barring a situation that hurts people or is unlawful), then they may see a valid reason for the situation. Perhaps if the organization changed the scope of volunteer work, then they feel volunteers can do the new work well anyway, or a situation came up that caused a major change in the organization's needs. An alternative or second step would be to openly communicate with the volunteer supervisor to address any concerns. This could assuage volunteers' concerns or give valid reasons for the change that volunteers did not think of from their perspective. Specifically, it would help to ask questions to clarify differences in expectations or to bring to light factors previously unaccounted for. Miscommunication can cause unnecessary issues with volunteering, and fixing miscommunication occurs through forthright conversation between the organization and volunteers.

Alternatively, what if the issue is not actually an issue but a cultural difference that volunteers did not know about? When volunteering domestically, volunteers know all the cultural norms of their community but the same cannot be said when visiting a new place to volunteer. These differences can seem glaring to a volunteer put into a new situation head first, but completely commonplace for the locals who run and partner with the organization. For instance, in many Latin American countries, such as Peru, Guatemala, Puerto Rico, Cuba and the Dominican Republic, I have met people who have, almost immediately after being introduced, expected me to follow them without explanation or get in their car without knowing them or where we would go. And once in the car, taxi drivers and people who became my friends would stop to show me places that we did not discuss. I have had taxi drivers stop to buy lunch and to give money to a friend while they took me to my destination. To individuals who grew up in a "stranger danger" culture, this can seem jarring. But in Latin America, acquaintances often go immediately and talk about where to go on the way, or enjoy the day without a plan. This constitutes part of the social fabric to make strong bonds quickly. Similarly, an issue may not be one at all if volunteers do not have an expert level of knowledge about the nonprofit's scope of work, such as norms for running a dog shelter or common practices in saving the rainforests. Learning more about why people do what they do can help shine a new light on something that volunteers felt unsure about.

However, some potential red flags really turn out to be red flags. If communicating about them does not satisfactorily solve the issue, then volunteers still have options. The first would be to have another conversation with the volunteer supervisor or the nonprofit's leaders to pinpoint volunteers' concerns. Volunteers can discuss how certain actions seem in contrast to best development methods and why. Volunteers can give examples of similar times where an alternative good development method worked and suggest a change. Sometimes people do not realize a better way exists, and this could fix the red flag. In extreme cases of falsehood, pressure to act unethically or behavior that makes volunteers uncomfortable that does not stop, know that the ends do not justify the means. In this situation, that means that volunteering for volunteering's sake could hurt the host community. Volunteers can ask to be reassigned or thank the organization and leave. Remember that this constitutes a last resort, since nonprofit organizations rely on their volunteers and count on their work.

Part 4

*Looking Toward the Future
with New International
Volunteering*

XI

Making Systemic Change

Globalization and Interconnectedness

Globalization is the phenomenon of connecting people all around the world to each other. With the growing connectivity from globalization, cultures, traditions, beliefs, and ways of life can mesh as people gain access to more information than ever before. Globalization has shaped our modern world, causing advances in technology and changing migratory patterns. It allows people to move freely using improved transportation over longer distances quicker than ever before. People who embrace globalization utilize technology to their advantage for personal learning, better communication and to grow their businesses. Globalization facilitates innovation at a rapid rate as people share ideas in subjects from entrepreneurship to healthcare. This can lead to greater efficiency and better quality of life.

Technology has brought important issues for communities around the world into the limelight. This occurred during the Arab Spring, a movement in several countries where people protested the status quo. The Arab Spring began in Tunisia when Mohamed Bouazizi, a fruit seller, set himself on fire after experiencing police humiliation while trying to make a living for his family. That started a chain of protests which eventually culminated in the resignation of Tunisia's and Egypt's presidents. The Arab Spring will be remembered for its massive protests in Tahrir Square in Cairo, Egypt. These were organized on social media by people like Esraa Abdel Fattah, aptly nicknamed "Facebook Girl" for her social media skills of organizing people with similar aims to protest. These protests, specifically social media's role in them, "g[ave] marginalized groups ... a voice ... to say 'Enough' and 'This is how I feel,'" according to Mona Eltahawy via *The Guardian*. The world saw this when the Arab Spring brought remote towns to the forefront of a global movement through citizen journalism. Citizen journalism showed the world the experiences of ordinary people involved in the Arab Spring through videos and images posted on social media sites.[1]

Globalization can help concerned citizens act as watchdogs to hold governments and businesses accountable. In 2017, Bolivia's government stripped protective status away from indigenous people in Tipnis in order to make a road through the Amazon. This occurred despite the fact that constitutionally, indigenous people have protective status for their land in Bolivia. In this age of globalization, international media including *The Guardian* and *Al Jazeera* broadcasted the Tipnis protests worldwide.[2] Similarly, the Lava Jato scandal in Brazil exposed a level of corruption and bribery in top businesses and highest levels of government. Ordinary Brazilians have taken matters into their own hands via the Social Observatory of Brazil movement. Concerned Brazilians in the Social Observatory of Brazil ensure that officials use public money correctly instead of favoring certain companies when giving contracts in order to stop corruption. They also check to be sure that none of the public money gets used personally by public officials. All one hundred and nine branches of the Social Observatory of Brazil check publicly available documents to make sure government money goes where it is supposed to go and that contractors do not overbill the government for materials. An estimate of the Observatory predicts that since 2016, citizens have saved 1.5 Billion Reais from going to corruption.[3]

International volunteers can help as witnesses. Gail Phares, co-founder of Witness for Peace Southeast, worked in Guatemala during the Guatemalan Civil War. The Guatemalan Civil War began after the U.S. government backed a coup ousting the first democratically elected president in the country's history. In the late 1970s and early 1980s the U.S. government did something similar in backing the Contras in Nicaragua, even though the Contras hurt their own people and violated human rights. Gail led a delegation of volunteers to Nicaraguan war zones to show them what actually occurred with the Contras in Nicaragua. Because of the volunteers' presence, the Contras stopped fighting simply because the group witnessed their actions. This led Gail to create several subsequent delegations of volunteers to Nicaraguan war zones in order to stop the killing and monitor fighting. During the delegations, volunteers documented Nicaraguans who were killed to show U.S. Congress members what happened. This documentation proved that the Contras murdered civilians and committed war crimes.[4]

Similarly, international volunteers can assist locals in coordinating community organization to bring communities together under a common issue they experience, such as witnessing war, preventing government corruption or protesting for human rights and against injustices. International volunteers can assist by setting the meetings, finding a meeting place, spreading the word about community organization and by liaising between the host community and the government (or private sector). Dr. Richard Slatta did this while serving as a Peace Corps volunteer in Panama, helping to organize approximately seventy thousand locals from nearby communities into a community assembly. The assembly had government representatives, which helped the community get potable water and roads. This model of organizing via support from international volunteers could work in many volunteering situations.

These advancements from globalization have positive applications for international volunteering. In fact, globalization helped international volunteering happen on the scale we see today. It has opened up opportunities to connect aid organizations with volunteers easier than ever before. Volunteers can fly to the project's location quickly thanks to the advent of fleets of commercial jets. Volunteers easily book tickets and accommodations on websites that aggregate hundreds of deals in seconds. Email and messenger services permit volunteers to communicate with the host community before arriving. For example, the volunteermatch.org website gives nonprofits a platform to advertise the volunteer help that they need and potential volunteers the search tools to find an ideal nonprofit to volunteer for. Volunteers can even connect directly with nonprofits through the website, making volunteering sign ups more convenient than ever before. Many volunteer opportunities on volunteermatch.org would connect volunteers to virtual assignments with international nonprofits, while others need traditional volunteers to come and help in person at a local organization. Over 14 million people have volunteered just through this site alone.[5]

In this way, globalization can be a positive international volunteering tool to spearhead change, growth and development. Globalization gives international volunteers the opportunity to do their part to help tackle problems they see on tv or online beyond the bounds of their community. When people see a disaster unfolding live on TV, they can use technology to quickly respond by donating online and signing up to volunteer there. Online communication abilities connect volunteers to communities around the world that could use their assistance. For example, in Urubamba, Peru, in the Andean mountains, a small, rural town partners with university student volunteers who go to Peru to study abroad in the summers. The community seeks their assistance to help keep the town's elementary school beautified and in good working order. Workers at the school contact the study abroad leaders to let them know what they would like done at the school when they arrive. In past years, students have built a wall, painted the school and installed toilets. Like in Urubamba, volunteers can go to rural areas and help connect people to the benefits of globalization. This will increase GDP, grow the economy and build better education and medical services.

I myself have felt the benefits of globalization as an international volunteer in Guatemala. I worked in a remote location that used to be difficult to reach, but now has technology to connect it. I utilized this technology by purchasing a USB WiFi stick that gave me access to the internet on my laptop wherever I brought it. Towns in that area used to have internet and computer access only in internet cafes, but now some people have computers and internet in their homes. Many cafes, restaurants and hotels have WiFi. Guatemalans in the area have their own smartphones, and they can refill phone minutes/text messaging capabilities at any convenience store.

Free Trade and Fair Trade

Free trade and fair trade do not often receive the limelight as important international development volunteering tools. Fair trade can be defined as trade where people who made the products receive a living wage and safe working conditions. Without fair trade, workers can be paid low wages without many benefits.[6] For example, without fair trade, coffee farmers might have to take out loans from a loan shark to purchase coffee tree seeds with an unreasonably high interest rate. Or big landowners could force growers to work all day without breaks. Fair trade helps ensure due monetary gain and ethical working conditions for the work of the coffee growers. Fair trade can prevent labor and borrowing problems by creating a safe and equitable environment in which to work. For instance, with fair trade, coffee growers could avoid loan sharks and sell coffee beans to international buyers for a fair profit. Because fair trade promotes reasonable work standards, fair trade remains the ethical way to trade with sellers, businesses and co-ops around the world.

Fair trade can improve the lives of farmers, and it already has. Companies like Andean Dream certify their products, such as quinoa pastas and quinoa cookies, as fair trade. As more consumers in industrialized markets demand that products they buy be fair trade, stores begin to deliver, especially health conscious stores. Some fair trade items carry a label that says certified fair trade, so consumers can ensure that the workers had fair treatment and wages. Many brands, such as Alter Eco, a chocolate company, proudly represent these ideals in their products, and so advertise with stories and statistics about the benefits of fair trade in their supply chain.[7]

Free trade is international trade without financial barriers such as tariffs or taxes that affect and hinder trade. National governments negotiate and agree on free trade agreements. Free trade, ideally, could be helpful for stimulating development by eliminating all barriers to trade.

With free trade, consumers would not have to absorb the costs of tariffs. Companies in host communities would be able to make more money by exporting their goods to major international markets. By exporting goods within free trade zones, workers can make a profit and reach more consumers in order to expand their business. This will create jobs and, over time, lift employees out of poverty.

However, in some situations, tariffs can aid in development by protecting workers in up-and-coming industries from having to compete with industrialized mega-companies who can sell the same product for cheaper. For example, after the implementation of the North American Free Trade Agreement (NAFTA) between the United States, Mexico, and Canada, many Mexican corn farmers could no longer compete with U.S. mega-farmers who produce corn in large batches for cheaper. The U.S. mega-farmers received large subsidies from the U.S. government, which meant that they had a competitive advantage over Mexican family farm operations. Since small corn farms in Mexico did not receive subsidies from the Mexican government to the same extent, they were no longer protected by high tariffs. Job losses impacted the industry heavily, leading to the destruction of the local corn markets in Mexico. Almost two million Mexican farmers have stopped farming since NAFTA was enacted and food prices in Mexico have increased during the same period. NAFTA did grow Mexico's manufacturing industry but many of the manufacturing plants pollute and do not give their employees fair wages or good working conditions. NAFTA mostly benefited the United States. It created jobs for American farmers because of the government subsidies. In fact, the United States exported four times more corn to Mexico after NAFTA and the prices of corn in Mexico dropped 66 percent during the first ten years after NAFTA.[8]

Parts of free trade agreements need to be replaced if many people lose their jobs and cannot find others, such as the Mexican farmers. When people lose their jobs, poverty will rise. If one person in a family does not have a job for at least six months, that household has a higher likelihood of transitioning into poverty than a similar family with no one unemployed, according to the Urban Institute. If someone remains unemployed for a long time, they have a higher likelihood of staying in poverty, because of the difficulty to gain employment after being without work for a long time. It can be even more difficult to leave poverty if someone experiences it before unemployment occurs. People in this situation tend to remain in poverty because they cannot afford to travel to interviews, do not have healthcare or money for childcare.[9]

If an industry loses many jobs under a free trade agreement, one solution would be for the government, volunteers and companies to team up to help people secure jobs in other industries. Volunteers can identify geographic areas where a lot of people are unemployed or where the main employment sector died out to teach people new job skills. Volunteers, local industries or governments can pay employees to take part in skills training programs at existing technical colleges or they could start their own teaching programs. This would give participants a fresh start and a viable way to bring in an income after an old industry collapsed from free trade. In some cases, it would be helpful if the job training focused on work for high skilled positions to increase participants' income. This program worked in Kentucky where ten laid off coal miners signed up to learn to code at a company called BitSource. The former miners got twenty-two weeks of paid training and then BitSource hired them. By learning to code, BitSource applies the coal miners' technology experience over to coding. At the time of writing, nine of the original ten employees still work there and over a thousand people applied to the initial program.[10]

Although free trade agreements may not directly impact each development project, it can help volunteers to be aware of consequences from them, such as lack of access to market due to free trade. Those consequences may factor into the development plan for fostering economic growth and job creation. Locals will have to find a competitive, unique product to make or service to perform that would be successful in the current international economy. The product can meet a need or be a service that gives customers a helpful experience. For instance, a call center could be based locally but meet an international need for customer service. It could also be a specialty or niche market special to the area, like how Costa Rica has a niche in sustainable tourism or how Guatemala exports handmade jewelry. Keep free trade in mind when thinking economically about international development, because workers in industrializing countries could benefit by exporting their products to other nations.[11]

Volunteers can help to create an exporting industry as a conduit or intermediary. For instance, a man I met in Guatemala works with a group of Guatemalan Civil War survivors. The survivors make beautiful handicrafts and this man takes several trips to the United States each year to sell the handicrafts at churches around the country. Each time he goes to a church, he gives a video presentation of the women telling how the war negatively impacted them. The presentation helps the women get a fair income for their work, tells their stories to an international audience and raises awareness to Americans about their government's involvement in the Guatemalan Civil War.[12]

Additionally, international volunteers could help the host community by supplying a demand they have. For example, Envirofit International Cookstoves makes safe stoves to replace harmful open fire cooking methods. They sell these to people with a consumer mindset. The cookstoves meet the customers' needs because the technology speeds the cooking process and acts as a greener alternative to cooking over an open flame. Cooking over an open fire, especially inside, causes over four million deaths each year, according to Envirofit. A high-quality product, the cookstove comes with a warranty and lowers fuel costs. By seeing people as consumers instead of charity beneficiaries, Envirofit formulated the cookstove to be something consumers like and find useful. Many times, charities would give a low quality cookstove that people would not be able to use. The beneficiaries could not give the charities adequate feedback on how the cookstoves did not meet their needs because the charities tended to donate and then leave. By using a market-based approach with a customer model, Envirofit gains feedback and makes product improvements like all businesses do. Envirofit created a market for selling cookstoves and by ensuring quality, it led them to sell over one million cookstoves.[13]

Climate Change Prevention

New international volunteering takes climate change into account because it causes worse natural disasters, which delay development efforts. Global warming, or the rise of ocean temperatures, causes ice glaciers to melt, which in turn causes sea levels to rise. The rising sea level and warmer sea temperatures contribute to worsening flooding and mudslides. This has become a problem in international development, especially because flooding and mudslides destroy infrastructure. Global warming also makes hurricanes stronger. Tropical storms form easier in warmer weather, and higher temperatures can strengthen the intensity of storms, causing more property damage. Global warming also increases moisture in the atmosphere, which leads to more rainfall with tropical cyclones. According to NASA, climate change also contributes to more severe heat waves, droughts and wildfires, all of which negatively impact food security worldwide.

Therefore, the new international volunteer focuses sustainability efforts on preventing and reversing human caused climate change. In development, stakeholders seek to preserve the planet and reduce the amount of human suffering. Earthlings (international volunteers included) need to reduce the impact of natural disasters. GDP takes a hit after a natural disaster and it makes life more economically and mentally difficult for the people affected. Good development tends to increase GDP and improve quality of life. To continue this trend, reducing the effects of climate change is a priority for new international volunteers. In this way, natural disasters caused by climate change will make many people have to go through unnecessary suffering. But there is hope if international volunteers and the international community at large prioritizes climate change prevention.

Natural disasters can put growing communities on a whole different trajectory than before. When a developing community gets impacted by a large-scale natural disaster, the community experiences hardship. They usually need to incorporate emergency relief just to get back to the economic development level they had prior to the disaster. As more frequent and stronger storms persist, and places deal with post-disaster relief efforts, they take away from other development projects that could help growth. The following chart shows this cycle. Development happens until a natural disaster occurs. After the natural disaster, the area's development resources get redirected to provide emergency relief. After a period of emergency relief, people begin to rebuild their homes and shared spaces in the community. Only after rebuilding can an area begin to develop again. Natural disasters represent a disrupting force that pauses development, making everyone worse off.

For example, global warming causes drought, which leads to famine. In too hot temperatures, livestock die and crops wither, causing people to die of hunger and thirst. If international volunteers spearheaded an initiative to grow micro-entrepreneurship before the famine, those resources may have to be reallocated to emergency food and medical relief during the famine. The money and resources would no longer contribute to growing local business, stalling economic growth. After the famine, the micro-entrepreneurship initiative could continue again, but perhaps after people picked up their lives again, so it would not continue exactly where it left off. This scenario could be preventable in some instances and less severe in others if climate change prevention efforts come into force.[14]

The approach the Cuban and American governments took after

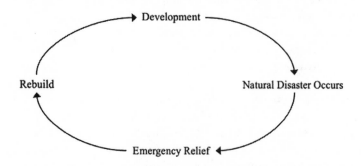

The cycle of natural disasters interrupting development.

similar hurricanes hit Cuba and Puerto Rico illustrates this concept further. Hurricanes Maria and Irma struck Puerto Rico and Cuba with considerable force and magnitude, leaving behind devastation in their wakes. Hurricane Maria, a Category Five hurricane with winds between 110–175 mph, brought damaging weather to the Caribbean. Over twenty inches of rain fell on Puerto Rico. Irma, a Category Five storm with winds reaching 125–160 mph when it hit land in Cuba, brought several feet of water into the streets of Havana. Maria and Irma brought the strongest winds in almost one hundred years to Puerto Rico and Cuba.

While both Cuba and Puerto Rico have infrastructure that is vulnerable to hurricanes, such as a prevalence for tin roofs, Hurricane Maria severely impacted the long-term future of Puerto Rico, while Cuba quickly repaired damage from Irma. In fact, professors from UC Berkeley estimate that in the next fifteen years Maria will lower incomes by 21 percent in Puerto Rico because of the damage it did to the infrastructure and electric grid on the entire island. Puerto Rico's electric grid incurred large damages due to Hurricane Maria, leaving the entire island without power for months. Before the hurricane, the old electric grid had not been well maintained, especially aboveground power lines. Additionally, a shortage of workers and little to no financing for repairs (due to the government's high debt load) exacerbated the situation. In fact, the utility went bankrupt along with the island's government just before Hurricane Maria.

In Cuba, the aftermath of Hurricane Irma looked quite different, largely due to Cuba's proactive climate change policies and aggressive post-hurricane response. While Puerto Rico went without power for months after Hurricane Maria, it took five days to restore power in Cuba after Hurricane Irma. After the storm had passed, thousands of Cuban first responders and government workers quickly cleared streets and beaches of debris and then advertised widely that the island could receive tourists once again. Puerto Rico did not see that kind of response, as whole towns were left isolated for days after the storm.

Preparation and prevention were key to Cuba's efforts that kept Hurricane Irma from destroying the island's future GDP. In fact, Cuba takes climate change seriously and seeks to prevent damage from climate change. Cubans strengthen the island's natural and manmade hurricane defenses with their Project Life program. This includes fortifying natural defenses, preventing coastal erosion, protecting coral reefs, restoring mangroves as a natural storm barrier and moving agriculture to plots of land that have not been inundated by seawater. The program also utilizes manmade coastal engineering principles like moving towns inland when necessary and not building in vulnerable seaside zones.[15]

The new international volunteer can prevent human-caused climate change by reducing their carbon footprint in many ways. A carbon footprint represents how much carbon a person or organization emits and can be calculated online by taking a quiz about one's lifestyle choices. A carbon footprint calculator can be found on the Environmental Protection Agency's website.[16] Specifically, while volunteering internationally, volunteers need to use green energy as much as possible, by sourcing windmills and solar panels. Volunteers can also reduce the project's demand for plastic and wood products, because plastic does not biodegrade and wood products require cutting down trees. To reduce the demand for these materials, volunteers can make conscious choices to pick alternative, locally available materials.

Reusable packaging also makes a difference in reducing the amount of trash a project generates. Decreasing waste from international volunteering projects can be implemented in simple ways, such as bringing a reusable bag to carry materials in instead of putting them in a single use plastic bag. If someone cannot replace plastic with an eco-friendly material, then recycling the plastic would make a good alternative. Volunteers can also offset their emissions, including from the flight and other transportation, by purchasing carbon offsets online. Additionally, volunteers can bring global attention to climate change to encourage more people to do their part to reduce their carbon footprint, both in and out of international volunteering.

After reducing the international volunteering project's carbon footprint, the new international volunteer can then take several actions to reverse human caused climate change. The simplest way to do this would be to plant trees that are native to the area when possible and appropriate. But it also involves careful planning and foresight before the project begins. When the new international volunteer thinks long term during the planning stage of a project, they can implement measures to counter climate change.

Urban planning helps reduce climate change from international volunteering as well. International volunteers can advocate for strong building codes so that infrastructure will not fail in a natural disaster. This can be done by not building on floodplains and not reducing natural marshes in city expansions. By advocating to incorporate climate change into city planning calculations, volunteers can make a difference in their field. Even small actions have major potential to help. In *Climate of Hope* by Michael Bloomberg and Carl Pope, the authors explain that painting rooftops white reflects sunlight instead of absorbing sunlight, which keeps buildings cooler. This reduces the need for air conditioning, a carbon emitter. Thinking long term about climate change does not apply only to projects in cities, however. Volunteers in every location can help members of the host community secure insurance to reduce the economic losses from natural disasters. After one does occur, the new international volunteer commits to rebuilding better than before (as opposed to rebuilding the same as before) to prevent destruction in the future.[17]

XII

Navigating the Future
of New International
Volunteering

Obstacles to Volunteering

International volunteers can face macro and geopolitical obstacles out of their control. These barriers can be difficult to change in order to create an environment suitable for international volunteering. For instance, political complications can make international volunteering difficult or even impossible. Sometimes, a country could need volunteers but international relations do not allow it, such as North Korea. A majority of people living in North Korea need food aid but political complications make it almost impossible for international volunteers to currently help, as many countries have a travel ban on North Korea.[1]

International volunteers cannot easily access several countries, like Iran, due to tense international relations and severe economic sanctions. International volunteering would be a near impossibility in those places until the political climate changes, or relations warm between countries, which can take a long time.[2] In other countries with diminished relations and economic sanctions, international volunteers can only help under certain special circumstances. This applies to international volunteers hoping to assist in Cuba. They have to do so under strict guidelines under the People to People program that the U.S. government put in place. People to People guidelines state that American citizens can only visit Cuba for a cultural exchange between Cuban and American citizens and they usually must do so in a group. In these cases, international volunteering can be more difficult, but doable. In order to jump through these hoops, potential international volunteers can either research an established organization that does volunteer work in the country, or they can research the government requirements to make sure their planned volunteering would be acceptable under the rules. Keep in mind that when volunteering internationally, both countries (the volunteer's home country and the host country) may have guidelines on what can be done during volunteering. Any international volunteering must comply with the rules of both countries. It can be helpful to reach out to others who have successfully volunteered in places such as Cuba for tips and advice on how to plan a successful international volunteering trip.[3]

As political situations evolve, so too can international volunteers' access to a country. Venezuela has descended into dictatorship under Nicolás Maduro. Venezuela now has one of the highest inflation rates in the world, currency with almost no value and a chronic shortage of food since the transition into dictatorship. Meanwhile, Venezuela has refused aid.[4] Similarly, unstable governments like Syria's regime, known to have violated the human rights of their citizens during the Syrian Civil War, has not allowed food aid into the country at times even though people have needed it.[5] It would be difficult for international volunteers to help during this situation of war, government oppression and changing political tides.

Safety can be a barrier to volunteers working. Medical and emergency aid volunteers often volunteer despite a major risk to their safety in an effort to help people living in extreme need. Some volunteers also risk their safety to help bring peace to conflict zones.[6] But volunteers can encounter safety risks in other places too, as crime levels rise in certain areas. Countries such as Brazil and the Northern Triangle countries of El Salvador, Honduras and Guatemala have experienced more violent crime in recent years.[7] In fact, Rio de Janeiro has descended into violence of such frequency and magnitude that Brazilians have created apps called Where There's Shooting and Crossfire to help people who live in Rio get home safely. These apps offer notifications of reported gun violence in real time to help people avoid dangerous shootouts on their commute. Violence like this can disrupt volunteering activities, but most importantly, the lives of people living in an area of increasing violence. For example, in Rio, the military has been called in to control the violence.[8] Or, international volunteers might come in contact with unexpected protests that compromise their safety and volunteer work. For example, after the President of Nicaragua, Daniel Ortega, cut pensions, protests erupted across the country that the government violently wiped out. Similarly, militant groups, like the ELN, and drug trafficking gangs have brought violence to isolated areas in Colombia that could benefit from a partnership with international volunteers.[9]

International volunteers can face obstacles at home too. Several countries, notably the United States, the United Kingdom, Brazil and Poland, have trended toward isolationism after electing populist leaders and the

Brexit referendum in the United Kingdom. Isolationism remains in contrast with the very idea of international volunteering and globalization. International volunteering functions successfully because the world has been more open than ever before, allowing the exchange of volunteers and locals—their work, lifestyles and ideas. With isolation, the very nature of international volunteering becomes challenged under a retreat within one's country.

International volunteers of past, present and future face obstacles of size and scale. Many issues volunteers would like to assist with seem huge, and can be intertwined with other problems to seem insurmountable. For example, AIDS devastates many people in countries around the world. When parents die of AIDS, they leave orphans behind. The increased rate of orphans and the human life taken by AIDS represent two intertwining problems that can seem difficult to improve. Increased rates of orphans and death from AIDS work together at the same time to cause harm on a large scale with a significant impact on the lives of those touched by them. When a disease like AIDS spreads to many countries and seems undefeatable, solutions may differ from country to country or even town to town because of location and other factors. Before beginning to volunteer, investigate customized solutions or special considerations the host community needs. Volunteers can join groups of locals working to reduce HIV infections and also taking care of orphans from AIDS concurrently.

Obstacles in international volunteering can alternatively be organizational by nature. Organizational and administrative problems can add up to undermine the positive effects of international volunteers' work. Organizational problems occur when several different organizations try to do the same thing in a scattered manner instead of joining forces and working together. When organizations work alone, they waste resources replicating each other's efforts. Those resources could be used much more effectively when pooled together. Organizations can also partner with regional bodies and major institutions, such as the Inter-American Development Bank or the United Nations for a joint effort. Cooperation and administrative efficiency can make a difference in most effectively tackling a large issue in international volunteering.

International volunteers of the future will face obstacles that today's volunteers have not encountered yet. Complications change over time as the world changes and as progress gets made toward ending poverty and spearheading economic development. Innovation and flexibility remain the keys to overcoming obstacles as they arise. The Brazilian safety apps, Where There's Shooting and Crossfire, represent examples of the kind of flexibility and innovation needed in changing situations. The apps are innovative solutions that meet the fluctuating nature of Rio de Janeiro's rising crime, utilizing technology in a way that could not have been done even just ten years ago.

Innovation in Volunteering

The new international volunteer is synonymous with the concept of innovation. Innovation breeds more innovation through the ideas of locals, volunteers and others. Innovation helps strengthen and evolve international volunteering. Innovation can be a tool volunteers can put into practice when solutions to problems remain unclear or when facing a new obstacle for the first time. Innovation can have a positive impact on host communities, such as when accessing a cutting-edge technology. Its beneficial for host communities to use the newest, innovative technology because it has a lasting impact and there is potential to use it in new ways. For example, locals can engage in distance learning for an untraditional but effective education. The skills learned in distance education, like a class for medical workers, teaches skills that will help the community directly, even after volunteers leave. The impact of this innovation happens in the long term and is sustainable.

Not every major world problem will end without innovative solutions. International volunteers can help facilitate innovation to most effectively meet challenges in economic development. The more volunteers learn about the issue at hand and the more they learn from people experiencing the problems, the easier it will be to innovate. The partnership between locals and volunteers will be a major source of innovation as they exchange ideas about solutions and what life entails for each of them. As locals and volunteers team up to innovate and implement together, success can more readily be found.

Distance education is one of the innovations that can have a positive impact on development. Benefits of distance education include classes that can be taken anywhere on a flexible schedule and people can apply what they learn in ways that make sense for them. Distance education can be an effective alternative to traditional brick and mortar education. It can solve problems of low-quality education and high teacher absenteeism because distance education can be reviewed to ensure quality. Students can also learn at any time. Distance education does need to be improved, however. Since most distance education teachers live in the West, their perspectives may not resonate with students around the world. Devex notes that "there must be a shift away from the narrative that the Global North is the teacher and the Global South is the student" because people in the Global South have a lot to teach people in the Global North as well. One part of the solution, according to Devex, is "increasing the number of instructors from developing countries who teach the courses and blending learning models."

Other potential pitfalls of distance education include "technology and internet connectivity, language barriers and the cultural relevance of the coursework," says Devex. One option for improvements, according to Devex, could be if the course hosts local office hours, in-person study sessions or parts of the course in person. Overall, distance education can improve the access of quality education for people around the world and improve the specialized skills of the workforce in industrializing areas. As pitfalls of distance education become addressed, it can be more effective for more people.[10]

Blockchain is a way to see digital currency transactions and a platform that hosts secure currency transactions. Because of the decentralized nature of blockchain, where data gets stored in multiple places for greater security, this emerging technology can have innovative applications in economic development. The Center for Global Development argues that blockchain "will help deliver money faster, more securely, and more transparently; that it will improve citizens' access to their rights; and reduce exploitation of the most vulnerable," making blockchain a potentially valuable tool for handling aid money securely without corruption. Devex predicts blockchain could be used for innovative banking solutions, such as making payments in places where individuals and businesses do not trust banks or do not have a strong banking network. People could use blockchain to send no fee remittances and for buying and selling solar energy from neighbors. Devex also mentions that there are international development applications for the data transparency feature of blockchain. This can help people verify the accuracy of land titles, access public project details for government accountability, create secure digital IDs for refugees and track aid money from sender to recipient. These applications could reduce corruption and promote government accountability around the world.[11]

Both businesses and nonprofits have already implemented drones in international development. Drones' purpose tends to be delivering vital supplies to isolated areas that vehicles cannot easily traverse. For example, the *Irish Examiner* reports that the Chinese business JD.com has delivered school supplies, such as books, to an Indonesian island.[12] Similarly, Bloomberg noted that Zipline International runs daily drone deliveries of blood for transfusions from Kigali to hospitals throughout Rwanda. The drones can still fly in the rain, making them a quicker and safer way to get blood to doctors without enough supplies. Zipline International employs local drone engineers and gives them a fair wage. They expanded drone deliveries into Ghana, according to CNBC, so they cover an area in which 22 million people live. They also extended their offering to include vaccines and medicines. The company aims to make technology accessible to all via drone deliveries.[13]

Drones can be used widely in international volunteering, depending on the purpose, scope and location of the project. For example, an isolated host community may ask volunteers to facilitate drone deliveries from a more central location in order to supply them with more goods. Drones could regularly make dropoffs to several host communities in the same region, such as deliveries for replacement well parts to keep potable well water running when mechanics need them. Drones can additionally replace certain volunteer efforts like a traveling library with book deliveries that a mobile library would normally visit.

Virtual reality is another cutting-edge technology beginning to be used in international development. Although virtual reality technology remains in its infancy, it has already benefited people around the world in the context of development. The World Bank's blog noted that virtual reality can help students practice something important before doing it, particularly those in the medical field. The blog stated that "virtual reality can enhance medical education, particularly in areas with a shortage of skilled doctors. HelpMeSee wants to train 30,000 people for a procedure to treat cataract blindness using a simulator that replicates the human eye and feel of live surgery." The benefit of practicing a medical procedure with virtual reality in a place with limited resources is that many students can use the machine multiple times and then pass it on to more students in neighboring areas. Virtual reality can facilitate the training of new entrants to the medical profession in rural or underserved areas. It can also give already practicing professionals more specialized training so they can help more people.[14]

However, innovation does not mean it has to be high tech. Innovation can come from out of the box thinking and creativity, using simple yet effective solutions. According to *The Economist*, a doctor in Bangladesh saw many children dying of pneumonia. The CPAP machine often used in the West to help save these children's lives can be prohibitively expensive in Bangladesh. The doctor, Mohamad Chisti, saw a different type of CPAP in Australia that uses bubbles to help babies with pneumonia breathe. He made his own version using a shampoo bottle for just $1.25 a device. The innovative CPAP alternative has reduced fatalities of pneumonia-stricken babies at his hospital by three quarters. This less expensive device can be just as innovative as new high-tech medical devices.[15]

International volunteers can spend their time helping to solve practical problems with big stakes for humanity. One issue in need of innovation has been an obstacle for many years but recently came into the spotlight during the Covid-19 pandemic: temperature requirements for vaccines. Some vaccines, such as the Covid-19 vaccines, need to be kept cold, and with special equipment instead of standard household refrigerators.[16] This has been an obstacle for getting vaccines in arms after they have been created, especially in places with hot climates or without a pre-existing infrastructure to transport and store the vaccines as they must be.

This problem could be solved in two ways. First, create a portable and cheap vaccine cooler and distribute it cheaply so no one who needs one goes without. Secondly, create a technology so that vaccines do not need to be cooled and can be stored at room temperature. Either solution would require volunteers, including engineers and scientists, to innovate by leveraging existing technology in novel ways or by creating new technologies that will aid humanity greatly.

Strengthening and Evolving International Volunteering

Creating a quality assurance mechanism for organizations that host international volunteering projects could strengthen the quality of international volunteering. This quality assurance mechanism already exists for the finances of nonprofits in some countries. For example, Charity Navigator rates the fiscal health of nonprofits in the United States based on their financial performance, accountability and transparency. For example, they establish how much money goes toward CEO pay and fundraising and how much financial data each nonprofit shares with the public. This gets the charity a rating and a number of stars, zero through four, to show how well they compare to others. Charity Navigator uses public tax documents to get the information from nonprofits. This transparency and data mining helps potential donors choose places to donate that will use their money well. They also give advisories about specific charities that may have acted illegally or unethically. The same accountability standards can be given for organizations that host international volunteering projects, and not just with finances. This rating can also consider how they treat the host community, their volunteers and how well they implement best practices in development.[17]

NGO Advisor has already started a quality control program for NGOs around the world. They rank NGOs based on "impact, innovation and sustainability." NGOs get a ranking out of ten for categories involving accountability, innovation and funding sources. The NGOs' profiles contain a detailed explanation to justify the ratings. However, it requires that users pay for access to lists of rankings and most NGO profiles. If NGO Advisor or a parallel website could provide a free version that focuses on volunteering ratings, then the system would have much more accountability and transparency.[18]

GiveWell and ImpactMatters bring a different measure of quality control in international anti-poverty efforts by calculating the efficiency per dollar for donations to international charity groups. This information can help international volunteers determine trustworthiness and impact before volunteering for those organizations. This is a good first step in accountability, but some of these rated organizations may not need international volunteers and only a small number of organizations have been rated thus far. Additionally, the ratings say nothing about the quality of volunteers' work specifically. A method called Randomized Control Trials (RCTs), pioneered by the 2019 Nobel Prize in Economics winners Michael Kremer, Esther Duflo and Abhijit Banerjee, has potential to evaluate the quality of international volunteers' work. Organizations like Innovations for Poverty Action already use RCTs to evaluate their anti-poverty efforts for quality assurance. In this way, Innovations for Poverty Action can be a guide for international volunteers desiring accountability and effectiveness in their work. Randomized Control Trials can be defined as rigorous and effective testing, using a control group against a group implementing an economic development initiative. Comparing the results and effects over time between the two groups measures the impact, or lack thereof, of the initiative.[19]

International volunteering could additionally be strengthened by creating qualification standards for the volunteers who participate in each international development project. This can be done in three steps. The first step would be to match volunteers to the needs of the project. Potential volunteers could go through an application and recruiting process to ensure they have the skills the project needs. The Peace Corps already implements this practice. Many Peace Corps applicants speak to a recruiter before applying and can choose to apply to where needs are high. This means they get placed based on where the Peace Corps thinks the applicant's skills will match best. Or they can apply to a specific project in a country that matches their skills and their application will be accepted or rejected. Potential volunteers can get an idea if their application will be accepted for a specific project because each Peace Corps project lists specific skills that a volunteer must have to be chosen. For instance, a recent posting for Community Service—Business Volunteer in Paraguay says that desired skills for volunteers include conversational Spanish skills, an MBA or master's in business, five years of work experience in business management, experience with business strategy, entrepreneurship, Information Communications Technology, event planning and working with youth.[20]

Some domestic nonprofits already have an application process in place. For instance, some pro bono legal volunteers have to submit their bar number and resume to show relevant experience and come to an interview before volunteering with non-profit law firms. Or potential volunteers sometimes must fill out an application and complete a background check before working at a literacy program at an elementary school. In international volunteering, a quality assurance standard for applications and a recruiting process will increase the quality of the team on each project. This will ensure that everyone has the skills needed to assist the host community in all the ways they request.

The second step to promote qualified international volunteers would be to give all selected volunteers a comprehensive training program. The training would occur before the project begins and would include a cultural and lingual immersion. The Peace Corps makes this immersion training a priority for volunteers before they begin their assignments. Before getting sworn in as a Peace Corps volunteer, individuals get trained and assessed on their language skills, technical, safety and health knowledge as well as project specific skills. After meeting basic language criteria, volunteers attend language classes five days a week. This includes doing homework assignments with their homestay families for stronger language immersion.[21] To apply the training process to all international volunteers would mean that long-term volunteers with any organization go through a pre-travel orientation period. For shorter trips, in addition to a thorough orientation, the immersion can be continual so volunteers' skills improve during the entire project. This can be done by setting aside time for advanced language lessons, group conversations or regularly conversing with a member of the host community. Some language schools employ this one-on-one time with a local to advance their students' skills. In this format, students spend the mornings in intensive language lessons, and in the afternoon, they participate in an activity with a local to build a relationship with them, learn about the culture and expand their conversational skills in the target language.

The final phase of assuring international volunteers begin work qualified could be an evaluation after the project's completion. An independent third party and the host community could complete evaluations of each volunteer's work for quality assurance and sustainability standards. These would be industry-wide quality standards that outline clear expectations for the end results of each international volunteering project. This incorporates the quality of the project, the performance of volunteers, sustainability and long-term follow-up. An example of the type of evaluation would be the host community satisfaction survey from Chapter III.

The evaluation would also have a portion to be completed by the volunteers who participated, giving organizations important data from their perspective. The evaluation could be a post-project debriefing or written feedback from volunteers. Helpful evaluations would ask about the project's successes and failures, along with any other feedback deemed relevant. The evaluation would need to take place immediately following the project but also include long-term follow-up at regular intervals. Long-term follow-up measures the quality of the project's long-term, sustainable objectives. A standard evaluation breeds a culture of accountability in international volunteering—both for the organization sponsoring the project and the volunteers who participate in it. These combined measures will further build up the reputation of international volunteering by showing that volunteers and the organizations they work with care about the host community and the sustainability of their efforts.

XIII

Where to Go from Here

Meeting Currently Unmet Needs

Even though the world saw poverty reduced more than ever before the pandemic, more progress still needs to be made to reach zero poverty. There were 652 million people who lived under the poverty line of $1.90 a day in 2018, according to the World Bank.[1] This section will present currently unmet needs, such as hunger and healthcare, that have not been fully addressed by the international community and international volunteers. In fact, the United Nations created the Sustainable Development Goals to tackle these gaps and raise awareness to what still needs to be done. Many non-profit organizations and Non-Governmental Organizations responded by creating strategies to work toward meeting the UN Goals. Some of the organizations doing good work in the areas of the Sustainable Development Goals will be mentioned in this chapter, along with ways international volunteers can pitch in.

Sometimes, several major unmet needs intersect among a population or in a certain situation. International volunteers can apply specific strategies when this occurs. For instance, international volunteers can work with one community at a time to help meet all of their intersecting needs at the same time. Or volunteers can devote themselves to one major need that people have around the world and partner with others that work on other corresponding needs to reduce them one by one. The goal, in either instance, would be to improve quality of life and help with anything else people may need. This can only be achieved if volunteers think about long-term sustainability plans so the gains will be permanent. If innovative solutions do not last, then people can fall back into poverty. For example, volunteers have dug wells that no longer work or get dirty, leaving people back at square one—walking miles to get water from unhealthy sources. At the time the volunteers installed the wells, people hoped they would stop getting sick from unpotable water and be able to free up their time to help their families in other ways. When the wells break or become contaminated, volunteers do not follow up, and locals do not have the tools to fix them, it ends that hope and things go back to the status quo.[2] International volunteering should never end hope, only increase it. Keep this in mind when thinking about the following big problems that still exist in the world today. Any progress toward eliminating them involves long-term follow-up. This way change can take root over time, leaving people permanently better off than before.

Hunger remains one of the most urgent and difficult issues people face. Hunger can be abated temporarily through food donations, but truly solving hunger would mean that everyone becomes food secure worldwide. The World Bank estimates that in 2019, 9 percent of the world's population experienced undernourishment.[3] The World Food Programme reduces undernourishment through the Zero Hunger Program. The Zero Hunger Program supports Goal Two of the United Nations' Sustainable Development Goals, to "end hunger, achieve food security and improved nutrition and promote sustainable agriculture."[4] The World Food Programme helps by providing emergency food aid, promoting good nutrition for children, preventing food waste and helping communities implement tactics to prevent food insecurity. The organization works with communities and governments to facilitate an "early-warning and preparedness system" so food insecurity can be mitigated before it happens. They help food insecure people eat in the short term while rebuilding long-term food assets with the Food Assistance for Assets program. The World Food Programme distributes emergency food aid through traditional aid, cash transfers and building a system where the national government can better feed its people.[5]

Potential international volunteers for the World Food Programme can contact them on its website to give their availability to volunteer in one of the program's many country offices around the world. They can also sign up to be a United Nations Volunteer as a World Food Programme assignment. The UN Volunteering Program lets potential volunteers directly apply if their skills meet the World Food Programme's needs. The application goes into the UN's Global Talent Pool where the organization contacts the volunteer. Alternatively, some in-demand projects get advertised on the UN Volunteer's website that volunteer candidates can apply for directly.[6]

Many people who do not have enough food to eat also do not have clean drinking water. Unpotable water makes people sick from waterborne illness. The World Health Organization states that "844 million people lack even a basic drinking-water service, including 159 million people who are dependent on surface water. Globally, at least 2 billion people use a drinking water source contaminated with feces. Contaminated water can transmit diseases such as diarrhea, cholera, dysentery, typhoid, and polio. Contaminated drinking water is estimated to cause 502,000 diarrheal deaths each year."[7] These deaths can be prevented by access to clean water. Pure Water for the World facilitates people having clean water in a customized way that works for their community. They do this through a partnership with communities in Central America and Haiti. Pure Water for the World begins partnering with a community who experiences health issues from unpotable water when the community declares an interest in the project and commits to assisting the clean water setup in various ways. Each family in the community donates money to the water solution, gets trained in the system and shares maintenance responsibilities. The host community works with Pure Water for the World during the project but 90 percent of the organization's employees live in the communities, making it a locally led project from all sides.

Pure Water for the World installs sanitation and clean water systems in all the homes and schools in the community. They partner with local health clinics to treat everyone for parasites, if needed. Community members no longer have to worry about contracting parasites after the water project because they will have sustainable, clean water for the long term. Before a family or school receives a water filter, they get educated on how to use it and how to maximize hygiene to prevent illnesses. Then, some community members volunteer to help the community keep their filters operational and support them with hygiene solutions as needed. After completing a community's water and sanitation system setup, Pure Water for the World goes back regularly to the community to ensure the effectiveness of the system. They do this by measuring a decrease in waterborne illness, asking if people followed through on hygiene practices and checking to see that the water filters still function as intended. If the community experiences any problems, Pure Water for the World adjusts to ensure the community gets the solutions they need.

This practice has worked in about two hundred towns with a population of seven hundred and fifty thousand people total. Pure Water for the World found that the people in these communities experience a better quality of life and decreased costs of medical bills because they no longer get sick from waterborne illnesses. Pure Water for the World needs volunteers domestically, internationally and virtually in many areas, depending on the volunteer's expertise. They need help with fundraising, marketing and in communities they support. The volunteer process begins by emailing them at info@purewaterfortheworld.org.[8]

Infrastructure continues to be a barrier to development as rural areas do not have the infrastructure to connect them to urban ones or crumbling infrastructure prevents people from easily selling their goods in other markets. The World Bank created a Global Infrastructure Outlook forecast of infrastructure needs in fifty countries by 2040. Most unfunded infrastructure projects consist of road building and electricity access in growing countries.[9] The United Nations and McKinsey Consulting Global Institute released a report in 2016 about world gaps in infrastructure. They found that "from 2016 through 2030, the world needs to invest about 3.8 percent of GDP, or an average of $3.3 trillion a year, in economic infrastructure just to support expected rates of growth. Emerging economies account for some 60 percent of that need. But if the current trajectory of underinvestment continues, the world will fall short by roughly 11 percent, or $350 billion a year. The size of the gap triples if we consider the additional investment required to meet the new UN Sustainable Development Goals."[10] This means that investment in infrastructure building can significantly help emerging economies and funding has not reached its full potential.

Engineers Without Borders focuses on gaps in infrastructure. Engineers Without Borders helps build projects that communities request in countries around the world. Volunteers plan, execute and follow up on each project. They promote relationship building with locals and sustainability by building field offices in countries they work in. Engineers Without Borders also brings in volunteers for technical help to support in-country engineers on their infrastructure projects, if they need a second opinion. Due to the technical aspects of engineering, Engineers Without Borders' volunteers need to have engineering skills for volunteering internationally. To begin volunteering, engineers or engineering students can become a member of Engineers Without Borders. Many colleges have their own chapters where students volunteer in the same project together. Similarly, engineering companies can have their own chapters where employees can do pro bono international volunteering projects together.[11]

Healthcare continues to be a complex issue in economic development and international volunteering. Healthcare is a multifaceted service that must meet varying needs for all people. For instance, people need access to clinics and hospitals, vaccinations, mental health care, treatment from disease, and research to find cures, among others. A strong healthcare system has the potential to extend the lifespan of the population and keep people healthy, improving their quality of life. However, currently, many people do not have reliable access to the medical care they need. For example, the World Bank calculated that in 2020, 17 percent of people are at risk of falling back into poverty because of the cost of surgical care.[12] Additionally, 17 babies died per 1,000 live births in 2020 and 211 mothers died from childbirth per 100,000 live births in 2017, according to the World Bank.[13] Many of the babies who survive birth die from a lack of vaccination availability.

According to Doctors Without Borders, "at least 1.5 million children die each year from vaccine-preventable diseases," and "tens of millions of people worldwide have not received the vaccines they need to be fully protected against vaccine-preventable diseases." This is due to barriers such as cost, location, and difficulties keeping vaccine temperatures low in hot environments.[14]

People experiencing mental health problems also need more care. The World Health Organization states, "Globally, more than 300 million people suffer from depression, the leading cause of disability. More than 260 million are living with anxiety disorders. Many of these people live with both. A recent WHO-led study estimates that depression and anxiety disorders cost the global economy US$ 1 trillion each year in lost productivity."[15] This does not include other mental health disorders such as schizophrenia, manic depression and post-traumatic stress disorder, among others.

Doctors Without Borders works to improve all these aspects of healthcare around the world. Doctors Without Borders gives people access to clinics and doctors by deploying emergency medical kits, including a pop-up hospital and surgical theater when necessary. In places with no healthcare, they start a system that helps treat people with chronic diseases, give emergency care for accidents, run ambulances and build health clinics. They also travel in a mobile health clinic to reach isolated places. To combat mother and child mortality, Doctors Without Borders set up a Mother and Child Care Center in Lebanon that provides family planning, prenatal, birthing, and post-delivery care for expecting mothers free of charge. Most of their clients are Syrian refugees who fled to Lebanon.[16]

To reach closer to the goal of universal vaccination, Doctors Without Borders vaccinates children in refugee camps and during outbreaks in urban settings. Their researchers try to adapt vaccines to tropical climates without the need for refrigeration. They aim to make vaccines cheaper so more people can get vaccinated for the same amount of funding. When an outbreak of disease happens, such as cholera, Doctors Without Borders trains local healthcare workers how to respond. They send in doctors with dehydration kits and antibiotics for treatment, and they map the outbreak to target care and prevent others from getting sick. Additionally, sanitation and water experts work to restore clean water and make sure the sanitation systems stay clean.[17]

Doctors Without Borders does not just focus on physical health, but on mental health too. They have been treating mental health disorders for over twenty years by training local health workers on how to help people with anxiety and depression. Trained locals especially help those who live with a disease or after a traumatic event occurs. The local workers then provide group and individual counseling sessions to people who need them.[18]

Doctors Without Borders and similar organizations have been on the frontlines of battling the Covid-19 pandemic as well. Doctors Without Borders initially pivoted to emergency Covid-19 treatment protocols at the beginning of the pandemic in over seventy countries before integrating Covid-19 services into their standard operations. Their Covid-19 response has included not only treatment and care, but prevention training, mental health treatment and vaccine equity advocacy.[19]

All Doctors Without Borders volunteers who want to help internationally in a medical capacity must have completed residency, giving them the two years of experience required by Doctors Without Borders. Nurses who want to volunteer need three years of experience. All doctors or nurses need training, teaching or management experience as well. The organization prefers their volunteers to have previous international experience since the volunteering can be demanding in many ways.[20]

Many people do not have access to adequate job opportunities or work full time without making a living wage. The World Bank estimates that only 53.6 percent of total employment included waged and salaried workers in 2020.[21] This means the remaining employed people do not receive a steady wage or salary and thus work informally in the gig economy, without reliable pay. This statistic also does not show how many waged and salaried workers obtain a sufficient salary. According to Fair Trade Campaigns, 2.6 billion people live on less than two dollars a day and 68 percent (1.768 billion) of those work as farmers. Fairtrade International helps increase the wages of farm workers through setting and monitoring fair trade practices. Fair trade helps raise the wages of famers by "endorsing an economic system that provides opportunities for international farmers, artisans and workers to lift themselves out of poverty." Many times, the people who harvest the world's food supply do not receive adequate benefits from global trade. Fair Trade Campaigns ensure agriculture workers get their due by "enabl[ing] economic development through equitable trading partnerships." Similarly, organizations like Fairtrade International and Fair Trade USA rate and certify products as fair trade, and provide oversight to verify that employers meet fair trade requirements over time. Some of these requirements include minimum price levels, fair contracts in each step of the supply chain, living wages for workers, workplace safety standards, workers' rights training, the ability for workers to unionize and reducing emissions during production. Fairtrade International gives a percentage of profit to a committee of local workers who invest the money in ways they deem beneficial to community development.[22]

Since fair trade organizations depend on global trade, interested volunteers mostly help locally instead of internationally to encourage their home community to maximize their purchasing power by buying fair trade certified products. Many people do not know the benefits farmers receive from working in a free trade certified company, so they do not seek out and demand fair trade products as consumers. Potential volunteers can help make their town or college a fair trade town or university by starting a fair trade campaign. This involves visiting local businesses or campus catering to ask them to stock more fair trade products and petitioning the local government or university leaders to pass a resolution advocating free trade.[23]

Proper shelter continues to be another basic need that many people around the world go without. The Terwilliger Center for Innovation in Shelter of Habitat for Humanity states that "more than 1.6 billion people across the globe ... still lack adequate and decent shelter." Habitat for Humanity builds affordable houses around the world. They also help revitalize neighborhoods and respond with emergency aid after natural disasters to help people who lost their housing. Additionally, Habitat researches innovative ways to help homeless people around the world acquire shelter and conducts financial training for families who will live in Habitat houses. With Habitat for Humanity, the families who will live in the houses work alongside volunteers to build them and will pay what they can afford on a mortgage. Habitat for Humanity tailors its work in each country to meet local housing needs. For example, in the Dominican Republic, building materials can be costly and some families have to make their own construction materials, which do not always function safely or durably. Habitat understands this reality, so, in the Dominican Republic, Habitat workers and volunteers replace homemade materials with safe alternatives on houses already built.[24]

Habitat for Humanity has two international volunteer programs—a short-term volunteering program called Global Village and a long-term international volunteer program. The long-term volunteer program needs international volunteers for three- to twelve-month durations. Those with construction skills can build houses while those with skills like grant writing, volunteer coordinating, researching and communications can volunteer internationally in an office setting. The Global Village does offer short-term trips but volunteers doing construction do not need previous experience and they do not typically finish building a house during that time. This can affect the house's final quality as volunteers without experience make mistakes and new volunteers cycle in on the same project.[25]

Every child needs an education but many do not get enough education or any at all. What education some kids do get may not be high quality, consistent or technology driven. Many girls remain excluded from the education system entirely because of their gender. The World Bank estimates that the worldwide primary school completion rate was 90 percent in 2020 and the lower secondary school completion rate was 77 percent in 2020 as well, leaving many students with an incomplete education.[26] Of adults aged fifteen and older, 87 percent could read in 2020, according to the World Bank.[27] International volunteers can help improve the education of children in several ways. For instance, some governments ask for international volunteers to assist them in bringing their educational goals to fruition. In this way, many governments invite international volunteers into their country to teach children fluency in English. Chile partners with the United Nations Development Programme to do this through their English Opens Doors Program. The international volunteers improve students' English speaking and listening skills by working with local teachers to plan lessons and by teaching. The program aims for volunteers to boost students' confidence by encouraging and motivating them with regards to English language learning. Volunteers live and eat for free with a homestay family. Each volunteer gets a stipend and health insurance. International volunteers only need to pay for their flight to and from Santiago. Volunteers also take a Spanish language class online and a teaching methods class in Santiago to improve their skills before getting in the classroom. Volunteers can be placed for one or two semesters in schools throughout Chile.[28]

The environment needs to be protected and the damage to it reversed. NASA notes that carbon dioxide in the atmosphere has increased to 408 parts per million, global temperatures have increased 1.8 degrees Fahrenheit since 1880, the arctic ice minimum decreased 13.2 percent per decade and the sea level has risen 3.2 millimeters per year. This puts species in risk of extinction and makes the planet vulnerable to consequences of climate change.[29] The Rainforest Foundation U.S. works to save the rainforests by supporting indigenous communities in South America who live in them. Indigenous communities who live in rainforests recognize and promote the value of preserving their ancestral lands, the rainforests. As the people who live there, indigenous communities know best how to protect lands from deforestation and support the variety of flora and fauna on their lands. The foundation helps support indigenous communities by lobbying for governments to formally recognize the indigenous peoples' rights to their land. Volunteers can contribute to the cause by not purchasing products made with palm oil and from trees commonly found in rainforests (such as mahogany). International volunteers can also support indigenous communities' rights to their lands when volunteering.[30]

Similarly, the World Wildlife Fund (WWF) focuses on wildlife protection, helping endangered species, preventing climate change and advocating for ethical practices with animals. The WWF prevents ivory trade and works with communities to address their particular animal habitat conservation challenges. Specifically, the WWF aims to double the tiger population by 2022 and fulfill the Paris Agreement on climate change. Volunteers can sign petitions, participate in a run to raise funds and be a Panda Ambassador. Panda Ambassadors educate others about the organization's work, recruit volunteers, fundraise and advocate to government leaders as needed. Individuals can also travel on WWF's conservation travel tours. The conservation tours give participants a carbon neutral, ethical way to see endangered species. For instance, a polar bear tour lets people see them in nature in a sustainable way that does not harm the bears' environment. During the tour, participants get to learn from Inuit and Metis leaders about the environment in which they live.[31]

The world still experiences a fundamental imbalance in gender equality, leaving women without the same economic opportunities as their male counterparts. In 2020, the World Bank's CPIA gender equality rating for the world was 3.3 on a scale of 1 to 6, one being the lowest and 6 the highest.[32] Similarly, 10 percent of female students did not attend primary school in 2020 compared to 8 percent of males, according to the World Bank.[33] The Malala Fund, the organization of Nobel Peace Prize winner Malala Yousafzai, brings awareness and fights to change the fact that 130 million girls do not go to school. The Gulmakai Network part of The Malala Fund supports girls around the world who advocate for education, especially girls' attendance in secondary school where they live. The activists work on breaking barriers specific to their countries, such as helping girls go to school despite pressure from Boko Haram in Nigeria or assisting girls to get back in school through re-enrollment campaigns in India. Volunteers can donate to the Malala Fund and write a piece about their life or ideas about gender equality for the publication *Assembly*. To increase the conversation about gender equality and raise awareness, volunteers can host a screening and discussion of the film He Named Me Malala or a book discussion of *I Am Malala: The Story of the Girl Who Stood Up for Education and Was Shot by the Taliban.*[34]

Another organization, He for She, tries to create a gender equal world and raise awareness about women's equality as a fundamental human right. He for She stems from a partnership between UN Women, the United Nations' gender equality arm, and actress Emma Watson. He for She focuses on achieving gender parity in the areas of education, health, identity, politics, violence and work. Their Impact 10x10x10 initiative engages leaders of governments, corporations and universities to prioritize equality by keeping track of and divulging their progress toward gender parity. Volunteers with He for She can help with specific issues of education, health, identity, politics, violence and work. Each topic has specific action steps volunteers can take to advance gender equality.

For example, with education, volunteers can stand up against gender biased language, help make the internet a safe space by sending positive messages to victims of cyberbullying and encourage teachers to use the UNESCO Guide for Gender Equality to bring equality to the learning environment. Volunteers can also become an Equalizer. The website features an Equalizer's Action Kit to help Equalizers host an event about gender equality. The event could be painting a mural with the theme of gender equality or a candle lighting event to raise awareness for gender equality. Volunteers can also sign a pledge online that they believe in the equality of people regardless of gender and that they will stand up to "Gender Bias, Discrimination and Violence to bring the benefits of equality to us all." International volunteers can take this principle with them as they volunteer around the world.[35]

Worldwide, everyone needs access to sanitation systems such as garbage and recycling collection and bathroom access. The World Bank estimates that 54 percent of the world's population used safely managed sanitation services in 2020.[36] WASH is UNICEF's program to help improve the lives of people affected by lack of sanitation systems. WASH stands for Water, Sanitation and Hygiene. According to UNICEF, "For children under five, water- and sanitation-related diseases are one of the leading causes of death. Every day, over 800 children die from preventable diseases caused by poor water, and a lack of sanitation and hygiene." This led UNICEF to help eleven million people get toilet access and fourteen million people get clean water in 2016 alone as part of their 2016–2030 strategy. To help more children and their families have the water, sanitation and hygiene they need, UNICEF's strategy includes reaching out to people living in urban areas who could use WASH.[37]

UNICEF needs volunteers in many countries. UNICEF Uniters help children in the United States by urging the government to pass legislation and funding on policies and programs that will help children. Uniters fundraise and teach people in their communities and their social media followers about the work UNICEF does. Since UNICEF is housed within the United Nations, UNICEF recruits international volunteers directly through the UN Volunteer system. Ideal volunteers have a minimum of an undergraduate degree and many years of work experience.[38]

In the twenty-first century, many people live without electricity, even though a large part of the world's population first accessed electricity in the twentieth century. In 2020, the World Bank calculated that 90.5 percent of the world's population had access to electricity.[39] An obstacle to electrification is that many rural areas are too far away from the grid to be easily connected to it. Additionally, the cost of connection can be prohibitively expensive in some areas. Off grid solutions, such as installing a microgrid or solar lanterns, can help bring electricity to parts of the world that still live without it. The organization Grid Alternatives does just that. Grid Alternatives installs solar powered systems in several countries for families and communities. The nonprofit uses solar as a clean and affordable solution as an alternative to a grid for non-electrified places. It estimates that, so far, it has installed over 79,000 kilowatts of power which will save families and communities over $600 million.

Internationally, Grid Alternatives installs solar systems in schools, clinics, orphanages, homes, small businesses and farms in the countries of Nepal, Nicaragua and Mexico. The organization trains locals on how to use and maintain the system. Locals also get continued support at an annual conference in Nicaragua. Trained locals can become solar installers so they can get employment in the growing clean energy industry. Grid Alternatives also regularly visits each solar installation to ensure it works properly. Grid Alternatives employs local workers and offers other locals paid internships so they can get a job in the industry afterward. Each community they partner with forms a gender balanced committee to help before, during and after solar installation.[40]

Grid Alternatives offers several ways for volunteers to participate. Domestically, volunteers can install solar panels, canvas, volunteer for special events and assist trainees with resume building and interview practice. They also offer alternative Winter and Spring break programs for college students to spend the week installing solar panels. Grid Alternatives hosts international programs where volunteers can install solar panels abroad. For instance, international volunteers helped install solar panels on the roof of a school in Nepal that did not have reliable and consistent electricity access due to the 2015 earthquake. This gave the children a reliable way to learn with computers at school. After the solar installation, the school powered computers, the internet and printers to improve students' learning tools and capabilities. Volunteers do not need prior solar industry skills because Grid Alternatives provides the necessary panel installation training before volunteers begin work.[41]

Lastly, the two major problems of violence and war go hand in hand. Many places in the world experience armed conflict or high murder rates in non-conflict zones. People around the world want safety and peace, and many international volunteers want to help. However, few options currently exist for international volunteers to dedicate their time to the issues of war and violence, except as emergency aid workers with organizations like the United Nations. Typically, the people who work toward peace and safety are those employed by governments, multi-national organizations and NGOs. Volunteers have few opportunities to assist in post-conflict peacebuilding or reducing murder rates in unsafe countries.[42]

Reducing Inequality

Globalization has the power to aid in eliminating poverty, or to keep the world's wealth in the hands of a small percentage of people. The outcome depends on if globalization's benefits will be spread to everyone or if only certain people can utilize them. Globalization has not yet been fully utilized for everyone, as the world's richest sixty-two people have the same wealth as the poorest 3.5 billion people, with the richest getting even richer over time, according to Oxfam and the World Economic Forum. Oxfam also shows that the world has become more unequal as time progresses so that the top 1 percent wealthiest people in the world make 82 percent of the total global wealth. To address inequality, the United Nations' Goal 10 of the UN Sustainable Development Goals focuses on reducing inequality in two ways. First, the UN aims to reduce intercountry inequality, or the inequality within a country's borders. Secondly, the UN would like to reduce inequality between countries. Inequality, according to the UN, can be felt not only in the amount of money a person makes but also in the quality and ease of access to services, like healthcare and education, that they have. Inequality can be nuanced, such as inequality of opportunity and differences of inequality in urban versus rural areas, with rural areas tending to be more unequal. According to the UN, inequality has gotten worse, especially in emerging economies, since 1990. In this way, inequality can be a problem when everyone cannot access the benefits in life that the richest people have.[43]

Inequality can be a bad thing when wealth becomes concentrated in the hands of a few people or companies, because they can also hold more power. Venezuela has experienced this problem firsthand in an unprecedented economic crisis. The government has defaulted on debt and currency inflation has skyrocketed to some of the highest levels in the world, creating a difficult economic situation for Venezuelans. During good economic times, Venezuela mostly exports oil and imports basic goods, however, the number of items being imported has gone down by 40 percent year on year, according to NPR. This signifies that the general population has access to less goods and only the richest can afford to purchase the few imports that still come into the country. Venezuela's economic mismanagement has produced a situation of scarcity for most of the population as their salaries and savings turned mostly worthless due to inflation. Store shelves sit empty of almost every product. Almost every Venezuelan has lost a significant amount of weight because of the unavailability and unaffordability of food. There have been food riots and people regularly line up for hours to try to get basic items, like toilet paper and milk. Many Venezuelans now do without laundry detergent and flour.

The average Venezuelan has lost 24 pounds in 2017 and 17.6 pounds in 2016 because they cannot access and pay for enough food, according to Reuters. Venezuelans call it the Maduro diet after the president, Nicolás Maduro, because his economic policies led to food shortages and high prices. *The Washington Post* found that between 2.3 and 4 million Venezuelans have fled the country in search of food and safety. This situation has made inequality much worse in Venezuela. Paradoxically, some of the richest people in Venezuela, such as powerful business people and high-level government officials can afford goods that the rest of the population makes do without. If the rich have money in dollars instead of Bolivars, the Venezuelan currency, they can cheaply buy items because of the inflation rate. The richest can also afford to buy goods in the black market so they do not have to live without food and basic necessities.[44]

China has taken a different approach to inequality. As a part of their development strategy, China has treated inequality as a good thing. Some top Chinese officials have thought that inequality can be positive overall if some people become better off (increasing inequality) and then more people eventually rise up to meet them (reducing inequality). To make the entire population rich, they have tried to lift up some in order to lift up all. In this way, China has focused on bringing everyone to the top so the entire country can be better off. But the rise to the top does not occur uniformly for everyone, based on their job and location to name a few. This strategy has had mixed success. China has made great strides in reducing country-wide poverty since introducing this new method of growing wealth even while actively increasing inequality.

However, some shortfalls to China's approach have become apparent. Today, China has a very high Gini Coefficient. The Gini coefficient measures the amount of inequality in a country from zero to one, with zero being no inequality and one being the most unequal. The actual Gini Coefficient can be hard to determine in China's case, as official numbers can be unreliable, but some analysts feel concerned at how high they project it to be. The difference in wealth between urban and rural residents constitutes a major part of the inequality China faces. Now China must address and correct intercountry inequality. Professor Fan Di thinks that China can reduce inequality by opening up state-owned enterprises and by giving regular people better access to capital and more equal educational opportunities.

Inequality has been reduced in locations that have opened up to trade, especially port areas by major waterways, according to Shang-Jin Wei and Yi Wu. These areas have increased their GDP through China's opening to trade. Coastal areas that have access to trade routes can make more money as they export products to other countries. Inequality has a higher risk of happening in landlocked areas that cannot fully participate in the benefits of global trade, according to the National Bureau of Economic Research. However, inequality in landlocked and rural areas can go down when towns industrialize to create valuable components in the global supply chain.[45]

On the other hand, Scandinavian and Nordic countries have made strong gains in reducing inequality by creating government policy aimed at reducing inequality. This government approach focused on a social safety net, a higher quality of life, improving productivity and higher wages, according to the Institute for Policy Studies. Protestors helped create an environment for policymakers to act on their inequality concerns, and the results largely worked as intended. This is one venue international volunteers could assist with if locals feel unsatisfied with levels of inequality in their country.[46]

Inequality reduces when workers switch from low skilled, low paying jobs to high skilled, higher paying jobs in areas where those jobs did not exist before globalization. Some global wages have increased but the people whose wages have not increased lose out on the benefits, according to The Economist.[47] To increase the wages of workers who have not experienced the rise in global average wages, international volunteers can provide job training that will help affected individuals find higher skilled positions. International volunteers can help in this way because a lot of workers who do not receive the global average wage cannot afford to pay for skills training themselves. Additionally, many employers will not invest in new training to increase wages for their employees, so international volunteers can fill in that gap. Alternatively, governments can take some of the profits from globalization and use them to fund healthcare, job training and job search services for the workers most negatively affected by globalization.[48]

Inequality can be reduced when people who live in an unequal area create successful businesses. For example, in Guatemala I met a husband-and-wife team of architects who had experience working and studying in America and Europe. They decided to move back to their hometown to raise a family and create growth in their community through their work. They designed and built a series of successful cafes with incredible food, good ambiance and fast WiFi. They hired local musicians to play live music on busy nights and hired many employees as they expanded to multiple locations in the area. Their business created a source of fair employment and raised the GDP for the area. Their business focused not only on creating beautiful cafes but also on creating a strong community pride. They made a public relations campaign for their hometown, highlighting the beauty of the town and the friendliness of the people. They raised up the community while stimulating economic growth.

Education is a key component in inequality reduction globally. Education serves two main purposes in inequality reduction. First, it alleviates short-term inequality with more information and training. Not only can education help stop intragenerational poverty, but it can also give students the knowledge to understand nutrition and health better. Informed choices can improve life immediately for students and their children. Since gender inequality persists, education can reduce it when girls become educated as well as boys. Similarly, when pregnant women get nutrition education during pregnancy, they have a better chance of staying healthy, reducing mother and child mortality rates. Learning to read helps people learn about sanitation. Literate parents can read pamphlets during health crises to learn about eliminating waterborne bacteria by boiling water and foodborne bacteria by keeping foods refrigerated after cooking. For example, during recent Zika and Ebola outbreaks, people read emergency notices about the diseases and how to prevent getting them. In this way, literacy and education can save lives.[49]

Secondly, education also can reduce inequality by increasing earning power. Secondary education can be a contributing factor to lowering poverty as people get more earning power with higher skilled jobs that pay greater wages. When a large amount of the population are educated individuals working high skilled jobs, the entire GDP of the country rises, helping economic growth on a large scale. The link between education and creating a healthier population means that healthcare costs decline. In fact, a study by the World Economic Program in Jamaica found that weekly sessions led by healthcare workers for toddlers and their families for two years led to the same children twenty years later earning 25 percent more than a control group.[50]

Education reduces inequality when it specifically focuses on teaching computer literacy to harness the power of the internet. Computer literacy opens up many jobs that can be done remotely so people who have internet access and computer literacy skills can do a variety of jobs with high pay all around the world. That reduces inequality when the workers live in rural areas but do their jobs remotely. The higher paying remote jobs give employees greater salary potential than they would otherwise have from jobs located in their area. In fact, a study by the telephone operator Vodafone found that smartphones can help reduce inequality, especially for "women, micro entrepreneurs and small farmers." By having internet access on smartphones, these groups can get access to information and create networking opportunities that would be impossible without digital literacy. Entrepreneurs can use smartphones to get information to utilize their business more effectively. In Kenya, the report found that over two thirds of businesswomen increased their incomes because of smartphone use. In Ghana, the study found that having smartphones helps businesses stay afloat in the short term and last in the long term because it provides access to "new ideas, information and tools." In fact, seven of the ten micro entrepreneurs had an easier time maintaining their businesses because of smartphone use. In India, the Vodafone study found that the information available from smartphones can lead to a 50 percent gain in small farmers' wages.[51]

International volunteers can help in reducing inequality. Reducing inequality via education makes students competitive in the global economy. Education acts as a key to development because when more students learn how to use the technology only previously available to the richest segment of the population, then people all over the world can share ideas and innovate together. When international volunteers have training, they can assist in schools as an added resource, especially for students left behind or learning at a slower pace. This helps reduce inequality by giving every student an equal chance at success, especially if volunteers form a strong bond with their students and consistently help them over time. Volunteers in schools can help to motivate students to go the extra mile and encourage them to enjoy learning more than ever before. Through one-on-one tutoring, international volunteers can break down barriers to learning. For example, many AmeriCorps volunteers work as tutors to help students improve their reading skills. They work with the same students multiple times a week to help them catch up to reading at grade level. International volunteers can use this AmeriCorps model to reduce inequality.[52]

The Journey Begins Here

As this book comes to an end, I encourage you to commit to the principles of the new international volunteer movement. Do this by pledging that all volunteering will be ethical, sustainable and without negative consequences. New international volunteers act on this pledge by adhering to the role of liaison and an extra set of helping hands for whatever locals need assistance with. New international volunteers fulfill their role by bringing resources to their projects and creating awareness as needed. They always listen to locals and adhere to their vision.

The new international volunteer does not recognize themself as a leader, but rather defers to locals in the host community as experts, creators and leaders.

The new international volunteer prepares for volunteering by communicating with locals and the volunteer team up front. They thoroughly research at home and in person, when possible. They choose the right project for them, considering the length and location, and ensure the organization and leaders follow ethical principles. Although volunteering focuses on people in the host community, new international volunteers take steps to mitigate any health risks they could encounter, be aware of safety and prepare for culture and reverse culture shock for their own wellbeing.

When volunteering, the new international volunteer utilizes all proven development tools—including development, relief, sustainability, incremental change and inclusion. They donate appropriately and use financial strategies wisely. The new international volunteer innovates in a changing world by utilizing globalization and social media to reduce inequality and climate change. They understand the benefits and pitfalls of international systems such as free trade, fair trade and international relations between countries.

After returning home, the new international volunteer follows up with the host community and strengthens long distance relationships with individuals they met there. They only post appropriate pictures of their trip that do not enforce negative stereotypes, take away privacy of children or portray themselves as saviors. The new international volunteer seeks to continue assisting the host community and building the bond between them over time. They follow up to ask questions about the long-term success of the project to make sure it functions sustainably as planned.

The world could be further toward the United Nations' Sustainable Development Goals if each person who volunteered internationally did so as a new international volunteer. If every person who volunteered internationally followed the principles of the new international volunteer, then it could make an impact on the micro level and the macro level, furthering economic growth, development and poverty reduction around the world. On the macro level, each helpful action new international volunteers make has a positive effect that maximizes the benefits of the volunteer project. On the micro level, the good outcome of all volunteers working as new international volunteers starts with the individual—both individuals in the host community and the individual volunteer.

If every international volunteer acted as a new international volunteer, there would be an impact on the smallest level that would have a big impact over time. This starts with the trips themselves. When volunteers choose to prioritize quality projects, unhelpful projects will disappear because volunteers do not demand them. Bad projects would then have to adjust their methods to become good or stop offering them completely. All international volunteers would choose projects that match their skill set, helping to achieve the volunteering goals effectively. Before beginning a project, new international volunteers would hone their abilities by learning specialized knowledge to apply their skills properly in the host community. This would increase the quality and accuracy of the volunteer work for the host community.

If all international volunteers became new international volunteers, the outcomes of projects would be optimized. Every project would permanently alter the future conditions in the host community by being long-lasting and sustainable. No volunteers nor host community would need to go back and redo projects that did not hold up after volunteers returned home. Similarly, the success rate of all projects would increase since volunteers would continually assist when needed and ensure past projects met quality assurance standards. In creating a world in which all international volunteers became new international volunteers, individuals in the host community would assume their proper role as leaders and innovators instead of volunteers taking on those roles. Locals would find empowerment and inclusion as volunteers stepped away from leadership to a role of supporting and assisting instead. As locals created projects and led them, engaging the whole community, especially women and minorities, the outcome of each project would be what locals want it to be instead of what international volunteers think would be helpful. Overall, when looking at all the combined projects new international volunteers would help with, there would be fewer negative outcomes and more positive outcomes, creating an overall positive development trajectory. This would replace a less positive trajectory currently in place that can, at times, trend neutral where good projects balance out bad results or where bad projects require fixing to get things back to their pre-project status.

Each host community as a whole would grow more due to a change to the new international volunteering methods because the projects would be more accurate and of a consistently high quality. Each host community would become more integrated with technology to take advantage of the benefits of globalization. As each community implemented regular technology use to further education and make money, economic growth could skyrocket and world inequality would decline. Even inter-country inequality could decline if the host communities located in rural areas align productivity and income averages close to urban ones. For the long term, host communities would benefit from projects by new international volunteers that mitigate danger from climate change because of the sustainable and climate-friendly volunteer priorities.

If every international volunteer acted as a new international volunteer, there would be a major impact from the combined changes, shifting global norms. Overall, people could expect less waste and duplication as organizations work together, concentrating their impact. Poverty would decline as volunteers listen to each host community and facilitate their needs as appropriate, following locals to implement customized solutions for poverty reduction. Projects could help eliminate some obstacles people in the host community experience, making economic growth and development easier. New international volunteers would forge a long-term partnership to continually support communities during any bumps in the road of economic growth. The major result from the new international volunteer approach will be fostering personalized economic development solutions instead of cookie cutter formulas that do not apply to every host community. The uniqueness of the new international volunteering approach in each place allows it to culminate into a large positive impact over time in many places.

For those of you reading this book and thinking that this is exactly what you need to be doing, the journey as a new international volunteer begins now. Start by spreading the word to family, friends, classmates and colleagues who also want to volunteer internationally, or have already, to disseminate the volunteering practices outlined in this book around. New international volunteers can begin researching potential projects that match their skill set. Then, when the time comes to go out and volunteer, be conscious every step of the way that the work meets the new international volunteer principles. After completing the project, make a long-term impact by following up with the host community and continuing a relationship with them. Finally, tell people on social media about the new international volunteering principles and how they too can get involved. With these few steps, the new international volunteering journey begins.

Chapter Notes

Preface

1. "Module 8: The Significant Harm of Worst Practices." *Unite for Sight*, Unite for Sight, www.uniteforsight.org/global-health-course/module8.

Chapter I

1. "Covid-19 to Add as Many as 150 Million Extreme Poor by 2021." *The World Bank*, 7 Oct. 2020, https://www.worldbank.org/en/news/press-release/2020/10/07/-covid-19-to-add-as-many-as-150-million-extreme-poor-by-2021.

2. "Poverty headcount ratio at $1.90 a day (2011 PPP) (% of population)." *The World Bank Data*, World Bank, data.worldbank.org/indicator/SI.POV.DDAY?view=chart.

3. "Prevalence of undernourishment (% of population)." *The World Bank Data*, World Bank, data.worldbank.org/indicator/SN.ITK.DEFC.ZS?view=chart.

4. "Pregnant women receiving prenatal care (%)." *The World Bank Data*, World Bank, data.worldbank.org/indicator/SH.STA.ANVC.ZS?view=chart.

5. "Access to Electricity (% of Population)." *The World Bank Data*, World Bank, data.worldbank.org/indicator/EG.ELC.ACCS.ZS?view=chart.

6. "Primary completion rate, total (% of relevant age group)." *The World Bank Data*, World Bank, data.worldbank.org/indicator/SE.PRM.CMPT.ZS?view=chart.

7. Wu, Guobao. "Ending Poverty in China: What Explains Great Poverty Reduction and a Simultaneous Increase in Inequality in Rural Areas?" *World Bank Blogs*, World Bank Group, 19 Oct. 2016, blogs.worldbank.org/eastasiapacific/ending-poverty-in-china-what-explains-great-poverty-reduction-and-a-simultaneous-increase-in-inequality-in-rural-areas.

8. "Why Does Kenya Lead the World in Mobile Money?" *The Economist*, The Economist Newspaper, 2 Mar. 2015, www.economist.com/blogs/economist-explains/2013/05/economist-explains-18.

9. Wetmore, Deanna. "How Technology Is Helping Economies in Developing Countries." *The Borgen Project*, The Borgen Project, 23 Nov. 2017, www.borgenproject.org/how-technology-is-helping-economies/.

10. "Upwardly Mobile: Kenya's Technology Start-up Scene Is about to Take Off." *The Economist*, The Economist Newspaper, 25 Aug. 2012, www.economist.com/node/21560912.

11. Singh, Malvinder Mohan. "The Rise Of The Services Sector Is Redefining India's Growth Narrative." *The Blog*, HuffPost India, 5 Aug. 2016, www.huffingtonpost.in/malvinder-mohan-singh/the-rise-of-the-services-sector-is-redefining-india-s-growth-nar_a_21445764/.

12. Das, Lawly, and Rajesh Raut. "Impact of Changes in Service Sector in India in Shaping the Future of Business & Society." *Procedia Economics and Finance*, vol. 11, 2014, pp. 795–803. *ScienceDirect*, doi:10.1016/s2212-5671(14)00243-3; Bhagat, Ram B. "Migration and Urban Transition in India: Implications for Development." *United Nations*, United Nations, 7 Sept. 2017, www.un.org/en/

development/desa/population/events/pdf/ expert/27/papers/V/paper-Bhagat-final. pdf.

13. Rosenberg, Tina. "In Rwanda, Health Care Coverage That Eludes the U.S." *Opinionator*, The New York Times, 3 July 2012, opinionator.blogs.nytimes. com/2012/07/03/rwandas-health-care-miracle/; Porter, Eduardo. "In Health Care, Republicans Could Learn From Rwanda." *The New York Times*, The New York Times, 18 July 2017, www.nytimes. com/2017/07/18/business/economy/-senate-obamacare-rwanda.html; "An African Trailblazer." *The Economist*, The Economist Newspaper, 15 Sept. 2016, www.economist.com/middle-east-and-africa/2016/09/15/an-african-trailblazer.

14. Bolterstein, Elyse. "Environmental Justice Case Study: Maquiladora Workers and Border Issues." *University of Michigan*, websites.umich.edu/~snre492/Jones/maquiladora.htm.

15. Blitzer, Jonathan. "The Deportees Taking Our Calls." *The New Yorker*, The New Yorker, 15 Jan. 2017, www.newyorker. com/magazine/2017/01/23/the-deportees-taking-our-calls.

16. Williams, Ollie A. "Corrupt Elites Siphon Aid Money Intended for World's Poorest." *Forbes*, Forbes Magazine, 20 Feb. 2020, https://www.forbes.com/sites/oliverwilliams1/2020/02/20/corrupt-elites-siphen-aid-money-intended-for-worlds-poorest/?sh=3715329c1565.

17. "Our Finances: Efficient and Verified." *UNICEF USA*, UNICEF USA, www. unicefusa.org/about/finances.

18. "About Us: Frequently Asked Questions." *UNICEF USA*, UNICEF USA, https://www.unicefusa.org/about/faq.

19. "Ethical Shoes Made in Africa." *soleRebels*, soleRebels, www.solerebels. com/pages/our-ethos; "Artisan Loomed Fabrics." *soleRebels*, soleRebels, www. solerebels.com/pages/artisan-loomed-fabrics; "Bethlehem Tilahun Alemu, soleRebels Founder." *soleRebels*, soleRebels, www.solerebels.com/pages/bethlehem-tilahun-alemu; Iwuoha, John-Paul. "SoleRebels—A Successful African Footwear Brand Made from Waste and Recycled Materials." *Smallstarter*, Smallstarter, 14 Mar. 2013, www.smallstarter.com/get-inspired/solerebels/.

20. Eulich, Whitney. "Months after Maria, Puerto Ricans Take Recovery into Their Own Hands." *The Christian Science Monitor*, The Christian Science Monitor, 7 May 2018, www.csmonitor.com/USA/Society/2018/0507/Months-after-Maria-Puerto-Ricans-take-recovery-into-their-own-hands.

21. "Latin Lessons: What Can We Learn from the World's Most Ambitious." *The Independent*, Independent Digital News and Media, 7 Nov. 2010, www.independent.co.uk/news/world/americas/latin-lessons-what-can-we-learn-from-the-worldrsquos-most-ambitious-literacy-campaign-2124433. html; "Cuba." *UNESCO*, UNESCO, en.unesco.org/countries/cuba.

22. Bianchi, Michele, and Lindsay Hedenskog. "What Home Is For A Refugee Without One." *IKEA /U.S./EN*, Ikea, 2016, www.ikea.com/ms/en_U.S./this-is-ikea/ikea-highlights/Home-for-a-refugee/index.html.

23. Saval, Malina. "Oprah Winfrey's Leadership Academy for Girls Marks 10 Years." *Variety*, Variety, 3 Aug. 2017, variety.com/2017/biz/news/oprah-winfrey-leadership-academy-for-girls-10-year-anniversary-1202510605/.

24. Lough, Benjamin J. "International Volunteering from the United States between 2004 and 2012." *Center for Social Development George Warren Brown School of Social Work*, Washington University in St. Louis, June 2013, web. archive.org/web/20170124173359/https://csd.wustl.edu/Publications/Documents/-RB13-14.pdf; Purvis, Katherine, and Lindsey Kennedy. "Volunteer Travel: Experts Raise Concerns over Unregulated Industry." *The Guardian*, Guardian News and Media, 13 Jan. 2016, https://www. theguardian.com/global-development-professionals-network/2016/jan/13/concerns-unregulated-volunteer-tourism-industry.

25. "Home- Australian Volunteers Program." *Australian Volunteers*, Australian Volunteers for International Development / Australian Aid, www. australianvolunteers.com/; Green, Lloyd. "Why More Europeans Are Volunteering in Asia." *GoAbroad.com*, GoAbroad. com, 14 June 2017, www.goabroad.com/articles/volunteer-abroad/why-more-europeans-are-volunteering-in-asia;

"Volunteering Abroad." *Travel.gc.ca*, Government of Canada, 27 Apr. 2016, travel.gc.ca/travelling/living-abroad/volunteering.

26. Baillie Smith, Matt, et al. "South–South Volunteering and Development." *The Geographical Journal*, Wiley Online Library, 1 Nov. 2017, https://rgs-ibg.onlinelibrary.wiley.com/doi/full/10.1111/geoj.12243.

27. Kahn, Carrie. "As 'Voluntourism' Explodes In Popularity, Who's It Helping Most?" *NPR*, NPR, 31 July 2014, www.npr.org/sections/goatsandsoda/2014/07/31/336600290/as-volunteerism-explodes-in-popularity-whos-it-helping-most.

28. "Human Mobility." *Casa De Los Amigos*, Casa De Los Amigos, www.casadelosamigos.org/en/migrationandasylum/.

29. "Volunteer Now: Become a Medical Volunteer in Haiti." *Midwives for Haiti*, Midwives for Haiti, midwivesforhaiti.org/volunteers/; "Volunteer Program: Volunteer With Us." *Midwives for Haiti*, Midwives for Haiti, midwivesforhaiti.org/volunteers/volunteer-program/; Galietta, Wendy. "'I Saw a Lot of Women Who Died during Delivery, but I Did Not Know How to Help Them." *The Washington Post*, WP Company, 24 July 2017, www.washingtonpost.com/news/in-sight/wp/2017/07/24/i-saw-a-lot-of-women-who-died-during-delivery-but-i-did-not-know-how-to-help-them/?utm_term=.3ff5657f6f49.

30. "UN Peacekeeping Partnering with UN Volunteers." *UN Volunteers*, United Nations, www.unv.org/partners/un-peacekeeping-partnering-un-volunteers.

31. Zamani, Marie. "Bringing Hope and Social Cohesion in Post-Conflict Côte D'Ivoire." *UN Volunteers*, United Nations, 1 Aug. 2016, www.unv.org/our-stories/-bringing-hope-and-social-cohesion-post-conflict-côte-d'ivoire.

32. "Seven Years Later, Life is Better." *American Red Cross*, ReliefWeb. 26 Dec 2011, reliefweb.int/report/indonesia/-seven-years-later-life-better; "Tsunami Recovery Program: Five Year Report." *American Red Cross*, Wayback Machine. 24 Aug 2012, web.archive.org/web/20120824015428/http://www.redcross.org/images/MEDIA_CustomPro

ductCatalog/m3140120_TsunamiRP5year Report.pdf.

33. Risteska, Aleksandra. "Volunteering to Prevent Famine in Somalia." *UN Volunteers*, United Nations, 28 June 2017, www.unv.org/our-stories/volunteering-prevent-famine-somalia.

34. Caron, Pierre-Louis. "Volunteers Map Some of the Earth's Most Remote Areas to Help Aid Workers." *VICE News*, VICE News, 15 Feb. 2016, news.vice.com/article/volunteers-map-the-planets-remote-areas-for-aid-workers; "Missing Maps." *Missing Maps*, Missing Maps, www.missingmaps.org/.

35. "Project Limón, Nicaragua." *FIMRC*, FIMRC, www.fimrc.org/nicaragua/.

36. Fujiwara, Lyla, and National Journal. "How I Used My Computer-Science Degree in the Peace Corps While Serving in Rural Africa." *The Atlantic*, Atlantic Media Company, 25 Apr. 2014, www.theatlantic.com/politics/archive/2014/04/-how-i-used-my-computer-science-degree-in-the-peace-corps-while-serving-in-rural-africa/430860/.

37. Peace Corps. "These 3 Volunteers Are Working to Feed the Future." *Peace Corps*, Peace Corps, 25 July 2013, www.peacecorps.gov/stories/photo-essay-how-pcvs-are-feeding-the-future/.

38. "Women Red Cross Volunteers Tackle Guinea Worm in Ghana." *The Carter Center*, The Carter Center, 26 Dec. 2003, www.cartercenter.org/news/documents/doc1572.html.

39. "Village Volunteer Viviana Kolong Works to Protect Her Community from Debilitating Disease." *The Carter Center*, The Carter Center, 10 May 2010, www.cartercenter.org/news/features/h/guinea_worm/profile-viviana-kolong.html.

40. "Sé Parte De Nuestros Programas." *Fundemar*, Fundemar, www.fundemardr.org/copy-of-programa-educativo; "Conservación de Arrecifes." *Fundemar*, Fundemar, www.fundemardr.org/copy-of-mamiferos-marinos.

41. "Module 8: The Significant Harm of Worst Practices." *Unite for Sight*, Unite for Sight, www.uniteforsight.org/global-health-course/module8.

42. Ravelo, Jenny Lei. "30 Percent of Aid Lost to Corruption—Ban Ki-Moon." *Devex*, Devex, 10 July 2012, www.devex.

com/news/30-percent-of-aid-lost-to-corruption-ban-ki-moon-78643.

43. Stupart, Richard. "7 Worst International Aid Ideas." *Matador Network*, Matador Network, 20 Feb. 2012, matadornetwork.com/change/7-worst-international-aid-ideas/.

44. Hall, A, et al. "Intensity of Reinfection with Ascaris Lumbricoides and Its Implications for Parasite Control." *National Institute of Health National Library of Medicine National Center for Biotechnology Information*, The Lancet, 23 May 1992, https://pubmed.ncbi.nlm.nih.gov/1349668/.

45. "Module 8: The Significant Harm of Worst Practices." *Unite for Sight*, Unite for Sight, www.uniteforsight.org/global-health-course/module8; Bauer, Irmgard. "More Harm than Good? the Questionable Ethics of Medical Volunteering and International Student Placements." *BioMed Central*, Tropical Diseases, Travel Medicine and Vaccines, 6 Mar. 2017, https://tdtmvjournal.biomedcentral.com/articles/10.1186/s40794-017-0048-y.

46. "Nobody Spends Enough on Mental Health." *The Economist*, The Economist Newspaper, 26 Apr. 2018, www.economist.com/special-report/2018/04/26/nobody-spends-enough-on-mental-health.

47. Kostopoulos, Ioannis, et al. "Volunteer Tourism as a Transformative Experience: A Mixed Methods Empirical Study." *SAGE Journals*, Journal of Travel Research, 8 Apr. 2020, https://journals.sagepub.com/doi/full/10.1177/0047287520913630.

48. Stupart, Richard. "Why You Shouldn't Participate in Voluntourism." *Matador Network*, Matador Network, 22 Aug. 2011, matadornetwork.com/change/why-you-shouldnt-participate-in-voluntourism/.

49. Jhingan, Rajit, et al. "Coping with Shortage of Ventilators in COVID-19 Pandemic: Indian Context and Exploring Effective Options in Countries with Limited Healthcare Resources." *Clinmed Journals International Library*, International Archives of Public Health and Community Medicine, 25 May 2020, https://www.clinmedjournals.org/articles/iaphcm/-international-archives-of-public-health-and-community-medicine-iaphcm-4-043.php?jid=iaphcm; "Covid-19: Schools for

More than 168 Million Children Globally Have Been Completely Closed for Almost a Full Year, Says UNICEF." *UNICEF*, 2 Mar. 2021, https://www.unicef.org/press-releases/schools-more-168-million-children-globally-have-been-completely-closed.

50. "Covid-19 to Add as Many as 150 Million Extreme Poor by 2021." *The World Bank*, 7 Oct. 2020, https://www.worldbank.org/en/news/press-release/2020/10/07/-covid-19-to-add-as-many-as-150-million-extreme-poor-by-2021.

51. "WHO Chief 'Appalled' by Rich Nations' COVID Vaccine Booster Talk with so Many Unvaccinated around the World." *CBS News*, 9 Sept. 2021, https://www.cbsnews.com/news/covid-vaccine-inequality-who-tedros-appalled-rich-nations-booster-shots/.

52. "UN Warns of 'Urgent Imperative' to Avoid Acute Afghan Food Insecurity." *United Nations*, United Nations, 7 Sept. 2021, https://news.un.org/en/story/2021/09/1099292.

53. Gharib, Malaka. "The Pandemic Changed the World of 'Voluntourism.' Some Folks like the New Way Better." *NPR*, 15 July 2021, https://www.npr.org/sections/goatsandsoda/2021/07/15/1009911082/the-pandemic-changed-the-world-of-voluntourism-some-folks-like-the-new-way-bette.

Chapter II

1. Walleigh, Rick. "6 Ways to Volunteer Abroad and Be Really Useful." *Forbes*, Forbes Magazine, 23 May 2016, https://www.forbes.com/sites/nextavenue/2016/05/23/6-ways-to-volunteer-abroad-and-be-really-useful/?sh=4d498ae061bd.

2. Loh, Lawrence. "Opinion: Volunteering Abroad Is Popular and Problematic. Let's Fix It." *NPR*, 12 Sept. 2019, https://www.npr.org/sections/goatsandsoda/2019/09/12/754347433/volunteering-abroad-is-popular-and-problematic-lets-fix-it.

3. Loh, Lawrence. "Opinion: Volunteering Abroad Is Popular and Problematic. Let's Fix It." *NPR*, 12 Sept. 2019, https://www.npr.org/sections/goatsandsoda/2019/09/12/754347433/volunteering-

abroad-is-popular-and-problematic-lets-fix-it.

4. Dubay, Alicia. "Voluntourism: The Good and the Bad." *World Vision Canada*, 21 June 2021, https://www.worldvision.ca/stories/voluntourism-the-good-and-the-bad.

Chapter III

1. "Goal 1 Targets." *UNDP*, United Nations, www.undp.org/content/undp/en/home/sustainable-development-goals/-goal-1-no-poverty/targets/.

2. Silver, Marc, and Malaka Gharib. "What's The Meaning Of The World Bank's New Poverty Lines?" *NPR*, NPR, 25 Oct. 2017, www.npr.org/sections/goatsandsoda/2017/10/25/558068646/whats-the-meaning-of-the-world-banks-new-poverty-lines.

3. Roser, Max. "Global Poverty in an Unequal World: Who Is Considered Poor in a Rich Country? and What Does This Mean for Our Understanding of Global Poverty?" *Our World in Data*, University of Oxford, 5 Mar. 2021, https://ourworldindata.org/higher-poverty-global-line.

4. "Abraham Maslow." *Pursuit of Happiness*, Pursuit of Happiness, www.pursuit-of-happiness.org/history-of-happiness/abraham-maslow/.

5. "Guinea Worm Eradication Program." *The Carter Center*, The Carter Center, https://www.cartercenter.org/health/guinea_worm/index.html.

6. Allers, Chris. "Why Major Donors Demand Measurement." *The Georgia Center for Nonprofits*, Apr. 2013, https://www.gcn.org/articles/Why-Major-Donors-Demand-Measurement.

7. Wade, Don. "Nonprofit Operators Told That Failure Can Bring Long-Term Success." *Memphis Daily News*, 12 May 2016, https://www.memphisdailynews.com/news/2016/may/12/nonprofit-operators-told-that-failure-can-bring-long-term-success/.

8. "Jordan: Healing Patients Wounded by Conflicts across the Middle East." *Doctors Without Borders*, Wayback Machine. 04 Jan 2018, web.archive.org/web/20180108124925/http://www.doctorswithoutborders.org/article/jordan-healing-patients-wounded-conflicts-across-middle-east.

9. Reid, Kathryn. "Child Labor: Facts, Faqs, and How to Help End It." *World Vision*, 22 June 2021, https://www.worldvision.org/child-protection-news-stories/child-labor-facts.

10. "Sharecropping." *PBS*, Public Broadcasting Service, https://www.pbs.org/tpt/slavery-by-another-name/themes/sharecropping/.

11. "Malnutrition." *World Health Organization*, World Health Organization, 9 June 2021, https://www.who.int/news-room/fact-sheets/detail/malnutrition.

12. Razzak, Junaid A., and Arthur L. Kellermann. "Emergency Medical Care in Developing Countries: Is It Worthwhile?" *WHO Bulletin*, World Health Organization, 2002, https://www.who.int/bulletin/archives/80(11)900.pdf.

13. "Lebanon: Huge Cost of Inaction in Trash Crisis." *Human Rights Watch*, 9 June 2020, https://www.hrw.org/news/2020/06/09/lebanon-huge-cost-inaction-trash-crisis.

14. Walleigh, Rick. "6 Ways to Volunteer Abroad and Be Really Useful." *Forbes*, Forbes Magazine, 23 May 2016, https://www.forbes.com/sites/nextavenue/2016/05/23/6-ways-to-volunteer-abroad-and-be-really-useful/?sh=4d498ae061bd.

Chapter IV

1. Rehberg, W. "Altruistic Individualists: Motivations for International Volunteering Among Young Adults in Switzerland." *Voluntas* 16, 109–122 (2005). https://doi.org/10.1007/s11266-005-5693-5

2. "IVHQ Social Network." *International Volunteer HQ*, https://www.volunteerhq.org/ivhq-social-network/.

3. "2011–Present: Disaster Response Programs." *Habitat for Humanity*, Habitat for Humanity, www.habitat.org/impact/-our-work/disaster-response/programs/-2011-present.

4. Gharib, Malaka. "Volunteering Abroad? Read This Before You Post That Selfie." *NPR*, NPR, 26 Nov. 2017, www.npr.org/sections/goatsandsoda/2017/11/26/565694874/volunteering-

abroad-read-this-before-you-post-that-selfie.

5. Dortonne, Nathalie. "The Dangers of Poverty Porn." *CNN*, Cable News Network, 8 Dec. 2016, www.cnn.com/2016/12/08/health/poverty-porn-danger-feat/index.html.

6. Quinn, Andrew. "Is There Any Space in the Development Debate for African Experts?" *The Guardian*, Guardian News and Media, 23 Aug. 2013, https://www.theguardian.com/global-development-professionals-network/2013/aug/23/-aspen-new-voices-africa-fellowship.

7. Lentfer, Jennifer. "Charities Want to Make an Impact. But Poverty Porn Is Not the Way." *The Guardian*, Guardian News and Media, 12 Jan. 2018, www.theguardian.com/voluntary-sector-network/2018/jan/12/charities-stop-poverty-porn-fundraising-ed-sheeran-comic-relief; Roenigk, Emily. "5 Reasons 'Poverty Porn' Empowers The Wrong Person." *The Huffington Post*, TheHuffingtonPost.com, 16 Apr. 2014, www.huffingtonpost.com/emily-roenigk/-poverty-charity-media_b_5155627.html; Dortonne, Nathalie. "The Dangers of Poverty Porn." *CNN*, Cable News Network, 8 Dec. 2016, www.cnn.com/2016/12/08/health/poverty-porn-danger-feat/index.html; Wooldridge, Leslie Quander. "Don't Post a Photo of Yourself with Strangers' Children in Your Tinder Profile." *The Washington Post*, WP Company, 26 Mar. 2018, www.washingtonpost.com/news/soloish/wp/2018/03/26/dont-post-a-photo-of-yourself-with-strangers-children-in-your-tinder-profile/?utm_term=.e014c3974806; Gharib, Malaka. "Volunteering Abroad? Read This Before You Post That Selfie." *NPR*, NPR, 26 Nov. 2017, www.npr.org/sections/goats andsoda/2017/11/26/565694874/-volunteering-abroad-read-this-before-you-post-that-selfie; Moore, Emma. "You Don't Know What's Best: The Overuse of Poverty Porn." *Brown Political Review*, Brown University, 28 Oct. 2013, https://brownpoliticalreview.org/2013/10/you-dont-know-whats-best-the-overuse-of-poverty-porn/.

8. "Radi- Aid." *Radi- Aid*, Norwegian Students' & Academics' International Assistance Fund, www.radiaid.com/.

9. "Barbie Savior." *Barbie Savior*, Barbie Savior, www.barbiesavior.com/.

10. "Virtual Volunteering." *Create the Good*, AARP, createthegood.org/articles/virtualvolunteering.

11. Bartley, Sylvia, and Emily Lauer-Bader. "Tapping the Power of Virtual Volunteers." *Stanford Social Innovation Review*, Stanford University, 2021, https://ssir.org/articles/entry/tapping_the_power_of_virtual_volunteers.

12. Aaron, Henry J. "The Social Safety Net: The Gaps That Covid-19 Spotlights." *Brookings*, The Brookings Institution, 23 June 2020, https://www.brookings.edu/blog/up-front/2020/06/23/the-social-safety-net-the-gaps-that-covid-19-spotlights/; "Frac's New Online Dashboard Reveals a Shocking Number of Households Don't Have Enough to Eat during the Pandemic." *Food Research & Action Center*, Food Research & Action Center, 15 July 2021, https://frac.org/news/fracs-new-online-dashboard-reveals-a-shocking-number-of-households-dont-have-enough-to-eat-during-the-pandemic.

13. Skovgaard-Smith, Irene. "The Complex World of the Global Citizen." *BBC Capital*, BBC, 10 Nov. 2017, www.bbc.com/capital/story/20171110-the-complex-world-of-the-global-citizen.

14. Rank, Mark Robert. *One Nation, Underprivileged: Why American Poverty Affects Us All*. Oxford University Press, 2005; "Poverty Facts: The Population of Poverty USA." *Poverty USA*, Poverty USA, povertyusa.org/facts.

15. "How We Work to End Hunger." *Feeding America*, Feeding America, www.feedingamerica.org/our-work/our-approach/; "Volunteer at Your Local Food Bank." *Feeding America*, Feeding America, www.feedingamerica.org/take-action/volunteer/; Yotopoulos, Amy. "Three Reasons Why People Don't Volunteer, and What Can Be Done About It." *Stanford Center on Longevity*, Stanford University, longevity.stanford.edu/three-reasons-why-people-dont-volunteer-and-what-can-be-done-about-it/; Grimm, Robert et al. "Volunteer Growth Since 1974: A Review of Trends Since 1974." *Nationalservice.gov*, Corporation for National & Community Service, Dec. 2006, www.nationalservice.gov/pdf/06_1203_volunteer_growth.pdf.

16. "A Profile of the Working Poor, 2018." *U.S. Bureau of Labor Statistics*, July 2020, https://www.bls.gov/opub/reports/-working-poor/2018/home.htm.

17. "The Number of People Forced to Flee Their Homes Due to Violence and Persecution Is Unprecedented in Human History. Of the 65 Million Currently Displaced, 20 Million Are Living Outside of Their Countries as Refugees." *Refugee Community Partnership*, Refugee Community Partnership, refugeecommunitypartnership.org/; "Volunteer." *Refugee Community Partnership*, Refugee Community Partnership, refugeecommunitypartnership.org/become-a-volunteer/.

18. Wpxi- Pittsburg. "500,000 Petitions Delivered to Mylan Headquarters in Protest of EpiPen Price Hike." *AJC*, Cox Media Group, 31 Aug. 2016, www.ajc.com/news/national/500-000-petitions-delivered-mylan-headquarters-protest-epipen-price-hike/JCblmmiGeO-EvgXfZEoEGNJ/.

Chapter V

1. Bailey, Jerome. "American Ideas on Volunteering Don't Resonate Worldwide." *The World from PRX*, Pri.org, 8 Mar. 2014, https://www.pri.org/stories/2014-03-08/american-ideas-volunteering-dont-resonate-worldwide.

2. "Conservation v Development along Indonesia's Longest River." *The Economist*, The Economist Newspaper, 23 Aug. 2018, www.economist.com/asia/2018/08/23/-conservation-v-development-along-indonesias-longest-river.

3. Walleigh, Rick. "6 Ways to Volunteer Abroad and Be Really Useful." *Forbes*, Forbes Magazine, 23 May 2016, https://www.forbes.com/sites/next avenue/2016/05/23/6-ways-to-volunteer-abroad-and-be-really-useful/?sh=4d498ae061bd.

4. "Players for Pits." *Playersforpits*, Players for Pits, www.playersforpits.com/.

5. Hall, Jenny. "Click Here to Support The Blueboys Christmas Appeal Organised by Jenny Hall." *Gofundme.com*, Go Fund Me, www.gofundme.com/theblueboysrescuechristmas.

6. Hall, Jenny. *Instagram*, The Blueboys, https://www.instagram.com/the_blue boys/?hl=en.

7. Ravsberg, Fernando. "Meet Papito, the 'Daddy' of Hairdressing in Havana." *Cuba | Al Jazeera*, Al Jazeera, 21 Oct. 2016, www.aljazeera.com/indepth/features/2016/09/meet-papito-daddy-hairdressing-havana-160926113009704.html.

8. Walleigh, Rick. "6 Ways to Volunteer Abroad and Be Really Useful." *Forbes*, Forbes Magazine, 23 May 2016, https://www.forbes.com/sites/next avenue/2016/05/23/6-ways-to-volunteer-abroad-and-be-really-useful/?sh=4d498ae061bd.

9. Bennett, Claire. "Common Assumptions Underlying Volunteer Travel." *ALTO Global Consulting*, https://www.altoglobalconsulting.com/altojournal/-common-assumptions-underlying-volunteer-travel.

10. "GNI per Capita, Atlas Method (Current U.S.$)." *World Bank Data*, The World Bank, data.worldbank.org/indicator/NY.GNP.PCAP.CD?locations=GT-XN.

11. Rus, Jan. "Comment: Financing Undocumented Migration and the Limits of Solidarity: Unsettling Findings from Guatemala." *Jstor*, Latin American Perspectives, Jan. 2010, https://www.jstor.org/stable/20684703.

12. Hellin, Jon, et al. "Maize Diversity, Market Access, and Poverty Reduction in the Western Highlands of Guatemala." *BioOne Complete*, International Mountain Society, 1 May 2017, https://bioone.org/journals/mountain-research-and-development/volume-37/issue-2/-MRD-JOURNAL-D-16-00065.1/Maize-Diversity-Market-Access-and-Poverty-Reduction-in-the-Western/10.1659/MRD-JOURNAL-D-16-00065.1.full.

13. "Welcome to Elephant Human Relations Aid in Namibia." *EHRA—Volunteer in Africa to Conserve the Desert Elephants of Namibia*, Elephant- Human Relations Aid, www.desertelephant.org/.

14. Walleigh, Rick. "6 Ways to Volunteer Abroad and Be Really Useful." *Forbes*, Forbes Magazine, 23 May 2016, https://www.forbes.com/sites/nextavenue/2016/05/23/6-ways-to-volunteer-abroad-and-be-really-useful/?sh=4d498ae061bd.

15. "Africa Unplugged." *The Economist*,

The Economist Newspaper, 29 Oct. 2016, www.economist.com/news/middle-east-and-africa/21709297-small-scale-solar-power-surging-ahead-africa-unplugged; "Mobile Phones Are Transforming Africa." *The Economist*, The Economist Newspaper, 10 Dec. 2016, www.economist.com/news/middle-east-and-africa/21711511-mobile-phones-are-transforming-africa-where-they-can-get-signal-mobile-phones; "On the Move." *The Economist*, The Economist Newspaper, 16 Apr. 2016, www.economist.com/news/-special-report/21696790-much-hangs-mobile-money-move.

16. Fernández, Pablo Armando. "Casa-Estudio De José Fuster." *Havana City Guide*, Lahabana.com, www.lahabana.com/guide/casa-estudio-de-jose-fuster/; "Jose Fuster: Painter-Sculptor." *Havana Club*, Havana Club, havana-club.com/en-ww/havana-cultura/josé-fuster; McClane, Dave. "Fusterlandia: Havana's Ceramic Fantasy World." *Man Vs. Globe*, Man Vs. Globe Travel Blog, 14 May 2017, www.manvsglobe.com/fusterlandia-havana/.

Chapter VI

1. Ellis, S, and S Barakat. "From relief to development: the long-term effects of 'temporary' accommodation on refugees and displaced persons in the Republic of Croatia." *Disasters* vol. 20,2 (1996): 111–24. doi:10.1111/j.1467–7717.1996.tb00521.x

2. "About the Ministry of Hope International." *Hope International*, Hope International, hope-international.us/about.php.

3. Lakhani, Nina. "The Hunger Industry: Does Charity Put a Band-Aid on American Inequality?" *The Guardian*, Guardian News and Media, 28 Apr. 2021, https://www.theguardian.com/environment/2021/apr/28/our-unequal-earth-food-insecurity-aid-corporate.

4. "About Us." *Food-Aid International*, Food-Aid International, food-aid.org/-about-us.html.

5. Giustra, Frank. "Without Long-Term Investment, Food Aid for Haiti Risks Being a Band-Aid." *Philanthropy News Digest*, Candid, 9 Sept. 2021, https://philanthropynewsdigest. org/commentary-and-opinion/without-long-term-investment-food-aid-for-haiti-risks-being-a-band-aid.

6. "About the Ministry of Hope International." *Hope International*, Hope International, hope-international.us/about.php.

7. Gharib, Malaka. "Humanitarian Aid Is 'Broken,' Says Former U.N. Official." *NPR*, 22 June 2017, https://www.npr.org/sections/goatsandsoda/2017/06/22/533639073/what-s-wrong-with-hu manitarian-aid.

8. Sheerin, Jude. "Malawi Windmill Boy with Big Fans." *BBC News*, BBC, 1 Oct. 2009, news.bbc.co.uk/2/hi/africa/8257153.stm.

9. "Guatemala." *Dol.gov*, U.S. Department of Labor, www.dol.gov/ilab/reports/-child-labor/findings/tda2007/guatemala.pdf.

10. Essossinam Ali, Aklesso Y.G. Egbendewe, Tahirou Abdoulaye & Daniel B. Sarpong (2020) Willingness to pay for weather index-based insurance in semi-subsistence agriculture: evidence from northern Togo, Climate Policy, 20:5,534–547, DOI: 10.1080/14693062.2020.1745742; Williamson, Shawn. "Do You Have Enough or Too Much Farm Insurance?" *Successful Farming*, Successful Farming, 11 May 2017, https://www.agriculture.com/farm-management/crop-insurance/do-you-have-enough-or-too-much-farm-insurance.

11. Bayeh, Endalcachew. "The Role of Empowering Women and Achieving Gender Equality to the Sustainable Development of Ethiopia." *Pacific Science Review B: Humanities and Social Sciences*, vol. 2, no. 1, Jan. 2016, pp. 37–42. *ScienceDirect*, doi:10.1016/j.psrb.2016.09.013.

12. UNDP Democratic Governance Group Bureau for Development Policy. "Marginalised Minorities in Development Programming." *Ohchr.org*, United Nations, May 2010, www.ohchr.org/Documents/Issues/Minorities/UNDPmarginalisedMinorities.pdf.

13. Orozco, Manuel, and Marcela Valdivia. "Educational Challenges in Guatemala and Consequences for Human Capital and Development." *Thedialogue.org*, The Dialogue, Feb. 2017, www.thedialogue.org/wp-content/

uploads/2017/02/Educational-Challenges-in-Guatemala-and-Consequences-for-Human-Capital-and-Development-1.pdf.

14. "Vaccine Equity." *World Health Organization*, World Health Organization, https://www.who.int/campaigns/vaccine-equity; Yamey G, Garcia P, Hassan F, Mao W, McDade K K, Pai M et al. It is not too late to achieve global covid-19 vaccine equity *BMJ* 2022; 376 :e070650 doi:10.1136/bmj-2022-070650

15. Peluffo, Nicoletta. "Breaking the 'Cultural Bubble' through the Immersive Model." *12th International Conference Innovation in Language Learning.* 2019.

Chapter VII

1. Brooks, Andrew. "The Hidden Trade in Our Second-Hand Clothes given to Charity." *The Guardian*, Guardian News and Media, 13 Feb. 2015, https://www.theguardian.com/sustainable-business/sustainable-fashion-blog/2015/feb/13/second-hand-clothes-charity-donations-africa.

2. "The One-for-One Business Model: Avoiding Unintended Consequences." *Knowledge@Wharton*, The Wharton School University of Pennsylvania, 16 Feb. 2015, https://knowledge.wharton.upenn.edu/article/one-one-business-model-social-impact-avoiding-unintended-consequences/; Murphy, Tom. "Do TOMS Shoes Harm Local Shoe Sellers?" *Humanosphere*, Humanosphere, 16 Sept. 2014, www.humanosphere.org/social-business/2014/09/toms-shoes-harm-local-shoe-sellers/; Chapin, Adele. "TOMS Shoe Donations Might Not Be Doing Any Good." *Racked.com*, Racked, 27 July 2015, www.racked.com/2015/7/27/9046207/-toms-shoes-charity-poverty; Montgomery, Mike. "What Entrepreneurs Can Learn From The Philanthropic Struggles Of TOMS Shoes." *Forbes*, Forbes Magazine, 28 Apr. 2015, www.forbes.com/sites/mikemontgomery/2015/04/28/-how-entrepreneurs-can-avoid-the-philanthropy-pitfalls/#19f2b6981c38.

3. Wydick, Bruce, et al. "Shoeing the Children: The Impact of the TOMS Shoe Donation Program in Rural El Salvador." *The World Bank Economic Review*, vol. 32,

no. 3, 20 Sept. 2016, pp. 727–751. *Oxford Academic*, doi:10.1093/wber/lhw042.

4. Chapin, Adele. "TOMS Shoe Donations Might Not Be Doing Any Good." *Racked.com*, Racked, 27 July 2015, www.racked.com/2015/7/27/9046207/toms-shoes-charity-poverty.

5. Dominick, Judy Wu. "Unpacking Operation Christmas Child." *Lifereconsidered.com* Judy Wu Dominick, 8 Nov. 2015, lifereconsidered.com/2015/11/08/-unpacking-operation-christmas-child/; Howell, Brian M. "Filling Millions of Shoe Boxes of Toys for Poor Kids Seems like a Great Idea. Here's Why It's Not." *The Washington Post*, WP Company, 20 Dec. 2017, www.washingtonpost.com/news/acts-of-faith/wp/2017/12/20/filling-millions-of-shoe-boxes-of-toys-for-poor-kids-seems-like-a-great-idea-heres-why-its-not/?utm_term=.82a8fab24e6d.

6. "Half the World's Refugee Children Not in School, UN Agency Finds." *UN News*, United Nations, 29 Aug. 2018, https://news.un.org/en/story/2018/08/1017962.

7. Leghtas, Izza. "Insecure Future: Deportations and Lack of Legal Work for Refugees in Turkey." *Refugees International*, 19 Sept. 2019, https://www.refugeesinternational.org/reports/2019/9/18/insecure-future-deportations-and-lack-of-legal-work-for-refugees-in-turkey.

8. Stanton, Brandon. *Humans of New York*, Humans of New York, www.humansofnewyork.com/post/171594811816/they-didnt-say-a-word-they-just-started-firing; Stanton, Brandon. "Click Here to Support Houses For Rohingya Refugees Organized by Brandon Stanton." *Gofundme.com*, Go Fund Me, www.gofundme.com/houses4rohingya.

9. "Refugees at Risk of Hunger and Malnutrition, as Relief Hit in Eastern Africa." *UN News*, United Nations, 26 Aug. 2020, https://www.unhcr.org/en-us/news/briefing/2000/8/3ae6b8274c/food-shortages-affecting-refugees.html.

10. "A refugee baker in Kenya helps provide school meals." *YouTube*, uploaded by International Finance Corporation, 6 Mar. 2018, youtu.be/uyG-NDkdISs.

11. "Carnival of Love." *The Wayfarer Foundation*, Wayfarer Studios, https://

www.wayfarerstudios.com/founda tion/carnival-of-love/.

12. "Low Income Housing Institute." *Low Income Housing Institute*, Low Income Housing Institute Seattle, lihi. org/.

13. "Child Hunger and Famine." *Save the Children*, Save the Children, www.savethechildren.org/site/c.8rK LIXMGIpI4E/b.9515661/k.6913/Hunger_ _Famine_Crisis.htm; "Response Summary: Save the Children Providing Relief to Massive Needs of Children in 8 Countries." *Save the Children*, Wayback Machine. Oct. 2017, web.archive.org/web/ 20171215001038/http://www.savethe children.org/atf/cf/%7B9def2ebe-10ae-432c-9bd0-df91d2eba74a%7D/STC_ HUNGER_FC_OCT17.PDF.

14. Freedman, John. "From Tragedy, Opportunity—A New Beginning for Haiti and the Dominican Republic." *The Permanente Journal*, vol. 14, no. 3, 2010, pp. 77–79. *PMC-NCBI*, www.ncbi.nlm.nih. gov/pmc/articles/PMC2937853/.

15. Singer, Peter. "Best Charities for Effective Giving." *The Life You Can Save*, https://www.thelifeyoucansave.org/.

16. "Connect Relief." *Connect Relief: Un Proyecto De Caras Con Causa*, Connect Relief, https://connectrelief.com/.

17. "Neglected Tropical Diseases." *National Institute of Allergy and Infectious Diseases*, U.S. Department of Health and Human Services, 11 July 2016, https:// www.niaid.nih.gov/research/neglected-tropical-diseases.

18. "River Blindness Elimination Program." *The Carter Center*, The Carter Center, www.cartercenter.org/health/ river_blindness/index.html.

19. "Guinea Worm Eradication Program." *The Carter Center*, The Carter Center, www.cartercenter.org/health/ guinea_worm/index.html.

20. "About Us." *Kiva*, Kiva, www.kiva. org/about.

21. Miller, Talea. "Lourdes's Dream: To Show the World a Woman's Worth." *Kiva Blog Posts*, Kiva, www.kiva.org/blog/-lourdess-dream-to-show-the-world-a-womans-worth.

22. Klapper, Leora, et al. *Income Biggest Barrier to Banking in Developing Countries.* Gallup, 19 Dec. 2012, https://news.gallup.com/poll/159380

/income-biggest-barrier-banking-develop ing-countries.aspx.

23. "About Us." *Kiva*, Kiva, www.kiva. org/about.

24. Kelly, Annie. "Money 'Wasted' on Water Projects in Africa." *The Guardian*, Guardian News and Media, 26 Mar. 2009, www.theguardian.com/society/ katineblog/2009/mar/26/water-projects-wasted-money.

25. Chalab, Nadine, et al. "Charitable Giving and Intermediation." *Monash Business School*, Nov. 2015, https:// www.monash.edu/business/economics/ research/publications/2015/1815-charitable-giving-and-intermediation. pdf.

Chapter VIII

1. University of Nebraska-Lincoln. "Why some parasitic worms persist in people." ScienceDaily. ScienceDaily, 22 May 2019. <www.sciencedaily.com/ releases/2019/05/190522101939.htm>.

2. "Avoid Contaminated Water during Travel." *Centers for Disease Control and Prevention*, 22 June 2021, https://wwwnc. cdc.gov/travel/page/water-disinfection.

3. "Travelers' Health: Food and Water Safety." *Centers for Disease Control and Prevention*, Centers for Disease Control and Prevention, 8 Jan. 2018, wwwnc.cdc. gov/travel/page/food-water-safety.

4. "Travelers' Health: Destinations." *Centers for Disease Control and Prevention*, Centers for Disease Control and Prevention, wwwnc.cdc.gov/travel/ destinations/list/.

5. "Foodborne Illness: Especially Dangerous for the Vulnerable." *U.S. Food and Drug Administration*, 4 June 2014, https:// www.fda.gov/consumers/consumer-updates/foodborne-illness-especially-dangerous-vulnerable.

6. Danise, Amy, and Jason Metz. "Best Covid-19 Travel Insurance Plans of May 2022." *Forbes Advisor*, Forbes Magazine, 12 May 2022, https://www.forbes.com/ advisor/travel-insurance/best-pandemic-travel-insurance/.

7. "Covid-19 Vaccine Effectiveness and Safety." *Centers for Disease Control and Prevention*, Centers for Disease Control and Prevention, 5 May 2022, https://www.

cdc.gov/mmwr/covid19_vaccine_safety. html.

8. "CDC Seasonal Flu Vaccine Effectiveness Studies." *Centers for Disease Control and Prevention*, Centers for Disease Control and Prevention, 11 Mar. 2022, https://www.cdc.gov/flu/vaccines-work/-effectiveness-studies.htm.

9. Mayo Clinic Staff. "How Well Do Face Masks Protect against Covid-19?" *Mayo Clinic*, Mayo Foundation for Medical Education and Research, 1 Mar. 2022, https://www.mayoclinic.org/diseases-conditions/coronavirus/in-depth/-coronavirus-mask/art-20485449.

10. "How to Protect Yourself & Others." *Centers for Disease Control and Prevention*, Centers for Disease Control and Prevention, 25 Feb. 2022, https://www.cdc.gov/coronavirus/2019-ncov/prevent-getting-sick/prevention.html.

11. Medez, Rich. "MIT Researchers Say Time Spent Indoors Increases Risk of Covid at 6 Feet or 60 Feet in New Study Challenging Social Distancing Policies." *CNBC*, CNBC, 27 Apr. 2021, https://www.cnbc.com/2021/04/23/mit-researchers-say-youre-no-safer-from-covid-indoors-at-6-feet-or-60-feet-in-new-study.html.

Chapter IX

1. "Country Information: Learn About Your Destination." *U.S. Passports & International Travel*, U.S. Department of State-Bureau of Consular Affairs, travel.state. gov/content/passports/en/country.html.

2. Archibold, Randal C. "Peace Corps to Scale Back in Central America." *The New York Times*, The New York Times, 21 Dec. 2011, www.nytimes.com/2011/12/22/world/americas/peace-corps-cuts-back-in-honduras-guatemala-and-el-salvador. html; "Countries." *Peace Corps*, Peace Corps, www.peacecorps.gov/countries/.

Chapter X

1. "Volunteer." *Engineers Without Borders USA*, Engineers Without Borders USA, www.ewb-usa.org/volunteer/.

2. "How to Tell That Your Volunteer Program Is Legitimate, and Not a Scam." *EveryNurse.org*, 15 Mar. 2020, https://

everynurse.org/volunteer-program-legitimate/.

3. "Extreme Makeover: Home Edition." *IMDb*, IMDb.com, www.imdb.com/title/tt0388595/.

4. Johnson, Meghan. "Pros and Cons of Short-Term Volunteer Programs." *Go Overseas*, 5 Mar. 2013, https://www.gooverseas.com/blog/pros-and-cons-short-term-volunteer-opportunities.

5. Kelly, Annie. "Money 'Wasted' on Water Projects in Africa." *The Guardian*, Guardian News and Media, 26 Mar. 2009, www.theguardian.com/society/katineblog/2009/mar/26/water-projects-wasted-money.

6. "Module 8: The Significant Harm of Worst Practices." *Unite for Sight*, Unite for Sight, www.uniteforsight.org/global-health-course/module8.

7. "Module 8: The Significant Harm of Worst Practices." *Unite for Sight*, Unite for Sight, www.uniteforsight.org/global-health-course/module8.

8. Johnson, Meghan. "Pros and Cons of Short-Term Volunteer Programs." *Go Overseas*, 5 Mar. 2013, https://www.gooverseas.com/blog/pros-and-cons-short-term-volunteer-opportunities.

9. Purvis, Katherine, and Lindsey Kennedy. "Volunteer Travel: Experts Raise Concerns over Unregulated Industry." *The Guardian*, Guardian News and Media, 13 Jan. 2016, www.theguardian.com/global-development-professionals-network/2016/jan/13/concerns-unregulated-volunteer-tourism-industry.

10. Popham, Gabriel. "Boom in 'Voluntourism' Sparks Concerns over Whether the Industry Is Doing Good." *Reuters*, Thomson Reuters, 29 June 2015, www.reuters.com/article/us-travel-volunteers-charities/boom-in-voluntourism-sparks-concerns-over-whether-the-industry-is-doing-good-idUSKCN0P91AX20150629.

11. "Countryside Experience." *Carnival Cruise Line*, Carnival Cruise Line, www.carnival.com/shore-excursions/la-romana/countryside-experience-428072.

12. "Hands On Chocolate Experience At Chocal." *Carnival Cruise Line*, Carnival Cruise Line, www.carnival.com/shore-excursions/amber-cove/-hands-on-chocolate-experience-at-chocal-445106.

13. "Tour With Locals: Sightseeing &

Lunch." *Carnival Cruise Line*, Carnival Cruise Line, www.carnival.com/shore-excursions/amber-cove/give-back-with-purpose-community-tour-445097.

14. Purvis, Katherine, and Lindsey Kennedy. "Volunteer Travel: Experts Raise Concerns over Unregulated Industry." *The Guardian*, Guardian News and Media, 13 Jan. 2016, www.theguardian.com/global-development-professionals-network/2016/jan/13/concerns-unregulated-volunteer-tourism-industry.

15. Stupart, Richard. "Why You Shouldn't Participate in Voluntourism." *Matador Network*, Matador Network, 22 Aug. 2011, matadornetwork.com/change/why-you-shouldnt-participate-in-voluntourism/.

16. Stupart, Richard. "Why You Shouldn't Participate in Voluntourism." *Matador Network*, Matador Network, 22 Aug. 2011, matadornetwork.com/change/why-you-shouldnt-participate-in-voluntourism/.

17. Stupart, Richard. "Why You Shouldn't Participate in Voluntourism." *Matador Network*, Matador Network, 22 Aug. 2011, matadornetwork.com/change/why-you-shouldnt-participate-in-voluntourism/.

18. Pycroft, Sara. "Teaching Abroad: 'Volunteers Had Little Educational Benefit to the Kids.'" *The Guardian*, Guardian News and Media, 13 Jan. 2016, https://www.theguardian.com/global-development-professionals-network/2016/jan/13/teaching-in-an-orphanage-abroad-volunteers-had-little-educational-benefit-to-the-kids.

19. "Supporting Peace, Justice, and Sustainable Economies in the Americas." *Witness for Peace*, Witness for Peace, witnessforpeace.org/.

Chapter XI

1. Stever, H. Guyford, and Janet H. Muroyama. "Globalization of Technology: International Perspectives." *National Academies Press: OpenBook*, The National Academies of Sciences Engineering Medicine, www.nap.edu/read/1101/chapter/2; Mitchell, Amy, et al. "The Role of Social Media in the Arab Uprisings." *Pew Research Center's Journalism Project*, Pew Research Center, 28 Nov. 2012, www.journalism.org/2012/11/28/role-social-media-arab-uprisings/; Beaumont, Peter. "The Truth about Twitter, Facebook and the Uprisings in the Arab World." *The Guardian*, Guardian News and Media, 25 Feb. 2011, www.theguardian.com/world/2011/feb/25/twitter-facebook-uprisings-arab-libya; "The Arab Spring: A Year Of Revolution." *NPR*, NPR, 17 Dec. 2011, www.npr.org/2011/12/17/143897126/-the-arab-spring-a-year-of-revolution.

2. Collyns, Dan. "Bolivia Approves Highway through Amazon Biodiversity Hotspot." *The Guardian*, Guardian News and Media, 15 Aug. 2017, www.theguardian.com/environment/2017/aug/15/bolivia-approves-highway-in-amazon-biodiversity-hotspot-as-big-as-jamaica; El Bardicy, Mohamad. "Protests in Bolivia against Plans for Tipnis Rainforest Highway." *Bolivia News | Al Jazeera*, Al Jazeera, 14 Aug. 2017, www.aljazeera.com/video/news/2017/08/protests-bolivia-renewed-plans-tipnis-rainforest-highway-170814055713885.html.

3. Dorcadie, Mathilde. "Brazil: Citizen Watchdogs Mobilise against Corruption." *Equal Times*, Equal Times, 27 July 2016, www.equaltimes.org/brazil-citizen-watchdogs-mobilise?lang=en#.WzIZm6dKjIU.

4. Hellerstein, Erica. "A Half-Century Ago, Gail Phares Went to Nicaragua. She Came Back a Radical." *INDY Week*, INDY Week, 22 Mar. 2017, www.indyweek.com/indyweek/a-half-century-ago-gail-phares-went-to-nicaragua-she-came-back-a-radical/Content?oid=5618612.

5. "About Us." *VolunteerMatch*, VolunteerMatch, www.volunteermatch.org/about/.

6. "The Difference That Fairtrade Makes." *Fairtrade.org*, Fairtrade Foundation, https://www.fairtrade.org.uk/what-is-fairtrade/the-impact-of-our-work/the-difference-that-fairtrade-makes/.

7. "Andean Dream Royal Quinoa." *Andean Dream*, Andean Dream Quinoa Products, www.andeandream.com/; "Organic Chocolate Bars, Truffles & Coconut Clusters." *Alter Eco*, Alter Eco, www.alterecofoods.com/.

8. Carlsen, Laura. "Under Nafta, Mexico Suffered, and the United States Felt Its

Pain." *The New York Times,* The New York Times, 24 Nov. 2013, www.nytimes.com/roomfordebate/2013/11/24/what-weve-learned-from-nafta/under-nafta-mexico-suffered-and-the-united-states-felt-its-pain; Darlington, Shasta, and Patrick Gillespie. "Mexican Farmer's Daughter: NAFTA Destroyed Us." *CNN Business,* Cable News Network, 9 Feb. 2017, money.cnn.com/2017/02/09/news/economy/nafta-farming-mexico-us-corn-jobs/index.html; Bolterstein, Elyse. "Environmental Justice Case Study: Maquiladora Workers and Border Issues." *University of Michigan,* websites.umich.edu/~snre492/Jones/maquiladora.htm.

9. Nichols, Austin, and Zachary J McDade. "Long-Term Unemployment and Poverty Produce a Vicious Cycle." *Urban Wire,* Urban Institute, 17 Sept. 2013, www.urban.org/urban-wire/long-term-unemployment-and-poverty-produce-vicious-cycle.

10. Field, Anne. "Turning Coal Miners Into Coders—And Preventing A Brain Drain." *Forbes,* Forbes Magazine, 30 Jan. 2017, www.forbes.com/sites/annefield/2017/01/30/turning-coal-miners-into-coders-and-preventing-a-brain-drain/#1c0e6da6f81d.

11. Glaser, Robert, et al. "What Does It Take to Create a Market?" *Yale Insights,* Yale School of Management, 23 Oct. 2007, insights.som.yale.edu/insights/what-does-it-take-to-create-market.

12. Barrett, David M. "Sterilizing a 'Red Infection' Congress, the CIA, and Guatemala, 1954." *Central Intelligence Agency,* Central Intelligence Agency, 3 Aug. 2011, www.cia.gov/library/center-for-the-study-of-intelligence/kent-csi/vol44no5/html/v44i5a03p.htm.

13. "Cookstoves." *Envirofit,* Envirofit Smarter Living, envirofit.org/; Bills, Ron. "Poor People Don't Need Your Charity—They Need You to Listen." *World Economic Forum,* World Economic Forum, 31 Mar. 2016, www.weforum.org/agenda/2016/03/poor-people-dont-need-charity-they-need-you-to-listen/; Milanovic, Nikola. "The Poor as Consumers." *The Stanford Progressive,* Stanford University, May 2010, web.stanford.edu/group/progressive/cgi-bin/?p=535.

14. "Global Warming and Hurricanes." *GFDL,* NOAA, 8 Feb. 2019, www.gfdl.noaa.gov/global-warming-and-hurricanes/; "Climate Change: How Do We Know?" *Global Climate Change: Vital Signs of the Planet,* NASA, climate.nasa.gov/evidence/; "Facts: A blanket around the Earth." *Global Climate Change: Vital Signs of the Planet,* NASA, climate.nasa.gov/causes/; "Facts: How climate is changing." *Global Climate Change: Vital Signs of the Planet,* NASA, climate.nasa.gov/effects/; Fawkes, Chris. "Is Climate Change Making Hurricanes Worse?" *BBC News,* BBC, 30 Dec. 2017, www.bbc.com/news/world-us-canada-42251921; Ernest, Emmalea. "Heat Effects on Vegetable and Fruit Crops." *Cooperative Extension in Delaware,* University of Delaware, 24 July 2015, extension.udel.edu/weeklycropupdate/?p=8354; Hawkes, Logan. "Summer Heat Poses Serious Problem for Cattle." *Southwest Farm Press,* Informa PLC, 13 July 2012, www.southwestfarmpress.com/livestock/summer-heat-poses-serious-problem-cattle.

15. Samenow, Jason. "Maria Regains Strength as It Pulls Away from Puerto Rico, Approaches Dominican Republic, Turks and Caicos." *The Washington Post,* WP Company, 21 Sept. 2017, www.washingtonpost.com/news/capital-weather-gang/wp/2017/09/20/as-maria-slowly-pulls-away-from-puerto-rico-the-u-s-east-coast-watches-and-awaits-its-next-move/?utm_term=.bf94e29ef032; Hanna, Jason, and Steve Almasy. "Hurricane Irma Becomes Category 5 Storm Again." *CNN,* Cable News Network, 8 Sept. 2017, www.cnn.com/2017/09/08/us/hurricane-irma-caribbean-florida/index.html; Smith-Spark, Laura, et al. "Cuba Cleans up after Hurricane Irma Tears through Caribbean." *CNN,* Cable News Network, 11 Sept. 2017, www.cnn.com/2017/09/10/americas/cuba-caribbean-hurricane-irma/index.html; Stone, Richard. "Cuba Embarks on a 100-Year Plan to Protect Itself from Climate Change." *Science,* AAAS, 10 Jan. 2018, www.sciencemag.org/news/2018/01/cuba-embarks-100-year-plan-protect-itself-climate-change; Grant, Will. "How Cuba and Puerto Rico Responded to Their Hurricanes." *BBC News,* BBC, 23 Sept. 2017, www.bbc.com/news/world-us-canada-41371793; Webber, Tim. "Why It's So Hard To Turn The Lights Back On

In Puerto Rico." NPR, NPR. 20 Oct 2017, www.npr.org/2017/10/20/558743790/why-its-so-hard-to-turn-the-lights-back-on-in-puerto; Hsiang, Solomon, and Trevor Houser. "Don't Let Puerto Rico Fall Into an Economic Abyss." *The New York Times*, The New York Times, 29 Sept. 2017, www.nytimes.com/2017/09/29/opinion/puerto-rico-hurricane-maria.html.

16. "Carbon Footprint Calculator." *EPA*, U.S. Environmental Protection Agency, www3.epa.gov/carbon-footprint-calculator/.

17. Bloomberg, M., and C. Pope, 2018: Climate of Hope: How Cities, Businesses, and Citizens Can Save the Planet. St. Martins Press, New York.

Chapter XII

1. "North Korea (Democratic People's Republic of Korea) Travel Advisory." *U.S. Department of State*, 28 June 2021, https://travel.state.gov/content/travel/en/traveladvisories/traveladvisories/north-korea-travel-advisory.html.

2. "Iran Travel Advisory." *U.S. Department of State*, 2 Aug. 2021, https://travel.state.gov/content/travel/en/traveladvisories/traveladvisories/iran-travel-advisory.html.

3. "Resource Center: Cuba Sanctions." *U.S. Department of the Treasury*, U.S. Department of the Treasury, 28 Feb. 2019, www.treasury.gov/resource-center/sanctions/programs/pages/cuba.aspx; "Frequently Asked Questions Related To Cuba." *U.S. Department of the Treasury*, U.S. Department of the Treasury Office of Foreign Assets Control, 8 Nov. 2017, www.treasury.gov/resource-center/sanctions/Programs/Documents/cuba_faqs_new.pdf.

4. Wyss, Jim. "Venezuelans Are Going Hungry. Why Won't the Country Accept Aid?" *Miami Herald*, Miami Herald, 8 Feb. 2018, www.miamiherald.com/news/nation-world/world/americas/venezuela/article199179509.html.

5. Ford, Robert, and Mark Ward. "Assad's Syria Plays Dirty with U.S. Humanitarian Aid." *The Hill*, The Hill, 12 Feb. 2018, thehill.com/opinion/national-security/373449-assads-syria-plays-dirty-with-us-humanitarian-aid.

6. Morris, Jeff. "Working in War Zones Overseas." *Transitions Abroad*, Transitions Abroad Magazine, https://www.transitionsabroad.com/publications/magazine/0201/warzone.shtml.

7. Licon, Adriana Gomez, and Freddy Cuevas. "Peace Corps Pullout a New Blow to Honduras." *NBCNews.com*, NBCUniversal News Group, 18 Jan. 2012, https://www.nbcnews.com/id/wbna46044373.

8. Nolen, Stephanie. "Getting Home in Rio: How Brazilians Rely on Crowdsourcing to Avoid Gun Battles on the Streets." *The Globe and Mail*, The Globe and Mail, 6 Sept. 2018, www.theglobeandmail.com/world/article-rios-killer-apps-how-brazilians-rely-on-crowdsourcing-to-stay-safe/.

9. "Nicaragua: Ortega Scraps Pension Reforms after Deadly Protests." *News | Al Jazeera*, Al Jazeera, 23 Apr. 2018, https://www.aljazeera.com/news/2018/4/23/nicaragua-ortega-scraps-pension-reforms-after-deadly-protests; Engels, Jorge, and Stefano Pozzebon. "Violence in Eastern Colombia Has Left 130 Dead This Year, UN and Catholic Church Say." *CNN*, Cable News Network, 30 Mar. 2022, https://www.cnn.com/2022/03/30/americas/colombia-violence-un-report-intl-latam/index.html.

10. Cheney, Catherine. "The Road to Real Results for Online Learning in Developing Countries." *Devex*, Devex, 3 Apr. 2017, www.devex.com/news/the-road-to-real-results-for-online-learning-in-developing-countries-89884.

11. Pisa, Michael. "Reassessing Expectations for Blockchain and Development." *Center For Global Development*, Center for Global Development, 17 May 2018, www.cgdev.org/publication/-reassessing-expectations-blockchain-and-development-cost-complexity; "Blockchain." *Center For Global Development*, Center for Global Development, www.cgdev.org/topics/blockchain; Thomason, Jane. "Opinion: 7 ways to use blockchain for international development." *Devex*, Devex, 11 Aug. 2017, www.devex.com/news/opinion-7-ways-to-use-blockchain-for-international-development-90839.

12. Stiffe, Rebecca. "Indonesia's First Official Drone Delivers Supplies to Village School." *Irish Examiner*, Irishexaminer.

com, 23 Jan. 2019, www.irishexaminer. com/breakingnews/technow/indonesias-first-official-drone-delivers-supplies-to-village-school-899654.html.

13. "In Rwanda, His Drones Are Saving Lives." *YouTube*, uploaded by Bloomberg, 16 Aug 2018, https://www.youtube.com/watch?v=NBdB3G9Qvqs&list=WL&index=4&t=0s; de Leon, Riley. "Zipline Takes Flight in Ghana, Making It the World's Largest Drone-Delivery Network." *CNBC*, CNBC, 24 Apr. 2019, www.cnbc.com/2019/04/24/with-ghana-expansion-ziplines-medical-drones-now-reach-22m-people.html.

14. Jagannathan, Sheila. "#9 From 2017: Virtual Reality—The Future of Immersive Learning for Development." *The World Bank Blog*, The World Bank, 14 Dec. 2017, blogs.worldbank.org/publicsphere/9--2017-virtual-reality-future-immersive-learning-development.

15. "How a Shampoo Bottle Is Saving Young Lives." *The Economist*, The Economist Newspaper, 6 Sept. 2018, www.economist.com/science-and-technology/2018/09/08/how-a-shampoo-bottle-is-saving-young-lives.

16. "Vaccine Storage and Handling Toolkit." *Centers for Disease Control and Prevention*, U.S. Department of Health and Human Services, 12 Apr. 2022, https://www.cdc.gov/vaccines/hcp/admin/storage/toolkit/index.html.

17. "Charity Navigator's Methodology." *Charity Navigator*, Charity Navigator, www.charitynavigator.org/index.cfm?bay=content.view&cpid=5593#rating.

18. "BRAC • NGO Advisor." *NGO Advisor*, 2019, https://www.ngoadvisor.net/ong/brac.

19. "About GiveWell." *GiveWell*, GiveWell, https://www.givewell.org/about; "ImpactMatters Methodology." *ImpactMatters*, ImpactMatters, https://www.impactmatters.org/methodology/index.html; "About." *Innovations for Poverty Action*, Innovations for Poverty Action, https://www.poverty-action.org/about; "IPA's 2025 Strategic Ambition." *Innovations for Poverty Action*, Innovations for Poverty Action, https://www.poverty-action.org/about/strategic-ambition.

20. "Application Process." *Peace Corps*, Peace Corps, www.peacecorps.gov/apply/application-process/; "Community Service-Business Volunteer." *Peace Corps*, Peace Corps, www.peacecorps.gov/volunteer/volunteer-openings/-community-services-business-volunteer-5340br/.

21. "Preparation and Training." *Peace Corps*, Peace Corps, www.peacecorps.gov/volunteer/preparation-and-training/.

Chapter XIII

1. "Poverty & Inequality Portal." *World Bank*, World Bank, https://pip.worldbank.org/home.

2. Kelly, Annie. "Money 'Wasted' on Water Projects in Africa." *The Guardian*, Guardian News and Media, 26 Mar. 2009, www.theguardian.com/society/katineblog/2009/mar/26/water-projects-wasted-money.

3. "Prevalence of Undernourishment (% of Population)." *World Bank Data*, World Bank, data.worldbank.org/indicator/sn.itk.defc.zs.

4. "Goal 2: End Hunger, Achieve Food Security and Improved Nutrition and Promote Sustainable Agriculture." *SDG Goals*, United Nations, unstats.un.org/sdgs/report/2016/goal-02/.

5. "Zero Hunger." *World Food Programme*, United Nations, www1.wfp.org/-zero-hunger.

6. "Volunteering." *World Food Programme*, United Nations, www1.wfp.org/careers/volunteers; "Volunteer Abroad." *UN Volunteers*, United Nations, www.unv.org/become-volunteer/volunteer-abroad; "Resilience building." *World Food Programme*, United Nations, www1.wfp.org/careers/resilience-building.

7. "Drinking-Water." *World Health Organization*, World Health Organization, 7 Feb. 2018, www.who.int/news-room/-fact-sheets/detail/drinking-water.

8. "We Partner With Communities." *Pure Water for the World*, Pure Water for the World, purewaterfortheworld.org/solutions/community-partnerships/; "Tools and Education." *Pure Water for the World*, Pure Water for the World, purewaterfortheworld.org/solutions/tools-and-education/; "Follow-up and Monitoring." *Pure Water for the World*, Pure Water for the World, purewaterfortheworld.org/solutions/follow-up-and-monitoring/;

"Our Results." *Pure Water for the World*, Pure Water for the World, purewaterfortheworld.org/our-results/; "Volunteer." *Pure Water for the World*, Pure Water for the World, purewaterfortheworld.org/donate/volunteer/.

9. Heathcote, Chris. "Forecasting Infrastructure Investment Needs for 50 Countries, 7 Sectors through 2040." *World Bank*, World Bank, 10 Aug. 2017, blogs.worldbank.org/ppps/forecasting-infrastructure-investment-needs-50-countries-7-sectors-through-2040.

10. "Bridging Global Infrastructure Gaps." *United Nations*, McKinsey & Company, June 2016, www.un.org/pga/71/wp-content/uploads/sites/40/2017/06/Bridging-Global-Infrastructure-Gaps-Full-report-June-2016.pdf.

11. "Approach & Solutions." *Engineers Without Borders USA*, Engineers Without Borders USA, www.ewb-usa.org/our-work/approach-solutions/; "Volunteer." *Engineers Without Borders USA*, Engineers Without Borders USA, www.ewb-usa.org/volunteer/.

12. "Risk of Impoverishing Expenditure for Surgical Care (% of People at Risk)." *World Bank Data*, World Bank, data.worldbank.org/indicator/SH.SGR.IRSK.ZS.

13. "Mortality rate, neonatal (per 1,000 live births)." *World Bank Data*, World Bank, data.worldbank.org/indicator/SH.DYN.NMRT; "Maternal mortality ratio (modeled estimate, per 100,000 live births)." *World Bank Data*, World Bank, data.worldbank.org/indicator/SH.STA.MMRT?end=2015&start=2015&view=bar.

14. "Vaccination." *Doctors Without Borders—USA*, Doctors Without Borders, www.doctorswithoutborders.org/what-we-do/medical-issues/vaccination.

15. "World Mental Health Day 2017." *World Health Organization*, World Health Organization, www.who.int/mental_health/world-mental-health-day/2017/en/.

16. "Maternal and Child Health." *Doctors Without Borders-Canada*, Doctors Without Borders, www.doctorswithoutborders.ca./issues/maternal-and-child-health; "Infant mortality." *Doctors Without Borders—Southern Africa*, Doctors Without Borders, www.msf.org.za/crisis-response/infant-mortality.

17. "Types of projects." *Doctors Without Borders—USA*, Doctors Without Borders, www.doctorswithoutborders.org/who-we-are/how-we-work/types-projects; "Cholera." *Doctors Without Borders—USA*, Doctors Without Borders, www.doctorswithoutborders.org/what-we-do/medical-issues/cholera.

18. "Mental health." *Doctors Without Borders—USA*, Doctors Without Borders, www.doctorswithoutborders.org/what-we-do/medical-issues/mental-health.

19. "Covid-19: Our Global Response." *Doctors Without Borders—USA*, Doctors Without Borders—USA, 6 May 2020, https://www.doctorswithoutborders.org/what-we-do/focus/covid-19.

20. "Essential Requirements." *Doctors Without Borders—USA*, Doctors Without Borders, www.doctorswithoutborders.org/careers/work-field/general-requirements.

21. "Wage and salaried workers, total (% of total employment) (modeled ILO estimate)." *World Bank Data*, World Bank, data.worldbank.org/indicator/SL.EMP.WORK.ZS.

22. "What Is Fair Trade?" *Fair Trade Campaigns*, Fair Trade Campaigns, fairtradecampaigns.org/about/faq/; "Workers' Rights & Trade Union Relations." *Fairtrade International*, Fairtrade International, www.fairtrade.net/programmes/workers-rights.html.

23. "Get Involved." *Fairtrade America*, Fairtrade America, www.fairtradeamerica.org/getinvolved/.

24. "Publications and Videos." *Habitat for Humanity*, Habitat for Humanity & Terwilliger Center for Innovation in Shelter, www.habitat.org/impact/our-work/terwilliger-center-innovation-in-shelter/publications-videos; "Dominican Republic." *Habitat for Humanity*, Habitat for Humanity, www.habitat.org/where-we-build/dominican-republic.

25. "Global Village: Volunteer abroad and immerse yourself in a new culture." *Habitat for Humanity*, Habitat for Humanity, www.habitat.org/volunteer/travel-and-build/global-village; "Long-term volunteer opportunities: We offer long-term volunteer opportunities

in the U.S. and around the world." *Habitat for Humanity*, Habitat for Humanity, www.habitat.org/volunteer/long-term-opportunities; "Global Village FAQs." *Habitat for Humanity*, Habitat for Humanity, www.habitat.org/volunteer/travel-and-build/global-village/faqs; "Our Work: How families partner with Habitat." *Habitat for Humanity*, Habitat for Humanity, www.habitat.org/volunteer/impact/our-work; "Habitat families: Who are the families who partner with Habitat for Humanity?" *Habitat for Humanity*, Habitat for Humanity, www.habitat.org/housing-help/habitat-families.

26. "Primary completion rate, total (% of relevant age group)." *World Bank Data*, World Bank, data.worldbank.org/indicator/SE.PRM.CMPT.ZS; "Lower secondary completion rate, total (% of relevant age group)." *World Bank Data*, World Bank, data.worldbank.org/indicator/SE.SEC.CMPT.LO.ZS.

27. "Literacy rate, total (% of people ages 15 and above)." *World Bank Data*, World Bank, data.worldbank.org/indicator/SE.ADT.LITR.ZS.

28. "English Opens Doors Program." *National Volunteer Center*, UNDP& Mineduc, centrodevoluntarios.cl/; "Volunteer Role & Benefits." *National Volunteer Center*, UNDP& Mineduc, centrodevoluntarios.cl/volunteer-role-benefits/.

29. "NASA: Climate Change and Global Warming." *Global Climate Change: Vital Signs of the Planet*, NASA, climate.nasa.gov/.

30. "10 Things You Can Do To Save The Rainforest." *Rainforest Foundation U.S.*, Rainforest Foundation U.S., rainforestfoundation.org/10-things-you-can-do-save-the-rainforest/; "What We Do." *Rainforest Foundation U.S.*, Rainforest Foundation U.S., rainforestfoundation.org/what-we-do/.

31. "Climate." *WWF*, World Wildlife Fund, www.worldwildlife.org/initiatives/climate; "Wildlife Conservation." *WWF*, World Wildlife Fund, www.worldwildlife.org/initiatives/wildlife-conservation; "Welcome To The Action Center." *Action Center*, World Wildlife Fund, support.worldwildlife.org/site/SPageServer?pagename=can_home&_ga=2.154398463.630396302.1536115369–850603967.1536115369; "Travel with WWF." *WWF*, World Wildlife Fund, www.worldwildlife.org/travel; "Panda Ambassador Program." *WWF*, World Wildlife Fund, support.worldwildlife.org/site/SPageServer?pagename=PandaAmbassadors; "Polar Bear Tour." *Natural Habitat Adventures*, Natural Habitat Adventures & WWF, www.nathab.com/polar-bear-tours/classic-polar-bear-expedition/.

32. "CPIA gender equality rating (1=low to 6=high)." *World Bank Data*, World Bank, data.worldbank.org/indicator/IQ.CPA.GNDR.XQ.

33. "Children out of school, female (% of female primary school age)." *World Bank Data*, World Bank, data.worldbank.org/indicator/SE.PRM.UNER.FE.ZS; "Children out of school, male (% of male primary school age)." *World Bank Data*, World Bank, data.worldbank.org/indicator/SE.PRM.UNER.MA.ZS.

34. "Join." *Malala Fund*, Malala Fund, www.malala.org/join; "About." *Malala Fund*, Malala Fund, www.malala.org/about; "Our Work." *Malala Fund*, Malala Fund, www.malala.org/gulmakai-network; Yousafzai, Malala, and Christina Lamb. *I Am Malala: The Girl Who Stood Up for Education and Was Shot By the Taliban*. First edition. New York: Little, Brown and Company, 2013.

35. "He For She." *HeForShe*, UN Women, www.heforshe.org/en; "Take Action: Education." *HeForShe*, Wayback Machine. web.archive.org/web/20180121182029/http://www.heforshe.org/en/take-action/education; "Our Mission." *HeForShe*, Wayback Machine. web.archive.org/web/20180205220745/http://www.heforshe.org/en/our-mission; "Impact." *HeForShe*, UN Women, www.heforshe.org/impact; "Take Action." *HeForShe*, UN Women, www.heforshe.org/en/action-kits.

36. "People using safely managed sanitation services (% of population)." *World Bank Data*, World Bank, data.worldbank.org/indicator/SH.STA.SMSS.ZS.

37. "Water, Sanitation and Hygiene." *UNICEF*, United Nations, www.unicef.org/wash; "Water, Sanitation and Hygiene: About WASH." *UNICEF*, United Nations, www.unicef.org/wash/3942_3952.html; "UNICEF's Strategy for Water, Sanitation and Hygiene 2016–2030." *UNICEF*, United Nations, Aug. 2016, www.unicef.org/

wash/files/WASH_Strategy_2016_2030_ At_A_Glance.PDF.

38. "Volunteering with UNICEF USA." *UNICEF USA*, United Nations, www. unicefusa.org/supporters/volunteers/- volunteering-faqs#q-what-us-fund- mission; "About UNICEF: Employment: Volunteers." *UNICEF*, United Nations, www.unicef.org/about/employ/index_ volunteers.html.

39. "Access to electricity (% of popu- lation)." *World Bank Data*, World Bank, data.worldbank.org/indicator/EG.ELC. ACCS.ZS.

40. "Our Model." *GRID Alternatives*, GRID Alternatives, gridalternatives. org/international-program/our-model; "International Program." *GRID Alter- natives*, GRID Alternatives, gridalter natives.org/what-we-do/international- program; "International Program FAQs." *GRID Alternatives*, GRID Alternatives, gridalternatives.org/ programs/international-program/FAQs?_ ga=2.31722558.1485809295.1538705917- 1947587059.1538705917; "Mission and History." *GRID Alternatives*, GRID Alter- natives, gridalternatives.org/who-we- are/mission-history; "Volunteer." *GRID Alternatives*, GRID Alternatives, grid- alternatives.org/get-involved/volunteer.

41. "Solar Spring Break." *GRID Alternatives*, GRID Alternatives, grid- alternatives.org/get-involved/solar- break; "Projects." *GRID Alternatives*, GRID Alternatives, gridalternatives. org/international-program/projects; "Bringing solar to the Shree Dumre Sec- ondary School in Palungtar, Nepal." *GRID Alternatives*, GRID Alternatives, gridalternatives.org/bringing-solar- shree-dumre-secondary-school-palnug tar-nepal.

42. Morris, Jeff. "Working in War Zones Overseas." *Transitions Abroad*, Transitions Abroad Magazine, https:// www.transitionsabroad.com/publica tions/magazine/0201/warzone.shtml.

43. Gray, Alex. "3 Charts That Explain Global Inequality." *World Economic Forum*, World Economic Forum, 20 Jan. 2016, www.weforum.org/agenda/2016/01/- 3-charts-that-explain-global-inequality/; "5 Shocking Facts about Extreme Global Inequality and How to Even It Up." *5 Shocking Facts about Extreme Global Inequality and How to Even It up | Oxfam International*, Oxfam International, www.oxfam.org/en/even-it/5-shocking- facts-about-extreme-global-inequality- and-how-even-it-davos; "Reduce Inequality within and among Countries." *United Nations Sustainable Develop- ment Goals*, United Nations, www.un.org/ sustainabledevelopment/inequality/.

44. Garcia-Navarro, Lulu. "Venezuela's Economic Implosion Exacerbates Inequal- ity." *NPR*, NPR, 7 July 2016, www.npr.org/ sections/parallels/2016/07/07/485058730/- venezuelas-economic-implosion- exacerbates-inequality; Sequera, Vivian. "Venezuelans Report Big Weight Losses in 2017 as Hunger Hits." *Reuters*, Thom- son Reuters, 21 Feb. 2018, www.reuters. com/article/us-venezuela-food/- venezuelans-report-big-weight-losses-in- 2017-as-hunger-hits-idUSKCN1G52HA; Tharoor, Ishaan. "Venezuela's Refugee Exodus Is the Biggest Crisis in the Hemi- sphere." *The Washington Post*, WP Com- pany, 23 Aug. 2018, www.washingtonpost. com/world/2018/08/23/venezuelas- refugee-exodus-is-biggest-crisis- hemisphere/?utm_term=.6916bc9ffd8f.

45. Lozada, Carlos. "Globaliza- tion Reduces Inequality in China." *The National Bureau of Economic Research*, The National Bureau of Economic Research, www.nber.org/digest/mar02/ w8611.html; Di, Fan. "Reflecting on Deng Xiaoping's 'Cat Theory' of Economic Reform." *The Epoch Times*, The Epoch Times, 18 Oct. 2016, www.theepochtimes. com/reflecting-on-deng-xiaopings-cat- theory-of-economic-reform_2173740. html.

46. "We Should Take a Lesson from the Nordic Countries on Inequality." *Institute for Policy Studies*, 18 July 2016, https://ips-dc.org/take-lesson-nordic- countries-inequality/.

47. "To Each According to His Abil- ities." *The Economist*, The Economist Newspaper, 31 May 2001, www.economist. com/node/639652.

48. Berger, Nahuel. "Theorist Eric Maskin: Globalization Is Increas- ing Inequality." *World Bank*, World Bank, 23 June 2014, www.worldbank. org/en/news/feature/2014/06/23/- theorist-eric-maskin-globalization-is- increasing-inequality; Birdsall, Nancy.

"Globalization Will Increase Inequality." *Global Policy Forum*, Global Policy Forum, 28 Feb. 2006, www.globalpolicy. org/component/content/article/218-injustice-and-inequality/46552.html; Wade, Robert Hunter. "Is Globalization Reducing Poverty and Inequality?" *International Journal of Health Services*, 1 July 2004. *Sage Journals*, doi:10.2190/G8F1--01FL-MEDW-JVG1; C.W. "Why Globalisation May Not Reduce Inequality in Poor Countries." *The Economist*, The Economist Newspaper, 3 Sept. 2014, www.economist. com/the-economist-explains/2014/09/02/-why-globalisation-may-not-reduce-inequality-in-poor-countries.

49. "Poverty and Education." *Child Fund International*, Child Fund International, www.childfund.org/poverty-and-education/; "The Benefits of Education." *Global Partnership for Education*, Global Partnership for Education, www.globalpartnership.org/education/-the-benefits-of-education.

50. Ming, Vivienne. "The Long-Term Benefits of Investing in Our Children's Future." *World Economic Forum*, World Economic Forum, 23 Nov. 2015, www. weforum.org/agenda/2015/11/the-long-term-benefits-of-investing-in-our-childrens-future/.

51. "Study Reveals Mobile Internet Access Reduces Inequality." *IT News Africa*, IT News Africa, 8 July 2016, www.itnewsafrica.com/2016/07/study-reveals-mobile-internet-access-reduces-inequality/.

52. Brown, Emma. "Can Volunteers Help Kids Read More Proficiently? New Research Says Yes." *The Washington Post*, WP Company, 28 Mar. 2015, www.washingtonpost.com/local/education/can-volunteers-help-kids-read-more-proficiently-new-research-says-yes/2015/03/28/7141c57c-c4ec-11e4-ad5c-3b8ce89f1b89_story.html?noredirect=on&utm_term=.8cf59ac67187; "Volunteers Are an Important Part of a System of Student and Learning Supports*." *UCLA School Mental Health Project*, UCLA, smhp.psych.ucla.edu/pdfdocs/vols.pdf.

Bibliography

Aaron, Henry J. "The Social Safety Net: The Gaps That Covid-19 Spotlights." *Brookings,* The Brookings Institution, 23 June 2020, https://www.brookings.edu/blog/up-front/2020/06/23/the-social-safety-net-the-gaps-that-covid-19-spotlights/.

"About." *Innovations for Poverty Action,* Innovations for Poverty Action, https://www.poverty-action.org/about.

"About." *Malala Fund,* Malala Fund, www.malala.org/about.

"About GiveWell." *GiveWell,* GiveWell, https://www.givewell.org/about.

"About the Ministry of Hope International." *Hope International,* Hope International, hope-international.us/about.php.

"About UNICEF: Employment: Volunteers." *UNICEF,* United Nations, www.unicef.org/about/employ/index_volunteers.html.

"About Us." *Food-Aid International,* Food-Aid International, food-aid.org/about-us.html.

"About Us." *Kiva,* Kiva, www.kiva.org/about.

"About Us." *VolunteerMatch,* VolunteerMatch, www.volunteermatch.org/about/.

"About Us: Frequently Asked Questions." *UNICEF USA,* UNICEF USA, https://www.unicefusa.org/about/faq.

"Abraham Maslow." *Pursuit of Happiness,* Pursuit of Happiness, www.pursuit-of-happiness.org/history-of-happiness/abraham-maslow/.

"Access to Electricity (% of Population)." *The World Bank Data,* World Bank, data.worldbank.org/indicator/EG.ELC.ACCS.ZS?view=chart.

"Africa Unplugged." *The Economist,* The Economist Newspaper, 29 Oct. 2016, www.economist.com/news/middle-east-and-africa/21709297-small-scale-solar-power-surging-ahead-africa-unplugged.

"An African Trailblazer." *The Economist,* The Economist Newspaper, 15 Sept. 2016, www.economist.com/middle-east-and-africa/2016/09/15/an-african-trailblazer.

Allers, Chris. "Why Major Donors Demand Measurement." *The Georgia Center for Nonprofits,* Apr. 2013, https://www.gcn.org/articles/Why-Major-Donors-Demand-Measurement.

"Andean Dream Royal Quinoa." *Andean Dream,* Andean Dream Quinoa Products, www.andeandream.com/.

"Application Process." *Peace Corps,* Peace Corps, www.peacecorps.gov/apply/application-process/.

"Approach & Solutions." *Engineers Without Borders USA,* Engineers Without Borders USA, www.ewb-usa.org/our-work/approach-solutions/.

"The Arab Spring: A Year Of Revolution." *NPR,* NPR, 17 Dec. 2011, www.npr.org/2011/12/17/143897126/the-arab-spring-a-year-of-revolution.

Archibold, Randal C. "Peace Corps to Scale Back in Central America." *The New York Times,* The New York Times, 21 Dec. 2011, www.nytimes.com/2011/12/22/world/americas/peace-corps-cuts-back-in-honduras-guatemala-and-el-salvador.html.

"Artisan Loomed Fabrics." *soleRebels,* soleRebels, www.solerebels.com/pages/artisan-loomed-fabrics.

"Avoid Contaminated Water during

Travel." *Centers for Disease Control and Prevention,* 22 June 2021, https://www.nc.cdc.gov/travel/page/water-disinfection.

Bailey, Jerome. "American Ideas on Volunteering Don't Resonate Worldwide." *The World from PRX,* Pri.org, 8 Mar. 2014, https://www.pri.org/stories/2014-03-08/american-ideas-volunteering-dont-resonate-worldwide.

Baillie Smith, Matt, et al. "South–South Volunteering and Development." *The Geographical Journal,* Wiley Online Library, 1 Nov. 2017, https://rgs-ibg.onlinelibrary.wiley.com/doi/full/10.1111/geoj.12243.

"Barbie Savior." *Barbie Savior,* Barbie Savior, www.barbiesavior.com/.

Barrett, David M. "Sterilizing a 'Red Infection' Congress, the CIA, and Guatemala, 1954." *Central Intelligence Agency,* Central Intelligence Agency, 3 Aug. 2011, www.cia.gov/library/center-for-the-study-of-intelligence/kent-csi/vol44no5/html/v44i5a03p.htm.

Bartley, Sylvia, and Emily Lauer-Bader. "Tapping the Power of Virtual Volunteers." *Stanford Social Innovation Review,* Stanford University, 2021, https://ssir.org/articles/entry/tapping_the_power_of_virtual_volunteers.

Bauer, Irmgard. "More Harm than Good? The Questionable Ethics of Medical Volunteering and International Student Placements." *BioMed Central,* Tropical Diseases, Travel Medicine and Vaccines, 6 Mar. 2017, https://tdtmvjournal.biomedcentral.com/articles/10.1186/s40794-017-0048-y.

Bayeh, Endalcachew. "The Role of Empowering Women and Achieving Gender Equality to the Sustainable Development of Ethiopia." *Pacific Science Review B: Humanities and Social Sciences,* vol. 2, no. 1, Jan. 2016, pp. 37–42. *ScienceDirect,* doi:10.1016/j.psrb.2016.09.013.

Beaumont, Peter. "The Truth about Twitter, Facebook and the Uprisings in the Arab World." *The Guardian,* Guardian News and Media, 25 Feb. 2011, www.theguardian.com/world/2011/feb/25/twitter-facebook-uprisings-arab-libya.

"The Benefits of Education." *Global Partnership for Education,* Global Partnership for Education, www.globalpartnership.org/education/the-benefits-of-education.

Bennett, Claire. "Common Assumptions Underlying Volunteer Travel." *ALTO Global Consulting,* https://www.altoglobalconsulting.com/altojournal/-common-assumptions-underlying-volunteer-travel.

Berger, Nahuel. "Theorist Eric Maskin: Globalization Is Increasing Inequality." *World Bank,* World Bank, 23 June 2014, www.worldbank.org/en/news/feature/2014/06/23/theorist-eric-maskin-globalization-is-increasing-inequality.

"Bethlehem Tilahun Alemu, soleRebels Founder." *soleRebels,* soleRebels, www.solerebels.com/pages/bethlehem-tilahun-alemu.

Bhagat, Ram B. "Migration and Urban Transition in India: Implications for Development." *United Nations,* United Nations, 7 Sept. 2017, www.un.org/en/development/desa/population/events/pdf/expert/27/papers/V/paper-Bhagat-final.pdf.

Bianchi, Michele, and Lindsay Hedenskog. "What Home Is For A Refugee Without One." *IKEA /U.S./EN,* Ikea, 2016, www.ikea.com/ms/en_U.S./this-is-ikea/ikea-highlights/Home-for-a-refugee/index.html.

Bills, Ron. "Poor People Don't Need Your Charity—They Need You to Listen." *World Economic Forum,* World Economic Forum, 31 Mar. 2016, www.weforum.org/agenda/2016/03/poor-people-dont-need-charity-they-need-you-to-listen/.

Birdsall, Nancy. "Globalization Will Increase Inequality." *Global Policy Forum,* Global Policy Forum, 28 Feb. 2006, www.globalpolicy.org/component/content/article/218-injustice-and-inequality/46552.html.

Blitzer, Jonathan. "The Deportees Taking Our Calls." *The New Yorker,* The New Yorker, 15 Jan. 2017, www.newyorker.com/magazine/2017/01/23/the-deportees-taking-our-calls.

"Blockchain." *Center For Global Development,* Center for Global Development, www.cgdev.org/topics/blockchain.

Bloomberg, M., and C. Pope, 2018: *Climate of Hope: How Cities, Businesses, and Citizens Can Save the Planet.* St. Martins Press, New York.

Bolterstein, Elyse. "Environmental Justice Case Study: Maquiladora Workers and Border Issues." *University of Michigan,* websites.umich.edu/~snre492/Jones/maquiladora.htm.

"BRAC • NGO Advisor." *NGO Advisor,* 2019, https://www.ngoadvisor.net/ong/brac.

"Bridging Global Infrastructure Gaps." *United Nations,* McKinsey & Company, June 2016, www.un.org/pga/71/wp-content/uploads/sites/40/2017/06/Bridging-Global-Infrastructure-Gaps-Full-report-June-2016.pdf.

"Bringing solar to the Shree Dumre Secondary School in Palungtar, Nepal." *GRID Alternatives,* GRID Alternatives, gridalternatives.org/bringing-solar-shree-dumre-secondary-school-palnugtar-nepal.

Brooks, Andrew. "The Hidden Trade in Our Second-Hand Clothes given to Charity." *The Guardian,* Guardian News and Media, 13 Feb. 2015, https://www.theguardian.com/sustainable-business/sustainable-fashion-blog/2015/feb/13/second-hand-clothes-charity-donations-africa.

Brown, Emma. "Can Volunteers Help Kids Read More Proficiently? New Research Says Yes." *The Washington Post,* WP Company, 28 Mar. 2015, www.washingtonpost.com/local/education/can-volunteers-help-kids-read-more-proficiently-new-research-says-yes/2015/03/28/7141c57c-c4ec-11e4-ad5c-3b8ce89f1b89_story.html?noredirect=on&utm_term=.8cf59ac67187.

"Carbon Footprint Calculator." *EPA,* U.S. Environmental Protection Agency, www3.epa.gov/carbon-footprint-calculator/.

Carlsen, Laura. "Under Nafta, Mexico Suffered, and the United States Felt Its Pain." *The New York Times,* The New York Times, 24 Nov. 2013, www.nytimes.com/roomfordebate/2013/11/24/what-weve-learned-from-nafta/under-nafta-mexico-suffered-and-the-united-states-felt-its-pain.

"Carnival of Love." *The Wayfarer Foundation,* Wayfarer Studios, https://www.wayfarerstudios.com/foundation/-carnival-of-love/.

Caron, Pierre-Louis. "Volunteers Map Some of the Earth's Most Remote Areas to Help Aid Workers." *VICE News,* VICE News, 15 Feb. 2016, news.vice.com/article/volunteers-map-the-planets-remote-areas-for-aid-workers; "Missing Maps." *Missing Maps,* Missing Maps, www.missingmaps.org/.

"CDC Seasonal Flu Vaccine Effectiveness Studies." *Centers for Disease Control and Prevention,* Centers for Disease Control and Prevention, 11 Mar. 2022, https://www.cdc.gov/flu/vaccines-work/effectiveness-studies.htm.

Chalab, Nadine, et al. "Charitable Giving and Intermediation." *Monash Business School,* Nov. 2015, https://www.monash.edu/business/economics/research/publications/2015/1815-charitable-giving-and-intermediation.pdf.

Chapin, Adele. "TOMS Shoe Donations Might Not Be Doing Any Good." *Racked.com,* Racked, 27 July 2015, www.racked.com/2015/7/27/9046207/toms-shoes-charity-poverty.

"Charity Navigator's Methodology." *Charity Navigator,* Charity Navigator, www.charitynavigator.org/index.cfm?bay=content.view&cpid=5593#rating.

Cheney, Catherine. "The Road to Real Results for Online Learning in Developing Countries." *Devex,* Devex, 3 Apr. 2017, www.devex.com/news/the-road-to-real-results-for-online-learning-in-developing-countries-89884.

"Child Hunger and Famine." *Save the Children,* Save the Children, www.savethechildren.org/site/c.8rKLIXMGIpI4E/b.9515661/k.6913/Hunger__Famine_Crisis.htm.

"Children out of school, female (% of female primary school age)." *World Bank Data,* World Bank, data.worldbank.org/indicator/SE.PRM.UNER.FE.ZS.

"Children out of school, male (% of male primary school age)." *World Bank Data,* World Bank, data.worldbank.org/indicator/SE.PRM.UNER.MA.ZS.

"Cholera." *Doctors Without Borders—USA,* Doctors Without Borders, www.doctorswithoutborders.org/what-we-do/medical-issues/cholera.

"Climate." *WWF,* World Wildlife Fund, www.worldwildlife.org/initiatives/climate.

"Climate Change: How Do We Know?" *Global Climate Change: Vital Signs of the Planet*, NASA, climate.nasa.gov/evidence/.

Collyns, Dan. "Bolivia Approves Highway through Amazon Biodiversity Hotspot." *The Guardian*, Guardian News and Media, 15 Aug. 2017, www.theguardian.com/environment/2017/aug/15/bolivia-approves-highway-in-amazon-biodiversity-hotspot-as-big-as-jamaica.

"Community Service-Business Volunteer." *Peace Corps*, Peace Corps, www.peacecorps.gov/volunteer/volunteer-openings/community-services-business-volunteer-5340br/.

"Connect Relief." *Connect Relief: Un Proyecto De Caras Con Causa*, Connect Relief, https://connectrelief.com/.

"Conservación de Arrecifes." *Fundemar*, Fundemar, www.fundemardr.org/copy-of-mamiferos-marinos.

"Conservation v Development along Indonesia's Longest River." *The Economist*, The Economist Newspaper, 23 Aug. 2018, www.economist.com/asia/2018/08/23/conservation-v-development-along-indonesias-longest-river.

"Cookstoves." *Envirofit*, Envirofit Smarter Living, envirofit.org/.

"Countries." *Peace Corps*, Peace Corps, www.peacecorps.gov/countries/.

"Country Information: Learn About Your Destination." *U.S. Passports & International Travel*, U.S. Department of State-Bureau of Consular Affairs, travel.state.gov/content/passports/en/country.html.

"Countryside Experience." *Carnival Cruise Line*, Carnival Cruise Line, www.carnival.com/shore-excursions/la-romana/countryside-experience-428072.

"Covid-19: Our Global Response." *Doctors Without Borders—USA*, Doctors Without Borders—USA, 6 May 2020, https://www.doctorswithoutborders.org/what-we-do/focus/covid-19.

"Covid-19: Schools for More than 168 Million Children Globally Have Been Completely Closed for Almost a Full Year, Says UNICEF." *UNICEF*, 2 Mar. 2021, https://www.unicef.org/press-releases/-schools-more-168-million-children-globally-have-been-completely-closed.

"Covid-19 to Add as Many as 150 Million Extreme Poor by 2021." *The World Bank*, 7 Oct. 2020, https://www.worldbank.org/en/news/press-release/2020/10/07/-covid-19-to-add-as-many-as-150-million-extreme-poor-by-2021.

"Covid-19 Vaccine Effectiveness and Safety." *Centers for Disease Control and Prevention*, Centers for Disease Control and Prevention, 5 May 2022, https://www.cdc.gov/mmwr/covid19_vaccine_safety.html.

"CPIA gender equality rating (1=low to 6=high)." *World Bank Data*, World Bank, data.worldbank.org/indicator/IQ.CPA.GNDR.XQ.

"Cuba." *UNESCO*, UNESCO, en.unesco.org/countries/cuba.

C.W. "Why Globalisation May Not Reduce Inequality in Poor Countries." *The Economist*, The Economist Newspaper, 3 Sept. 2014, www.economist.com/-the-economist-explains/2014/09/02/-why-globalisation-may-not-reduce-inequality-in-poor-countries.

Danise, Amy, and Jason Metz. "Best Covid-19 Travel Insurance Plans of May 2022." *Forbes Advisor*, Forbes Magazine, 12 May 2022, https://www.forbes.com/advisor/travel-insurance/best-pandemic-travel-insurance/.

Darlington, Shasta, and Patrick Gillespie. "Mexican Farmer's Daughter: NAFTA Destroyed Us." *CNN Business*, Cable News Network, 9 Feb. 2017, money.cnn.com/2017/02/09/news/economy/nafta-farming-mexico-us-corn-jobs/index.html.

Das, Lawly, and Rajesh Raut. "Impact of Changes in Service Sector in India in Shaping the Future of Business & Society." *Procedia Economics and Finance*, vol. 11, 2014, pp. 795–803. *ScienceDirect*, doi:10.1016/s2212-5671(14)00243-3.

de Leon, Riley. "Zipline Takes Flight in Ghana, Making It the World's Largest Drone-Delivery Network." *CNBC*, CNBC, 24 Apr. 2019, www.cnbc.com/2019/04/24/with-ghana-expansion-ziplines-medical-drones-now-reach-22m-people.html.

Di, Fan. "Reflecting on Deng Xiaoping's 'Cat Theory' of Economic Reform." *The Epoch Times*, The Epoch Times, 18 Oct. 2016, www.theepochtimes.com/reflecting-on-deng-xiaopings-cat-theory-of-economic-reform_2173740. html.

"The Difference That Fairtrade Makes." *Fairtrade.org,* Fairtrade Foundation, https://www.fairtrade.org.uk/what-is-fairtrade/the-impact-of-our-work/the-difference-that-fairtrade-makes/.

"Dominican Republic." *Habitat for Humanity,* Habitat for Humanity, www.habitat.org/where-we-build/-dominican-republic.

Dominick, Judy Wu. "Unpacking Operation Christmas Child." *Lifereconsidered.com,* 8 Nov. 2015, lifereconsidered.com/2015/11/08/unpacking-operation-christmas-child/.

Dorcadie, Mathilde. "Brazil: Citizen Watchdogs Mobilise against Corruption." *Equal Times,* 27 July 2016, www.equaltimes.org/brazil-citizen-watchdogs-mobilise?lang=en#.WzIZm6dKjIU.

Dortonne, Nathalie. "The Dangers of Poverty Porn." *CNN,* 8 Dec. 2016, www.cnn.com/2016/12/08/health/poverty-porn-danger-feat/index.html.

"Drinking-Water." *World Health Organization,* World Health Organization, 7 Feb. 2018, www.who.int/news-room/-fact-sheets/detail/drinking-water.

Dubay, Alicia. "Voluntourism: The Good and the Bad." *World Vision Canada,* 21 June 2021, https://www.worldvision.ca/stories/voluntourism-the-good-and-the-bad.

El Bardicy, Mohamad. "Protests in Bolivia against Plans for Tipnis Rainforest Highway." *Bolivia News | Al Jazeera,* 14 Aug. 2017, www.aljazeera.com/video/news/2017/08/protests-bolivia-renewed-plans-tipnis-rainforest-highway-170814055713885.html.

Ellis, S, and S Barakat. "From relief to development: the long-term effects of 'temporary' accommodation on refugees and displaced persons in the Republic of Croatia." *Disasters* vol. 20,2 (1996): 111–24. doi:10.1111/j.1467–7717.1996.tb00521.x

Engels, Jorge, and Stefano Pozzebon. "Violence in Eastern Colombia Has Left 130 Dead This Year, UN and Catholic Church Say." *CNN,* 30 Mar. 2022, https://www.cnn.com/2022/03/30/americas/colombia-violence-un-report-intl-latam/index.html.

"English Opens Doors Program." *National Volunteer Center,* UNDP& Mineduc, centrodevoluntarios.cl/.

Ernest, Emmalea. "Heat Effects on Vegetable and Fruit Crops." *Cooperative Extension in Delaware,* University of Delaware, 24 July 2015, extension.udel.edu/weeklycropupdate/?p=8354.

"Essential Requirements." *Doctors Without Borders—USA,* Doctors Without Borders, www.doctorswithoutborders.org/careers/work-field/general-requirements.

Essossinam Ali, Aklesso Y.G. Egbendewe, Tahirou Abdoulaye & Daniel B. Sarpong (2020) Willingness to pay for weather index-based insurance in semi-subsistence agriculture: evidence from northern Togo, *Climate Policy,* 20:5,534–547, DOI: 10.1080/1469 3062.2020.1745742

"Ethical Shoes Made in Africa." *soleRebels,* soleRebels, www.solerebels.com/pages/-our-ethos.

Eulich, Whitney. "Months after Maria, Puerto Ricans Take Recovery into Their Own Hands." *The Christian Science Monitor,* 7 May 2018, www.csmonitor.com/USA/Society/2018/0507/Months-after-Maria-Puerto-Ricans-take-recovery-into-theirown-hands.

"Extreme Makeover: Home Edition." *IMDb,* IMDb.com, www.imdb.com/title/tt0388595/.

"Facts: A blanket around the Earth." *Global Climate Change: Vital Signs of the Planet,* NASA, climate.nasa.gov/causes/.

"Facts: How climate is changing." *Global Climate Change: Vital Signs of the Planet,* NASA, climate.nasa.gov/effects/.

Fawkes, Chris. "Is Climate Change Making Hurricanes Worse?" *BBC News,* BBC, 30 Dec. 2017, www.bbc.com/news/-world-us-canada-42251921.

Fernández, Pablo Armando. "Casa-Estudio De José Fuster." *Havana City Guide,* Lahabana.com, www.lahabana.com/guide/casa-estudio-de-jose-fuster/.

Field, Anne. "Turning Coal Miners Into Coders—And Preventing A Brain Drain." *Forbes,* 30 Jan. 2017, www.forbes.com/sites/annefield/2017/01/30/turning-coal-miners-into-coders-and-preventing-a-brain-drain/#1c0e6da6f81d.

"5 Shocking Facts about Extreme Global Inequality and How to Even It Up." *5 Shocking Facts about Extreme Global*

Inequality and How to Even It up | *Oxfam International,* Oxfam International, www.oxfam.org/en/even-it/5-shocking-facts-about-extreme-global-inequality-and-how-even-it-davos.

"Follow-up and Monitoring." *Pure Water for the World,* Pure Water for the World, purewaterfortheworld.org/solutions/follow-up-and-monitoring/.

"Foodborne Illness: Especially Dangerous for the Vulnerable." *U.S. Food and Drug Administration,* 4 June 2014, https://www.fda.gov/consumers/consumer-updates/foodborne-illness-especially-dangerous-vulnerable.

Ford, Robert, and Mark Ward. "Assad's Syria Plays Dirty with U.S. Humanitarian Aid." *The Hill,* The Hill, 12 Feb. 2018, thehill.com/opinion/national-security/-373449-assads-syria-plays-dirty-with-us-humanitarian-aid.

"Frac's New Online Dashboard Reveals a Shocking Number of Households Don't Have Enough to Eat during the Pandemic." *Food Research & Action Center,* Food Research & Action Center, 15 July 2021, https://frac.org/news/fracs-new-online-dashboard-reveals-a-shocking-number-of-households-dont-have-enough-to-eat-during-the-pandemic.

Freedman, John. "From Tragedy, Opportunity—A New Beginning for Haiti and the Dominican Republic." *The Permanente Journal,* vol. 14, no. 3, 2010, pp. 77–79. *PMC-NCBI,* www.ncbi.nlm.nih.gov/pmc/articles/PMC2937853/.

"Frequently Asked Questions Related To Cuba." *U.S. Department of the Treasury,* U.S. Department of the Treasury Office of Foreign Assets Control, 8 Nov. 2017, www.treasury.gov/resource-center/sanctions/Programs/Documents/cuba_faqs_new.pdf.

Fujiwara, Lyla, and National Journal. "How I Used My Computer-Science Degree in the Peace Corps While Serving in Rural Africa." *The Atlantic,* Atlantic Media Company, 25 Apr. 2014, www.theatlantic.com/politics/archive/2014/04/how-i-used-my-computer-science-degree-in-the-peace-corps-while-serving-in-rural-africa/430860/.

Galietta, Wendy. "I Saw a Lot of Women Who Died during Delivery, but I Did Not Know How to Help Them." *The Washington Post,* WP Company, 24 July 2017, www.washingtonpost.com/news/in-sight/wp/2017/07/24/i-saw-a-lot-of-women-who-died-during-delivery-but-i-did-not-know-how-to-help-them/?utm_term=.3ff5657f6f49.

Garcia-Navarro, Lulu. "Venezuela's Economic Implosion Exacerbates Inequality." *NPR,* NPR, 7 July 2016, www.npr.org/sections/parallels/2016/07/07/485058730/venezuelas-economic-implosion-exacerbates-inequality.

"Get Involved." *Fairtrade America,* Fairtrade America, www.fairtradeamerica.org/get involved/.

Gharib, Malaka. "Humanitarian Aid Is 'Broken,' Says Former U.N. Official." *NPR,* 22 June 2017, https://www.npr.org/sections/goatsandsoda/2017/06/22/533639073/what-s-wrong-with-humanitarian-aid.

Gharib, Malaka. "The Pandemic Changed the World of 'Voluntourism.' Some Folks like the New Way Better." *NPR,* 15 July 2021, https://www.npr.org/sections/goatsandsoda/2021/07/15/1009911082/the-pandemic-changed-the-world-of-voluntourism-some-folks-like-the-new-way-bette.

Gharib, Malaka. "Volunteering Abroad? Read This Before You Post That Selfie." *NPR,* 26 Nov. 2017, www.npr.org/sections/goatsandsoda/2017/11/26/565694874/volunteering-abroad-read-this-before-you-post-that-selfie.

Giustra, Frank. "Without Long-Term Investment, Food Aid for Haiti Risks Being a Band-Aid." *Philanthropy News Digest,* Candid, 9 Sept. 2021, https://philanthropynewsdigest.org/commentary-and-opinion/-without-long-term-investment-food-aid-for-haiti-risks-being-a-band-aid.

Glaser, Robert, et al. "What Does It Take to Create a Market?" *Yale Insights,* Yale School of Management, 23 Oct. 2007, insights.som.yale.edu/insights/what-does-it-take-to-create-market.

"Global Village FAQs." *Habitat for Humanity,* Habitat for Humanity, www.habitat.org/volunteer/travel-and-build/-global-village/faqs.

"Global Village: Volunteer abroad and immerse yourself in a new culture." *Habitat for Humanity,* Habitat for Humanity, www.habitat.org/

volunteer/travel-and-build/global-village.

"Global Warming and Hurricanes." *GFDL*, NOAA, 8 Feb. 2019, www.gfdl.noaa.gov/-global-warming-and-hurricanes/.

"GNI per Capita, Atlas Method (Current U.S.$)." *World Bank Data*, The World Bank, data.worldbank.org/indicator/NY.GNP.PCAP.CD?locations=GT-XN.

"Goal 1 Targets." *UNDP*, United Nations, www.undp.org/content/undp/en/home/-sustainable-development-goals/goal-1-no-poverty/targets/.

"Goal 2: End Hunger, Achieve Food Security and Improved Nutrition and Promote Sustainable Agriculture." *SDG Goals*, United Nations, unstats.un.org/sdgs/report/2016/goal-02/.

Grant, Will. "How Cuba and Puerto Rico Responded to Their Hurricanes." *BBC News*, BBC, 23 Sept. 2017, www.bbc.com/news/world-us-canada-41371793.

Gray, Alex. "3 Charts That Explain Global Inequality." *World Economic Forum*, World Economic Forum, 20 Jan. 2016, www.weforum.org/agenda/2016/01/3-charts-that-explain-global-inequality/.

Green, Lloyd. "Why More Europeans Are Volunteering in Asia." *GoAbroad.com*, GoAbroad.com, 14 June 2017, www.goabroad.com/articles/volunteer-abroad/why-more-europeans-are-volunteering-in-asia.

Grimm, Robert et al. "Volunteer Growth Since 1974: A Review of Trends Since 1974." *Nationalservice.gov*, Corporation for National & Community Service, Dec. 2006, www.nationalservice.gov/pdf/06_1203_volunteer_growth.pdf.

"Guatemala." *Dol.gov*, U.S. Department of Labor, www.dol.gov/ilab/reports/child-labor/findings/tda2007/guatemala.pdf.

"Guinea Worm Eradication Program." *The Carter Center*, The Carter Center, www.cartercenter.org/health/guinea_worm/index.html.

"Habitat families: Who are the families who partner with Habitat for Humanity?" *Habitat for Humanity*, Habitat for Humanity, www.habitat.org/housing-help/habitat-families.

"Half the World's Refugee Children Not in School, Un Agency Finds." *UN News*, United Nations, 29 Aug. 2018, https://news.un.org/en/story/2018/08/1017962.

Hall, A, et al. "Intensity of Reinfection with Ascaris Lumbricoides and Its Implications for Parasite Control." *National Institute of Health National Library of Medicine National Center for Biotechnology Information*, The Lancet, 23 May 1992, https://pubmed.ncbi.nlm.nih.gov/1349668/.

Hall, Jenny. "Click Here to Support The Blueboys Christmas Appeal Organised by Jenny Hall." *Gofundme.com*, Go Fund Me, www.gofundme.com/theblueboysrescuechristmas.

Hall, Jenny. *Instagram*, The Blueboys, https://www.instagram.com/the_blueboys/?hl=en.

"Hands On Chocolate Experience At Chocal." *Carnival Cruise Line*, Carnival Cruise Line, www.carnival.com/shore-excursions/amber-cove/hands-on-chocolate-experience-at-chocal-445106.

Hanna, Jason, and Steve Almasy. "Hurricane Irma Becomes Category 5 Storm Again." *CNN*, Cable News Network, 8 Sept. 2017, www.cnn.com/2017/09/08/us/hurricane-irma-caribbean-florida/index.html.

Hawkes, Logan. "Summer Heat Poses Serious Problem for Cattle." *Southwest Farm Press*, Informa PLC, 13 July 2012, www.southwestfarmpress.com/livestock/summer-heat-poses-serious-problem-cattle.

"He For She." *HeForShe*, UN Women, www.heforshe.org/en.

Heathcote, Chris. "Forecasting Infrastructure Investment Needs for 50 Countries, 7 Sectors through 2040." *World Bank*, World Bank, 10 Aug. 2017, blogs.worldbank.org/ppps/forecasting-infrastructure-investment-needs-50-countries-7-sectors-through-2040.

Hellerstein, Erica. "A Half-Century Ago, Gail Phares Went to Nicaragua. She Came Back a Radical." *INDY Week*, INDY Week, 22 Mar. 2017, www.indyweek.com/indyweek/a-half-century-ago-gail-phares-went-to-nicaragua-she-came-back-a-radical/Content?oid=5618612.

Hellin, Jon, et al. "Maize Diversity, Market Access, and Poverty Reduction in the Western Highlands of Guatemala." *BioOne Complete*, International Mountain Society, 1 May 2017, https://bioone.org/journals/mountain-research-and-development/volume-37/issue-2/MRD-JOURNAL-D-16-

00065.1/Maize-Diversity-Market-Access-and-Poverty-Reduction-in-the-Western/10.1659/MRD-JOURNAL-D-16-00065.1.full.

"Home-Australian Volunteers Program." *Australian Volunteers,* Australian Volunteers for International Development / Australian Aid, www.australian volunteers.com/.

"How a Shampoo Bottle Is Saving Young Lives." *The Economist,* The Economist Newspaper, 6 Sept. 2018, www.economist.com/science-and-technology/2018/09/08/how-a-shampoo-bottle-is-saving-young-lives.

"How to Protect Yourself & Others." *Centers for Disease Control and Prevention,* Centers for Disease Control and Prevention, 25 Feb. 2022, https://www.cdc.gov/coronavirus/2019-ncov/prevent-getting-sick/prevention.html.

"How to Tell That Your Volunteer Program Is Legitimate, and Not a Scam." *EveryNurse.org,* 15 Mar. 2020, https://everynurse.org/volunteer-program-legitimate/.

"How We Work to End Hunger." *Feeding America,* Feeding America, www.feedingamerica.org/our-work/our-approach/.

Howell, Brian M. "Filling Millions of Shoe Boxes of Toys for Poor Kids Seems like a Great Idea. Here's Why It's Not." *The Washington Post,* WP Company, 20 Dec. 2017, www.washingtonpost.com/news/acts-of-faith/wp/2017/12/20/filling-millions-of-shoe-boxes-of-toys-for-poor-kids-seems-like-a-great-idea-heres-why-its-not/?utm_term=.82a8fab24e6d.

Hsiang, Solomon, and Trevor Houser. "Don't Let Puerto Rico Fall Into an Economic Abyss." *The New York Times,* The New York Times, 29 Sept. 2017, www.nytimes.com/2017/09/29/opinion/-puerto-rico-hurricane-maria.html.

"Human Mobility." *Casa De Los Amigos,* Casa De Los Amigos, www.casadelos amigos.org/en/migrationandasylum/.

"Impact." *HeForShe,* UN Women, www.heforshe.org/impact.

"ImpactMatters Methodology." *Impact-Matters,* ImpactMatters, https://www.impactmatters.org/methodology/index.html.

"In Rwanda, His Drones Are Saving Lives." *YouTube,* uploaded by Bloomberg, 16 Aug 2018, https://www.youtube.com/watch?v=NBdB3G9Qvqs&list=WL&index=4&t=0s.

"Infant mortality." *Doctors Without Borders—Southern Africa,* Doctors Without Borders, www.msf.org.za/crisis-response/infant-mortality.

"International Program." *GRID Alternatives,* GRID Alternatives, gridalter natives.org/what-we-do/international-program.

"International Program FAQs." *GRID Alternatives,* GRID Alternatives, gridalternatives.org/programs/international-program/FAQs?_ga=2.3172 2558.1485809295.1538705917-194758 7059.1538705917.

"IPA's 2025 Strategic Ambition." *Innovations for Poverty Action,* Innovations for Poverty Action, https://www.poverty-action.org/about/strategic-ambit ion.

"Iran Travel Advisory." *U.S. Department of State,* 2 Aug. 2021, https://travel.state.gov/content/travel/en/traveladvisories/traveladvisories/iran-travel-advisory.html.

"IVHQ Social Network." *International Volunteer HQ,* https://www.volunteer hq.org/ivhq-social-network/.

Iwuoha, John-Paul. "SoleRebels—A Successful African Footwear Brand Made from Waste and Recycled Materials." *Smallstarter,* Smallstarter, 14 Mar. 2013, www.smallstarter.com/get-inspired/solerebels/.

Jagannathan, Sheila. "#9 From 2017: Virtual Reality—The Future of Immersive Learning for Development." *The World Bank Blog,* The World Bank, 14 Dec. 2017, blogs.worldbank.org/publicsphere/9-2017-virtual-reality-future-immersive-learning-develop ment.

Jhingan, Rajit, et al. "Coping with Shortage of Ventilators in COVID-19 Pandemic: Indian Context and Exploring Effective Options in Countries with Limited Healthcare Resources." *Clinmed Journals International Library,* International Archives of Public Health and Community Medicine, 25 May 2020, https://www.clinmedjournals.org/articles/iaphcm/international-archives-of-public-health-and-com munity-medicine-iaphcm-4-043. php?jid=iaphcm.

Johnson, Meghan. "Pros and Cons of Short-Term Volunteer Programs." *Go Overseas,* 5 Mar. 2013, https://www. gooverseas.com/blog/pros-and-cons-short-term-volunteer-opportunities.

"Join." *Malala Fund,* Malala Fund, www. malala.org/join.

"Jordan: Healing Patients Wounded by Conflicts across the Middle East." *Doctors Without Borders,* Wayback Machine. 04 Jan 2018, web.archive. org/web/20180108124925/http://www. doctorswithoutborders.org/article/-jordan-healing-patients-wounded-conflicts-across-middle-east.

"Jose Fuster: Painter-Sculptor." *Havana Club,* Havana Club, havana-club.com/-en-ww/havana-cultura/josé-fuster.

Kahn, Carrie. "As 'Voluntourism' Explodes In Popularity, Who's It Helping Most?" *NPR,* NPR, 31 July 2014, www.npr.org/sections/goatsandsoda/2014/07/31/336600290/as-volunteerism-explodes-in-popularity-whos-it-helping-most.

Kelly, Annie. "Money 'Wasted' on Water Projects in Africa." *The Guardian,* Guardian News and Media, 26 Mar. 2009, www.theguardian.com/society/katineblog/2009/mar/26/water-projects-wasted-money.

Klapper, Leora, et al. *Income Biggest Barrier to Banking in Developing Countries.* Gallup, 19 Dec. 2012, https:// news.gallup.com/poll/159380/income-biggest-barrier-banking-developing-countries.aspx.

Kostopoulos, Ioannis, et al. "Volunteer Tourism as a Transformative Experience: A Mixed Methods Empirical Study." *SAGE Journals,* Journal of Travel Research, 8 Apr. 2020, https:// journals.sagepub.com/doi/full/10. 1177/0047287520913630.

Lakhani, Nina. "The Hunger Industry: Does Charity Put a Band-Aid on American Inequality?" *The Guardian,* Guardian News and Media, 28 Apr. 2021, https://www.theguardian. com/environment/2021/apr/28/our-unequal-earth-food-insecurity-aid-corporate.

"Latin Lessons: What Can We Learn from the World's Most Ambitious."

The Independent, Independent Digital News and Media, 7 Nov. 2010, www.independent.co.uk/news/world/americas/latin-lessons-what-can-we-learn-from-the-worldrsquos-most-ambitious-literacy-campaign-2124433. html.

"Lebanon: Huge Cost of Inaction in Trash Crisis." *Human Rights Watch,* 9 June 2020, https://www.hrw.org/news/2020/06/09/lebanon-huge-cost-inaction -trash-crisis.

Leghtas, Izza. "Insecure Future: Deportations and Lack of Legal Work for Refugees in Turkey." *Refugees International,* 19 Sept. 2019, https:// www.refugeesinternational.org/reports/2019/9/18/insecure-future-deportations-and-lack-of-legal-work-for-refugees-in-turkey.

Lentfer, Jennifer. "Charities Want to Make an Impact. But Poverty Porn Is Not the Way." *The Guardian,* Guardian News and Media, 12 Jan. 2018, www.theguardian.com/voluntary-sector-network/2018/jan/12/charities-stop-poverty-porn-fundraising-ed-sheeran-comic-relief.

Licon, Adriana Gomez, and Freddy Cuevas. "Peace Corps Pullout a New Blow to Honduras." *NBCNews.com,* NBCUniversal News Group, 18 Jan. 2012, https:// www.nbcnews.com/id/wbna46044373.

"Literacy rate, total (% of people ages 15 and above)." *World Bank Data,* World Bank, data.worldbank.org/indicator/SE.ADT.LITR.ZS.

Loh, Lawrence. "Opinion: Volunteering Abroad Is Popular and Problematic. Let's Fix It." *NPR,* 12 Sept. 2019, https://www.npr.org/sections/goatsandsoda/2019/09/12/754347433/-volunteering-abroad-is-popular-and-problematic-lets-fix-it.

"Long-term volunteer opportunities: We offer long-term volunteer opportunities in the U.S. and around the world." *Habitat for Humanity,* Habitat for Humanity, www.habitat.org/volunteer/long-term-opportunities.

Lough, Benjamin J. "International Volunteering from the United States between 2004 and 2012." *Center for Social Development George Warren Brown School of Social Work,* Washington University in St. Louis, June 2013, web.archive.org/

web/20170124173359/https://csd.wustl.
edu/Publications/Documents/RB13-14.
pdf.

"Low Income Housing Institute." *Low Income Housing Institute,* Low Income Housing Institute Seattle, lihi.org/.

"Lower secondary completion rate, total (% of relevant age group)." *World Bank Data,* World Bank, data.worldbank.org/indicator/SE.SEC.CMPT.LO.ZS.

Lozada, Carlos. "Globalization Reduces Inequality in China." *The National Bureau of Economic Research,* The National Bureau of Economic Research, www.nber.org/digest/mar02/w8611.html.

"Malnutrition." *World Health Organization,* World Health Organization, 9 June 2021, https://www.who.int/news-room/fact-sheets/detail/malnutrition.

"Maternal and Child Health." *Doctors Without Borders—Canada,* Doctors Without Borders, www.doctorswithoutborders.ca./issues/maternal-and-child-health.

"Maternal mortality ratio (modeled estimate, per 100,000 live births)." *World Bank Data,* World Bank, data.worldbank.org/indicator/SH.STA.MMRT?end=2015&start=2015&view=bar.

Mayo Clinic Staff. "How Well Do Face Masks Protect against Covid-19?" *Mayo Clinic,* Mayo Foundation for Medical Education and Research, 1 Mar. 2022, https://www.mayoclinic.org/diseases-conditions/coronavirus/in-depth/coronavirus-mask/art-20485449.

McClane, Dave. "Fusterlandia: Havana's Ceramic Fantasy World." *Man Vs. Globe,* Man Vs. Globe Travel Blog, 14 May 2017, www.manvsglobe.com/fusterlandia-havana/.

Medez, Rich. "MIT Researchers Say Time Spent Indoors Increases Risk of Covid at 6 Feet or 60 Feet in New Study Challenging Social Distancing Policies." *CNBC,* CNBC, 27 Apr. 2021, https://www.cnbc.com/2021/04/23/mit-researchers-say-youre-no-safer-from-covid-indoors-at-6-feet-or-60-feet-in-new-study.html.

"Mental health." *Doctors Without Borders—USA,* Doctors Without Borders, www.doctorswithoutborders.org/what-we-do/medical-issues/mental-health.

Milanovic, Nikola. "The Poor as Consumers." *The Stanford Progressive,* Stanford University, May 2010, web.stanford.edu/group/progressive/cgi-bin/?p=535.

Miller, Talea. "Lourdes's Dream: To Show the World a Woman's Worth." *Kiva Blog Posts,* Kiva, www.kiva.org/blog/lourdess-dream-to-show-the-world-a-womans-worth.

Ming, Vivienne. "The Long-Term Benefits of Investing in Our Children's Future." *World Economic Forum,* World Economic Forum, 23 Nov. 2015, www.weforum.org/agenda/2015/11/the-long-term-benefits-of-investing-in-our-childrens-future/.

"Mission and History." *GRID Alternatives,* GRID Alternatives, gridalternatives.org/who-we-are/mission-history.

Mitchell, Amy, et al. "The Role of Social Media in the Arab Uprisings." *Pew Research Center's Journalism Project,* Pew Research Center, 28 Nov. 2012, www.journalism.org/2012/11/28/role-social-media-arab-uprisings/.

"Mobile Phones Are Transforming Africa." *The Economist,* The Economist Newspaper, 10 Dec. 2016, www.economist.com/news/middle-east-and-africa/21711511-mobile-phones-are-transforming-africa-where-they-can-get-signal-mobile-phones.

"Module 8: The Significant Harm of Worst Practices." *Unite for Sight,* Unite for Sight, www.uniteforsight.org/global-health-course/module8.

Montgomery, Mike. "What Entrepreneurs Can Learn From The Philanthropic Struggles Of TOMS Shoes." *Forbes,* Forbes Magazine, 28 Apr. 2015, www.forbes.com/sites/mikemontgomery/2015/04/28/how-entrepreneurs-can-avoid-the-philanthropy-pitfalls/#19f2b6981c38.

"Months after Maria, Puerto Ricans Take Recovery into Their Own Hands." *The Christian Science Monitor,* The Christian Science Monitor, 7 May 2018, www.csmonitor.com/USA/Society/2018/0507/Months-after-Maria-Puerto-Ricans-take-recovery-into-their-own-hands.

Moore, Emma. "You Don't Know What's Best: The Overuse of Poverty Porn." *Brown Political Review,* Brown University, 28 Oct. 2013, https://brownpoliticalreview.org/2013/10/you-dont-know-whats-best-the-overuse-of-poverty-porn/.

Morris, Jeff. "Working in War Zones Overseas." *Transitions Abroad,* Transitions Abroad Magazine, https://www.transitionsabroad.com/publications/magazine/0201/warzone.shtml.

"Mortality rate, neonatal (per 1,000 live births)." *World Bank Data,* World Bank, data.worldbank.org/indicator/SH.DYN.NMRT.

Murphy, Tom. "Do TOMS Shoes Harm Local Shoe Sellers?" *Humanosphere,* Humanosphere, 16 Sept. 2014, www.humanosphere.org/social-business/2014/09/toms-shoes-harm-local-shoe-sellers/.

"NASA: Climate Change and Global Warming." *Global Climate Change: Vital Signs of the Planet,* NASA, climate.nasa.gov/.

"Neglected Tropical Diseases." *National Institute of Allergy and Infectious Diseases,* U.S. Department of Health and Human Services, 11 July 2016, https://www.niaid.nih.gov/research/neglected-tropical-diseases.

"Nicaragua: Ortega Scraps Pension Reforms after Deadly Protests." *News | Al Jazeera,* Al Jazeera, 23 Apr. 2018, https://www.aljazeera.com/news/2018/4/23/nicaragua-ortega-scraps-pension-reforms-after-deadly-protests

Nichols, Austin, and Zachary J McDade. "Long-Term Unemployment and Poverty Produce a Vicious Cycle." *Urban Wire,* Urban Institute, 17 Sept. 2013, www.urban.org/urban-wire/long-term-unemployment-and-poverty-produce-vicious-cycle.

"Nobody Spends Enough on Mental Health." *The Economist,* The Economist Newspaper, 26 Apr. 2018, www.economist.com/special-report/2018/04/26/nobody-spends-enough-on-mental-health.

Nolen, Stephanie. "Getting Home in Rio: How Brazilians Rely on Crowdsourcing to Avoid Gun Battles on the Streets." *The Globe and Mail,* The Globe and Mail, 6 Sept. 2018, www.theglobeandmail.com/world/article-rios-killer-apps-how-brazilians-rely-on-crowdsourcing-to-stay-safe/.

"North Korea (Democratic People's Republic of Korea) Travel Advisory." *U.S. Department of State,* 28 June 2021, https://travel.state.gov/content/travel/en/traveladvisories/traveladvisories/-north-korea-travel-advisory.html.

"The Number of People Forced to Flee Their Homes Due to Violence and Persecution Is Unprecedented in Human History. Of the 65 Million Currently Displaced, 20 Million Are Living Outside of Their Countries as Refugees." *Refugee Community Partnership,* Refugee Community Partnership, refugeecommunitypartnership.org/.

"On the Move." *The Economist,* The Economist Newspaper, 16 Apr. 2016, www.economist.com/news/special-report/-21696790-much-hangs-mobile-money-move.

"1 NO POVERTY: End Poverty in all its forms everywhere." *Data Topics,* World Bank Group, datatopics.worldbank.org/sdgatlas/SDG-01-no-poverty.html.

"The One-for-One Business Model: Avoiding Unintended Consequences." *Knowledge@Wharton,* The Wharton School University of Pennsylvania, 16 Feb. 2015, https://knowledge.wharton.upenn.edu/article/one-one-business-model-social-impact-avoiding-unintended-consequences/.

"Organic Chocolate Bars, Truffles & Coconut Clusters." *Alter Eco,* Alter Eco, www.alterecofoods.com/.

Orozco, Manuel, and Marcela Valdivia. "Educational Challenges in Guatemala and Consequences for Human Capital and Development." *Thedialogue.org,* The Dialogue, Feb. 2017, www.thedialogue.org/wp-content/uploads/2017/02/Educational-Challenges-in-Guatemala-and-Consequences-for-Human-Capital-and-Development-1.pdf.

"Our Finances: Efficient and Verified." *UNICEF USA,* UNICEF USA, www.unicefusa.org/about/finances.

"Our Mission." *HeForShe,* Wayback Machine. web.archive.org/web/20180205220745/http://www.heforshe.org/en/our-mission.

"Our Model." *GRID Alternatives,* GRID Alternatives, gridalternatives.org/-international-program/our-model.

"Our Results." *Pure Water for the World,* Pure Water for the World, purewaterfortheworld.org/our-results/.

"Our Work." *Malala Fund,* Malala Fund, www.malala.org/gulmakai-network.

"Our Work: How families partner with Habitat." *Habitat for Humanity,* Habitat for Humanity, www.habitat.org/volunteer/impact/our-work.

"Panda Ambassador Program." *WWF,* World Wildlife Fund, support.worldwildlife.org/site/SPageServer?pagename=PandaAmbassadors.

Peace Corps. "These 3 Volunteers Are Working to Feed the Future." *Peace Corps,* Peace Corps, 25 July 2013, www.peacecorps.gov/stories/photo-essay-how-pcvs-are-feeding-the-future/.

Peluffo, Nicoletta. "Breaking the 'Cultural Bubble' through the Immersive Model." *12th International Conference Innovation in Language Learning.* 2019.

"People using safely managed sanitation services (% of population)." *World Bank Data,* World Bank, data.worldbank.org/indicator/SH.STA.SMSS.ZS.

Pisa, Michael. "Reassessing Expectations for Blockchain and Development." *Center For Global Development,* Center for Global Development, 17 May 2018, www.cgdev.org/publication/reassessing-expectations-blockchain-and-development-cost-complexity.

"Players for Pits." *Playersforpits,* Players for Pits, www.playersforpits.com/.

"Polar Bear Tour." *Natural Habitat Adventures,* Natural Habitat Adventures & WWF, www.nathab.com/polar-bear-tours/classic-polar-bear-expedition/.

Popham, Gabriel. "Boom in 'Voluntourism' Sparks Concerns over Whether the Industry Is Doing Good." *Reuters,* Thomson Reuters, 29 June 2015, www.reuters.com/article/us-travel-volunteers-charities/boom-in-voluntourism-sparks-concerns-over-whether-the-industry-is-doing-good-idUSKCN0P91AX20150629.

Porter, Eduardo. "In Health Care, Republicans Could Learn From Rwanda." *The New York Times,* The New York Times, 18 July 2017, www.nytimes.com/2017/07/18/business/economy/senate-obamacare-rwanda.html.

"Poverty and Education." *Child Fund International,* Child Fund International, www.childfund.org/poverty-and-education/.

"Poverty & Inequality Portal." *World Bank,* World Bank, https://pip.worldbank.org/home.

"Poverty Facts: The Population of Poverty USA." *Poverty USA,* Poverty USA, povertyusa.org/facts.

"Poverty headcount ratio at $1.90 a day (2011 PPP) (% of population)." *The World Bank Data,* World Bank, data.worldbank.org/indicator/SI.POV.DDAY?view=chart.

Poverty Reduction in the Western Highlands of Guatemala." *BioOne Complete,* International Mountain Society, 1 May 2017, https://bioone.org/journals/-mountain-research-and-development/-volume-37/issue-2/MRD-JOURNAL-D-16-00065.1/Maize-Diversity-Market-Access-and-Poverty-Reduction-in-the-Western/10.1659/MRD-JOURNAL-D-16-00065.1.full.

"Pregnant women receiving prenatal care (%)." *The World Bank Data,* World Bank, data.worldbank.org/indicator/SH.STA.ANVC.ZS?view=chart.

"Preparation and Training." *Peace Corps,* Peace Corps, www.peacecorps.gov/volunteer/preparation-and-training/.

"Prevalence of Undernourishment (% of Population)." *World Bank Data,* World Bank, data.worldbank.org/indicator/sn.itk.defc.zs.

"Primary completion rate, total (% of relevant age group)." *World Bank Data,* World Bank, data.worldbank.org/indicator/SE.PRM.CMPT.ZS.

"A Profile of the Working Poor, 2018." *U.S. Bureau of Labor Statistics,* July 2020, https://www.bls.gov/opub/reports/-working-poor/2018/home.htm.

"Project Limón, Nicaragua." *FIMRC,* FIMRC, www.fimrc.org/nicaragua/.

"Projects." *GRID Alternatives,* GRID Alternatives, gridalternatives.org/-international-program/projects.

"Publications and Videos." *Habitat for Humanity,* Habitat for Humanity & Terwilliger Center for Innovation in Shelter, www.habitat.org/impact/our-work/terwilliger-center-innovation-in-shelter/publications-videos.

Purvis, Katherine, and Lindsey Kennedy. "Volunteer Travel: Experts Raise Concerns over Unregulated Industry." *The Guardian,* Guardian News and Media, 13 Jan. 2016, www.theguardian.com/global-development-professionals-network/2016/jan/13/-concerns-unregulated-volunteer-tourism-industry.

Pycroft, Sara. "Teaching Abroad: 'Volunteers Had Little Educational Benefit to the Kids.'" *The Guardian*, Guardian News and Media, 13 Jan. 2016, https://www.theguardian.com/global-development-professionals-network/2016/jan/13/teaching-in-an-orphanage-abroad-volunteers-had-little-educational-benefit-to-the-kids.

"Radi-Aid." *Radi-Aid*, Norwegian Students' & Academics' International Assistance Fund, www.radiaid.com/.

Rank, Mark Robert. *One Nation, Underprivileged: Why American Poverty Affects Us All*. Oxford University Press, 2005.

Ravelo, Jenny Lei. "30 Percent of Aid Lost to Corruption—Ban Ki-Moon." *Devex*, Devex, 10 July 2012, www.devex.com/news/30-percent-of-aid-lost-to-corruption-ban-ki-moon-78643.

Ravsberg, Fernando. "Meet Papito, the 'Daddy' of Hairdressing in Havana." *Cuba | Al Jazeera*, Al Jazeera, 21 Oct. 2016, www.aljazeera.com/indepth/features/2016/09/meet-papito-daddy-hairdressing-havana-160926113009704.html.

Razzak, Junaid A., and Arthur L. Kellermann. "Emergency Medical Care in Developing Countries: Is It Worthwhile?" *WHO Bulletin*, World Health Organization, 2002, https://www.who.int/bulletin/archives/80(11)900.pdf.

"Reduce Inequality within and among Countries." *United Nations Sustainable Development Goals*, United Nations, www.un.org/sustainabledevelopment/inequality/.

"A refugee baker in Kenya helps provide school meals." *YouTube*, uploaded by International Finance Corporation, 6 Mar. 2018, youtu.be/uyG-NDkdISs.

"Refugees at Risk of Hunger and Malnutrition, as Relief Hit in Eastern Africa." *UN News*, United Nations, 26 Aug. 2020, https://www.unhcr.org/en-us/news/briefing/2000/8/3ae6b8274c/food-shortages-affecting-refugees.html.

Rehberg, W. "Altruistic Individualists: Motivations for International Volunteering Among Young Adults in Switzerland." *Voluntas* 16, 109–122

(2005). https://doi.org/10.1007/s11266-005-5693-5

Reid, Kathryn. "Child Labor: Facts, Faqs, and How to Help End It." *World Vision*, 22 June 2021, https://www.worldvision.org/child-protection-news-stories/-child-labor-facts.

"Resilience building." *World Food Programme*, United Nations, www1.wfp.org/careers/resilience-building.

"Resource Center: Cuba Sanctions." *U.S. Department of the Treasury*, U.S. Department of the Treasury, 28 Feb. 2019, www.treasury.gov/resource-center/sanctions/programs/pages/cuba.aspx.

"Response Summary: Save the Children Providing Relief to Massive Needs of Children in 8 Countries." *Save the Children*, Wayback Machine. Oct 2017, web.archive.org/web/20171215001038/http://www.savethechildren.org/atf/cf/%7B9def2ebe-10ae-432c-9bd0-df91d2eba74a%7D/STC_HUNGER_FC_OCT17.PDF.

"Risk of Impoverishing Expenditure for Surgical Care (% of People at Risk)." *World Bank Data*, World Bank, data.worldbank.org/indicator/SH.SGR.IRSK.ZS.

Risteska, Aleksandra. "Volunteering to Prevent Famine in Somalia." *UN Volunteers*, United Nations, 28 June 2017, www.unv.org/our-stories/volunteering-prevent-famine-somalia.

"River Blindness Elimination Program." *The Carter Center*, The Carter Center, www.cartercenter.org/health/river_blindness/index.html.

Roenigk, Emily. "5 Reasons 'Poverty Porn' Empowers The Wrong Person." *The Huffington Post*, TheHuffingtonPost.com, 16 Apr. 2014, www.huffingtonpost.com/emily-roenigk/poverty-charity-media_b_5155627.html.

Rosenberg, Tina. "In Rwanda, Health Care Coverage That Eludes the U.S." *Opinionator*, The New York Times, 3 July 2012, opinionator.blogs.nytimes.com/2012/07/03/rwandas-health-care-miracle/.

Roser, Max. "Global Poverty in an Unequal World: Who Is Considered Poor in a Rich Country? and What Does This Mean for Our Understanding of Global Poverty?" *Our World in*

Data, University of Oxford, 5 Mar. 2021, https://ourworldindata.org/higher-poverty-global-line.

Rus, Jan. "Comment: Financing Undocumented Migration and the Limits of Solidarity: Unsettling Findings from Guatemala." *Jstor,* Latin American Perspectives, Jan. 2010, https://www.jstor.org/stable/20684703.

Samenow, Jason. "Maria Regains Strength as It Pulls Away from Puerto Rico, Approaches Dominican Republic, Turks and Caicos." *The Washington Post,* WP Company, 21 Sept. 2017, www.washingtonpost.com/news/capital-weather-gang/wp/2017/09/20/as-maria-slowly-pulls-away-from-puerto-rico-the-u-s-east-coast-watches-and-awaits-its-next-move/?utm_term=.bf94e29ef032.

Saval, Malina. "Oprah Winfrey's Leadership Academy for Girls Marks 10 Years." *Variety,* Variety, 3 Aug. 2017, variety.com/2017/biz/news/oprah-winfrey-leadership-academy-for-girls-10-year-anniversary-1202510605/.

"Sé Parte De Nuestros Programas." *Fundemar,* Fundemar, www.fundemardr.org/-copy-of-programa-educativo.

Sequera, Vivian. "Venezuelans Report Big Weight Losses in 2017 as Hunger Hits." *Reuters,* Thomson Reuters, 21 Feb. 2018, www.reuters.com/article/-us-venezuela-food/venezuelans-report-big-weight-losses-in-2017-as-hunger-hits-idUSKCN1G52HA.

"Seven Years Later, Life is Better." *American Red Cross,* ReliefWeb. 26 Dec 2011, reliefweb.int/report/indonesia/seven-years-later-life-better.

"Sharecropping." *PBS,* Public Broadcasting Service, https://www.pbs.org/tpt/slavery-by-another-name/themes/sharecropping/.

Sheerin, Jude. "Malawi Windmill Boy with Big Fans." *BBC News,* BBC, 1 Oct. 2009, news.bbc.co.uk/2/hi/africa/8257153.stm.

Silver, Marc, and Malaka Gharib. "What's The Meaning Of The World Bank's New Poverty Lines?" *NPR,* NPR, 25 Oct. 2017, www.npr.org/sections/goatsandsoda/2017/10/25/558068646/whats-the-meaning-of-the-world-banks-new-poverty-lines.

Singer, Peter. "Best Charities for Effective Giving." *The Life You Can Save,* https://www.thelifeyoucansave.org/.

Singh, Malvinder Mohan. "The Rise Of The Services Sector Is Redefining India's Growth Narrative." *The Blog,* HuffPost India, 5 Aug. 2016, www.huffingtonpost.in/malvinder-mohan-singh/the-rise-of-the-services-sector-is-redefining-india-s-growth-nar_a_21445764/.

Skovgaard-Smith, Irene. "The Complex World of the Global Citizen." *BBC Capital,* BBC, 10 Nov. 2017, www.bbc.com/capital/story/20171110-the-complex-world-of-the-global-citizen.

Smith-Spark, Laura, et al. "Cuba Cleans up after Hurricane Irma Tears through Caribbean." *CNN,* Cable News Network, 11 Sept. 2017, www.cnn.com/2017/09/10/americas/cuba-caribbean-hurricane-irma/index.html.

"Solar Spring Break." *GRID Alternatives,* GRID Alternatives, gridalternatives.org/get-involved/solar-break.

Stanton, Brandon. "Click Here to Support Houses For Rohingya Refugees Organized by Brandon Stanton." *Gofundme.com,* Go Fund Me, www.gofundme.com/houses4rohingya.

Stanton, Brandon. *Humans of New York,* Humans of New York, www.humansofnewyork.com/post/171594811816/they-didnt-say-a-word-they-just-started-firing.

Stever, H. Guyford, and Janet H. Muroyama. "Globalization of Technology: International Perspectives." *National Academies Press: OpenBook,* The National Academies of Sciences Engineering Medicine, www.nap.edu/read/1101/chapter/2.

Stiffe, Rebecca. "Indonesia's First Official Drone Delivers Supplies to Village School." *Irish Examiner,* Irish examiner.com, 23 Jan. 2019, www.irishexaminer.com/breakingnews/technow/indonesias-first-official-drone-delivers-supplies-to-village-school-899654.html.

Stone, Richard. "Cuba Embarks on a 100-Year Plan to Protect Itself from Climate Change." *Science,* AAAS, 10 Jan. 2018, www.sciencemag.org/news/2018/01/cuba-embarks-100-year-plan-protect-itself-climate-change.

"Study Reveals Mobile Internet Access Reduces Inequality." *IT News Africa,* IT

News Africa, 8 July 2016, www.itnews africa.com/2016/07/study-reveals-mobile-internet-access-reduces-inequality/.

Stupart, Richard. "7 Worst International Aid Ideas." *Matador Network,* Matador Network, 20 Feb. 2012, matadornetwork.com/change/7-worst-international-aid-ideas/.

Stupart, Richard. "Why You Shouldn't Participate in Voluntourism." *Matador Network,* Matador Network, 22 Aug. 2011, matadornetwork.com/change/-why-you-shouldnt-participate-in-voluntourism/.

"Supporting Peace, Justice, and Sustainable Economies in the Americas." *Witness for Peace,* Witness for Peace, witnessforpeace.org/.

"Take Action." *HeForShe,* UN Women, www.heforshe.org/en/action-kits.

"Take Action: Education." *HeForShe,* Wayback Machine. web.archive.org/web/20180121182029/http://www.hefor she.org/en/take-action/education.

"10 Things You Can Do To Save The Rainforest." *Rainforest Foundation U.S.,* Rainforest Foundation U.S., rainforest-foundation.org/10-things-you-can-do-save-the-rainforest/.

Tharoor, Ishaan. "Venezuela's Refugee Exodus Is the Biggest Crisis in the Hemisphere." *The Washington Post,* WP Company, 23 Aug. 2018, www.washingtonpost.com/world/2018/08/23/venezuelas-refugee-exodus-is-biggest-crisis-hemisphere/?utm_term=.6916bc9ffd8f.

Thomason, Jane. "Opinion: 7 ways to use blockchain for international development." *Devex,* Devex, 11 Aug. 2017, www.devex.com/news/opinion-7-ways-to-use-blockchain-for-international-development-90839.

"To Each According to His Abilities." *The Economist,* The Economist Newspaper, 31 May 2001, www.economist.com/node/639652.

"Tools and Education." *Pure Water for the World,* Pure Water for the World, pure-waterfortheworld.org/solutions/tools-and-education/.

"Tour With Locals: Sightseeing & Lunch." *Carnival Cruise Line,* Carnival Cruise Line, www.carnival.com/shore-excursions/amber-cove/give-back-with-purpose-community-tour-445097.

"Travel with WWF." *WWF,* World Wildlife Fund, www.worldwildlife.org/travel.

"Travelers' Health: Destinations." *Centers for Disease Control and Prevention,* Centers for Disease Control and Prevention, wwwnc.cdc.gov/travel/destinations/list/.

"Travelers' Health: Food and Water Safety." *Centers for Disease Control and Prevention,* Centers for Disease Control and Prevention, 8 Jan. 2018, wwwnc.cdc.gov/travel/page/food-water-safety.

"Tsunami Recovery Program: Five Year Report." *American Red Cross,* Wayback Machine. 24 Aug. 2012, web.archive.org/web/20120824015428/http://www.redcross.org/images/MEDIA_CustomProductCatalog/m3140120_TsunamiRP5yearReport.pdf.

"2011–Present: Disaster Response Programs." *Habitat for Humanity,* Habitat for Humanity, www.habitat.org/impact/our-work/disaster-response/programs/2011-present.

"Types of projects." *Doctors Without Borders—USA,* Doctors Without Borders, www.doctorswithoutborders.org/who-we-are/how-we-work/types-projects.

"UN Peacekeeping Partnering with UN Volunteers." *UN Volunteers,* United Nations, www.unv.org/partners/-un-peacekeeping-partnering-un-volunteers.

"UN Warns of 'Urgent Imperative' to Avoid Acute Afghan Food Insecurity." *United Nations,* United Nations, 7 Sept. 2021, https://news.un.org/en/story/2021/09/1099292.

UNDP Democratic Governance Group Bureau for Development Policy. "Marginalised Minorities in Development Programming." *Ohchr.org,* United Nations, May 2010, www.ohchr.org/Documents/Issues/Minorities/UNDPmarginalisedMinorities.pdf.

"UNICEF's Strategy for Water, Sanitation and Hygiene 2016–2030." *UNICEF,* United Nations, Aug. 2016, www.unicef.org/wash/files/WASH_Strategy_2016_2030_At_A_Glance.PDF.

University of Nebraska–Lincoln. "Why some parasitic worms persist in people." ScienceDaily. ScienceDaily, 22

May 2019. <www.sciencedaily.com/releases/2019/05/190522101939.htm>.

"Upwardly Mobile: Kenya's Technology Start-up Scene Is about to Take Off." *The Economist,* The Economist Newspaper, 25 Aug. 2012, www.economist.com/node/21560912.

"Vaccination." *Doctors Without Borders—USA,* Doctors Without Borders, www.doctorswithoutborders.org/what-we-do/medical-issues/vaccination.

"Vaccine Equity." *World Health Organization,* World Health Organization, https://www.who.int/campaigns/vaccine-equity.

"Vaccine Storage and Handling Toolkit." *Centers for Disease Control and Prevention,* U.S. Department of Health and Human Services, 12 Apr. 2022, https://www.cdc.gov/vaccines/hcp/admin/storage/toolkit/index.html.

"Village Volunteer Viviana Kolong Works to Protect Her Community from Debilitating Disease." *The Carter Center,* The Carter Center, 10 May 2010, www.cartercenter.org/news/features/h/guinea_worm/profile-viviana-kolong.html.

"Virtual Volunteering." *Create the Good,* AARP, createthegood.org/articles/virtualvolunteering.

"Volunteer." *Engineers Without Borders USA,* Engineers Without Borders USA, www.ewb-usa.org/volunteer/.

"Volunteer." *GRID Alternatives,* GRID Alternatives, gridalternatives.org/get-involved/volunteer.

"Volunteer." *Pure Water for the World,* Pure Water for the World, purewaterfortheworld.org/donate/volunteer/.

"Volunteer." *Refugee Community Partnership,* Refugee Community Partnership, refugeecommunitypartnership.org/become-a-volunteer/.

"Volunteer Abroad." *UN Volunteers,* United Nations, www.unv.org/become-volunteer/volunteer-abroad.

"Volunteer at Your Local Food Bank." *Feeding America,* Feeding America, www.feedingamerica.org/take-action/volunteer/.

"Volunteer Now: Become a Medical Volunteer in Haiti." *Midwives for Haiti,* Midwives for Haiti, midwivesforhaiti.org/volunteers/.

"Volunteer Program: Volunteer With Us." *Midwives for Haiti,* Midwives for Haiti, midwivesforhaiti.org/volunteers/-volunteer-program/.

"Volunteer Role & Benefits." *National Volunteer Center,* UNDP& Mineduc, centrodevoluntarios.cl/volunteer-role-benefits/.

"Volunteering." *World Food Programme,* United Nations, www1.wfp.org/careers/volunteers.

"Volunteering Abroad." *Travel.gc.ca,* Government of Canada, 27 Apr. 2016, travel.gc.ca/travelling/living-abroad/volunteering.

"Volunteering with UNICEF USA." *UNICEF USA,* United Nations, www.unicefusa.org/supporters/volunteers/-volunteering-faqs#q-what-us-fund-mission.

"Volunteers Are an Important Part of a System of Student and Learning Supports*." *UCLA School Mental Health Project,* UCLA, smhp.psych.ucla.edu/pdfdocs/vols.pdf.

Wade, Don. "Nonprofit Operators Told That Failure Can Bring Long-Term Success." *Memphis Daily News,* 12 May 2016, https://www.memphisdailynews.com/news/2016/may/12/nonprofit-operators-told-that-failure-can-bring-long-term-success/.

Wade, Robert Hunter. "Is Globalization Reducing Poverty and Inequality?" *International Journal of Health Services,* 1 July 2004. *Sage Journals,* doi:10.2190/G8F1–01FL-MEDW-JVG1.

"Wage and salaried workers, total (% of total employment) (modeled ILO estimate)." *World Bank Data,* World Bank, data.worldbank.org/indicator/SL.EMP.WORK.ZS.

Walleigh, Rick. "6 Ways to Volunteer Abroad and Be Really Useful." *Forbes,* Forbes Magazine, 23 May 2016, https://www.forbes.com/sites/nextavenue/2016/05/23/6-ways-to-volunteer-abroad-and-be-really-useful/?sh=4d498ae061bd.

"Water, Sanitation and Hygiene." *UNICEF,* United Nations, www.unicef.org/wash.

"Water, Sanitation and Hygiene: About WASH." *UNICEF,* United Nations, www.unicef.org/wash/3942_3952.html.

"We Partner With Communities." *Pure Water for the World,* Pure Water for the World, purewaterfortheworld.org/solutions/community-partnerships/.

"We Should Take a Lesson from the Nordic Countries on Inequality." *Institute for Policy Studies,* 18 July 2016, https://ips-dc.org/take-lesson-nordic-countries-inequality/.

Webber, Tim. "Why It's So Hard To Turn The Lights Back On In Puerto Rico." NPR, NPR. 20 Oct 2017, www.npr.org/2017/10/20/558743790/why-its-so-hard-to-turn-the-lights-back-on-in-puerto.

"Welcome to Elephant Human Relations Aid in Namibia." *EHRA—Volunteer in Africa to Conserve the Desert Elephants of Namibia,* Elephant- Human Relations Aid, www.desertelephant.org/.

"Welcome To The Action Center." *Action Center,* World Wildlife Fund, support.worldwildlife.org/site/SPageServer?pagename=can_home&_ga=2.154398463.630396302.1536115369-850603967.1536115369.

Wetmore, Deanna. "How Technology Is Helping Economies in Developing Countries." *The Borgen Project,* The Borgen Project, 23 Nov. 2017, www.borgenproject.org/how-technology-is-helping-economies/.

"What Is Fair Trade?" *Fair Trade Campaigns,* Fair Trade Campaigns, fairtradecampaigns.org/about/faq/.

"What We Do." *Rainforest Foundation U.S.,* Rainforest Foundation U.S., rainforestfoundation.org/what-we-do/.

"WHO Chief 'Appalled' by Rich Nations' COVID Vaccine Booster Talk with so Many Unvaccinated around the World." *CBS News,* 9 Sept. 2021, https://www.cbsnews.com/news/covid-vaccine-inequality-who-tedros-appalled-rich-nations-booster-shots/.

"Why Does Kenya Lead the World in Mobile Money?" *The Economist,* The Economist Newspaper, 2 Mar. 2015, www.economist.com/blogs/economist-explains/2013/05/economist-explains-18.

"Wildlife Conservation." *WWF,* World Wildlife Fund, www.worldwildlife.org/initiatives/wildlife-conservation.

Williams, Ollie A. "Corrupt Elites Siphon Aid Money Intended for World's Poorest." *Forbes,* Forbes Magazine, 20 Feb. 2020, https://www.forbes.com/sites/oliverwilliams1/2020/02/20/corrupt-elites-siphen-aid-money-intended-for-worlds-poorest/?sh=3715329c1565.

Williamson, Shawn. "Do You Have Enough or Too Much Farm Insurance?" *Successful Farming,* Successful Farming, 11 May 2017, https://www.agriculture.com/farm-management/-crop-insurance/do-you-have-enough-or-too-much-farm-insurance.

"Women Red Cross Volunteers Tackle Guinea Worm in Ghana." *The Carter Center,* The Carter Center, 26 Dec. 2003, www.cartercenter.org/news/documents/doc1572.html.

Wooldridge, Leslie Quander. "Don't Post a Photo of Yourself with Strangers' Children in Your Tinder Profile." *The Washington Post,* WP Company, 26 Mar. 2018, www.washingtonpost.com/news/soloish/wp/2018/03/26/dont-post-a-photo-of-yourself-with-strangers-children-in-your-tinder-profile/?utm_term=.e014c3974806.

"Workers' Rights & Trade Union Relations." *Fairtrade International,* Fairtrade International, www.fairtrade.net/programmes/workers-rights.html.

"World Mental Health Day 2017." *World Health Organization,* World Health Organization, www.who.int/mental_health/world-mental-health-day/2017/en/.

WPXI-Pittsburgh. "500,000 Petitions Delivered to Mylan Headquarters in Protest of EpiPen Price Hike." *AJC,* Cox Media Group, 31 Aug. 2016, www.ajc.com/news/national/500-000-petitions-delivered-mylan-headquarters-protest-epipen-price-hike/JCblmmiGeOEvgXfZEoEGNJ/.

Wu, Guobao. "Ending Poverty in China: What Explains Great Poverty Reduction and a Simultaneous Increase in Inequality in Rural Areas?" *World Bank Blogs,* World Bank Group, 19 Oct. 2016, blogs.worldbank.org/eastasiapacific/ending-poverty-in-china-what-explains-great-poverty-reduction-and-a-simultaneous-increase-in-inequality-in-rural-areas.

Wydick, Bruce, et al. "Shoeing the Children: The Impact of the TOMS Shoe Donation Program in Rural El Salvador." *The World Bank Economic Review,* vol. 32, no. 3, 20 Sept. 2016, pp. 727–751. *Oxford Academic,* doi:10.1093/wber/lhw042.

Wyss, Jim. "Venezuelans Are Going

Hungry. Why Won't the Country Accept Aid?" *Miami Herald,* Miami Herald, 8 Feb. 2018, www.miamiherald.com/news/nation-world/world/americas/venezuela/article199179509.html.

Yamey G, Garcia P, Hassan F, Mao W, McDade K K, Pai M et al. It is not too late to achieve global covid-19 vaccine equity *BMJ* 2022; 376 :e070650 doi:10.1136/bmj-2022–070650

Yotopoulos, Amy. "Three Reasons Why People Don't Volunteer, and What Can Be Done About It." *Stanford Center on Longevity,* Stanford University, longevity.stanford.edu/three-reasons-why-people-dont-volunteer-and-what-can-be-done-about-it/.

Yousafzai, Malala, and Christina Lamb. *I Am Malala: The Girl Who Stood Up for Education and Was Shot By the Taliban.* First edition. New York: Little, Brown and Company, 2013.

Zamani, Marie. "Bringing Hope and Social Cohesion in Post-Conflict Côte D'Ivoire." *UN Volunteers,* United Nations, 1 Aug. 2016, www.unv.org/our-stories/bringing-hope-and-social-cohesion-post-conflict-côte-d'ivoire.

"Zero Hunger." *World Food Programme,* United Nations, www1.wfp.org/zero-hunger.

Index